Wolfhilde's Hitler Youth Diary
1939 – 1946

Written by
Wolfhilde von König

Translated by
Dr. Hedwig Hamer
Monika Trujillo

iUniverse, Inc.
Bloomington

Wolfhilde's Hitler Youth Diary 1939-1946

iUniverse books may be ordered through booksellers or by contacting:

iUniverse
1663 Liberty Drive
Bloomington. IN 47403
www.iuniverse.com
1-800-Authors (1-800-288-4677)

ISBN: 978-1-4759-6855-2 (sc)
ISBN: 978-1-4759-6854-5 (hc)
ISBN: 978-1-4759-6856-9 (ebk)

Library of Congress Control Number: 2012924035

Printed in the United States of America

iUniverse rev. date: 01/09/2013

Munich Marienplatz and Salvatorkirche photos printed by license agreement with *Süddeutsche Verlag*.

Translated by Dr. Hedwig Hamer and Monika Trujillo

Cover design by Cori Hatheway

Layout by Charles H. Long, Ph. D.

DEDICATION

This book, which evolved around the *Kriegestagebuch* (War Diary),
is dedicated, with special honor,
to our father Emanuel and to our aunt Wolfhilde.

The nickname given our father by his parents was *Manü*,
which readily translated into English as Manny. Wolfhilde, too, had a
nickname, but its origin is a bit more obscure. Her mother, Elise
Jadoul, was born and raised in Liege, Belgium, where a dialect of
French is spoken. Wolf is *Lu*. Wolfhilde was Elise's Little Wolf; hence
the diminutive form, *Lulu*. Her full legal name was

Wolfhilde Oktavia Emma Elisabeth König von Paumbshausen.

Our father's full name, prefaced by a title meaning Noble Knight,
was
Edler Ritter Emanuel Anton Felix Ludwig König von Paumbshausen.

In Germany, for non-legal daily use, everyone in the family
was allowed to use the abbreviated surname von König. When our
father was granted United States citizenship, he chose to eliminate
three of his four first names, leaving not even a middle initial; to
declare as legal the German surname of daily use; to capitalize the V
and to adopt the Anglicized oe in place of ö.

Three of us bear, as middle names, one of those names from
his own. One of us chooses to retain the surname form given to all
of us at birth, honoring his father's choice in that matter. Three of us
have reverted to the small v, in conscious acknowledgment and
appreciation of our age-old German heritage.

Douglas Ludwig von Koenig, 1957 –
Jeffrey Emanuel von Koenig, 1959 –
Edward Frederick von Koenig, 1962 –
Curtis Anton Von Koenig, 1965 –

CONTENTS

DISCOVERY OF THE MANUSCRIPT

by

Douglas von Koenig
Jeffrey von Koenig
Edward von Koenig
Curtis Von Koenig

Our father, Emanuel Von Koenig, is the younger brother of Wolfhilde von König. When he died in 2009, we found among his papers this *Kriegestagebuch,* or *War Diary,* written by our aunt. The discovery came as a complete surprise, since its existence had never been mentioned to us, even though it must have come to him upon her death in 1993. Dad was thorough, meticulous to a fault. He must have examined all of her bequeathed papers and must certainly have known this was among them. That he did not speak of the *Diary* suggests the difficulty he had with the intensity and immediacy inherent in its subject matter.

After years of prodding for more information about his war time experiences, he responded in 2005 with 15 pages of material he had written. His account of imprisonment in a Russian camp, his escape and making his way home to Munich are included in this publication.

Wolfhilde's handwritten *War Diary* entries date from 22 August 1939, when she was just 13 years of age, through her 21st birthday on 8 November 1946. They are inscribed in five volumes; the first three being self-constructed bound books; the fourth, a purchased, smaller bound notebook; and the last, just an assembly of cut-edged loose sheets which appear to have originally been part of yet another bound notebook.

IN SEARCH OF A TRANSLATOR

In 2009, when we recognized the manuscript for what it was, the only family member who could have read it—our father—had just died.

We suspected that the writing would contain material we would find sensitive; therefore, shied away from agencies which provide professional translation. Our idea of the perfect person was German-born Walt Hammerling, who had been our German teacher while we were students in Michigan's St. Joseph School District. All of us held him in high esteem.

Walt, however, had long since moved to Sarasota and gone into the real estate business. We weren't quite sure how to approach him. Fortunately for us, our mother's good friend Marian O'Meara Evans, who is his mother-in-law, had no such reservations.

Walt could not read the Old German Script in which the manuscript is written, his parents having brought him to America when he was very young; nonetheless, he took it upon himself to find for us someone who could. He recalled knowing that a colleague, Monika Trujillo, was fluent in German, as well as Spanish as suggested by her last name. Monika could decipher very little of the archaic form, but volunteered that her mother, *Frau Dr. med.* Hedwig Hamer, born in Germany the same year as the *Diary*'s author and who, like Wolfhilde, became a medical doctor, most likely could.

TRANSLATORS

Dr. Hedwig Hamer, *b.* 1925, Würzburg, Bavaria, Germany —
Monika Turjillo, *b.* 1962, Fulda, Bavaria, Germany —

Dr. Hamer's eyes were the first to open wider in wonder at the narrative revealed in the handwritten diary discovered in 2009 because she could read the Old German *Sütterlin* Script used by her 13-year-old cohort, Wolfhilde von König, when she began writing in 1939.

IN HEDWIG HAMER'S OWN WORDS

Three years ago my daughter, Monika, asked me for help in reading a German diary, written in a script incomprehensible to her, which she had been requested to translate—if she could. She was enthused by the challenge and confident she could accomplish such a task, if only, first of all, she could read it. She was sure I could read it, and asked me if I would. After obtaining the von Koenigs' permission, I began the task of reading aloud to Monika from the original Old Script, making it possible for her to type what she heard into modern German form.

This type of handwriting, *Sütterlin*, was faded out of the school system during my elementary school years. We were then taught to write in the Latin style. It amazes me that Wolfhilde chose to write in the old style when she, too, must have learned the Latin; nonetheless, the Old Script is what we have here.

While Wolfhilde's writings are in good penmanship, over the years she wrote the letters smaller and narrower—harder to decipher. With any handwritten material there can be difficulty making out proper names or other unknown words. If not every single letter is clearly legible, it can be difficult to identify the exact word. The translation process can be very time consuming.

When we started the procedure, we did not realize that it would take us almost two years to complete the entire project. As we became more and more involved in thinking about this important time in history, always new questions arose. All in all, it was a great challenge for Monika and me, but also a great pleasure since it brought us both great satisfaction.

Monika came to my house nearly every afternoon, after her work as a rental manager at a condominium on Siesta Key in Florida, and I had to be prepared for dictating everything to her correctly, especially all the proper names which I had spent hours researching on the internet. The internet was of immeasurable help in verifying the names of villages, towns and regions where German troops had come and gone; as well as the names and ranks of both German and foreign military personnel and politicians.

Then, Monika started with the translation into English. The first difficulties appeared when the military ranks had to be translated. Our German friend, Helmut, who had served in the American Army, was a great help. He also knew most of the names of the great battlegrounds and battleships and the different ammunitions used by the Germans and the Allies.

My initial excitement about the project was heightened when I learned that Wolfhilde was just one month older than I, and that we had both been born in the German state of Bavaria, in cities separated by a mere 135 miles. Yet what a difference there was between my experiences as a Hitler Youth, an organization of which all youngsters were compulsory members—I know of no exceptions—and Wolfhilde's daily life!

Wolfhilde's upbringing in Munich had an intensity lacking in mine. As far as I remember, Hitler visited my small (100,000 inhabitants) hometown of Würzburg only once, and I never saw him close-up. Munich, on the other hand, was the "City of the Hitler Movement," where the Nazi Party began and where Hitler himself was ever-present, either physically or psychologically, to maintain and heighten fervor of the ever-increasing number of Party adherents.

Würzburg is most notable for being a very Catholic town, with a bishop, and as home of one of Germany's oldest and most traditional centers of learning, the Julius Maximilian University, founded in 1402, where my father was a professor of old Greek language, history and religion.

A highlight, if not **the** highlight of any year, was the great Procession on *Fronleichnam* (German name for Corpus Christi) staged on the Thursday occurring 60 days after Easter. Religiosity and erudition united for this occasion, with most of our friends—who were teachers and university professors—joining the Procession wearing their colorful official gowns and robes, every faculty a different color. Our family was not Catholic, but we were avid spectators. Würzburg found this, and related traditions, much more interesting than any Military Parade or SS March.

My father's occupation placed him outside Party scrutiny, whereas Wolfhilde's, as a civil servant, would have had to watch his every step and control every potential slip-of-tongue.

What further distanced me from the core of the Movement in which Wolfhilde was embedded, was my family's ongoing access to outside information and development, especially in the Arts. We spent most of our summer vacations with our grandmother and my mother's sister, our beloved *Tante* Erna, who lived in the north German city of Lübeck, near the Baltic Sea. *Tante* Erna was assistant to the director of the Lübeck Museums and very much engaged in Modern Art. When Hitler, in 1933, declared *Tante* Erna's specialty to be *Entartete Kunst*, Degenerated Art, her boss lost his position and she was demoted to a lower job at the public library. (They were both reinstated after the war.)

Every summer of my youth, I spent seeing and appreciating forbidden art and reading forbidden authors. Wolfhilde felt that she was being lavished with the best of German art, literature, music and theater—without realizing that she experienced only what was left after Nazi censorship; or, worse, knowing it was censored and already trained into agreement with that practice.

My parents did not talk much about politics. There was no visible resistance in our family, but nobody believed or even hoped that we would win the war. Their only hope was for an end of the Nazi Regime. They were not members of the NSDAP, the official and only party of the Third Reich, but were not immune to its dictates and on two occasions had to find ways to circumvent them.

I was the third-born child in our family, with two sisters who were five and three years older than I. When my brother, the fourth child, was born in 1934, my mother was to be honored with the *Mutterkreuz*, the medal for mothers who bear four or more children for the Reich. My mother refused to be counted as one of these and was adamant, within the family circle, in refusing the invitation to the bestowment ceremony. This was dangerous behavior and would have been interpreted as a great insult to the Party and to Hitler, personally. Diplomatically, my father appeared there to fetch the medal for his "ill" wife.

A few years later, it was my father who refused—and somehow "got away with it"—to send his blue-eyed and blond son to the NAPOLA (*National Politische Lehranstalt*, National Political Academy); special schools for politically indoctrinating children who look strikingly Aryan, training them to become the true master race.

Social life among the academic circles gradually dwindled after Hitler's takeover in 1933. Some of our Jewish friends moved to foreign countries. Those who stayed lived more or less in isolation. I remember my mother leaving after dark to visit those friends, until they "disappeared" and just weren't there anymore. I remember the *Kristallnacht*, Crystal Night, over the night of 9-10 November 1938 when the Nazis inspired the ravaging of Jewish homes, businesses and synagogues, which resulted in much broken glass. Wolfhilde would have turned 13 just the day before; I not quite yet. It would be another 10 months before she started writing her *Diary*.

On that night, I was standing in front of an apartment which was first being looted and then destroyed by a mob, when my mother hurriedly fetched me home muttering about how terrible this was. From that day on, there was a lot of whispering among my parents and their friends, but we children never knew exactly what they were talking about.

I graduated from high school early in the year of 1944, as did Wolfhilde; like her, I served the following year doing one form or another of National Labor Service.

During the heavy bombings in March 1945, Würzburg was nearly completely destroyed. My family lost our home, but was able to move into a ranger's house near Würzburg, where I also lived when I returned home from Service in July 1945.

We could register for the first post-war semester at the University of Würzburg in winter 1945, but since nearly all buildings were at least burnt, if not completely demolished, all students had to help in the reconstruction. We girls had to clean the still reusable bricks that had been removed from the rubble. While I was doing this voluntarily in Würzburg, Wolfhilde was similarly engaged in Munich as part of the de-Nazification program she was required to complete before she would be allowed to matriculate at the University of Munich. Had she not been "required" to "de-Nazify" I'm sure she would have, nonetheless, worked as willingly as I did to restore our beautiful cities.

Classes for the Medical School in Würzburg opened in the spring of 1946, just as did those in Munich, where Wolfhilde enrolled. We each graduated from our respective Medical School in the spring of 1952.

Over 1950-1951, with a US scholarship, I had the great experience of studying for two semesters at the University of Indiana Medical School in Indianapolis. This would not be relevant to this narrative except for a circumstance which came to light over the Memorial Day weekend of 2010. Monika and I were to be visiting relatives in Chicago and inquired of the von Koenigs if we might come to St. Joseph, Michigan, where they live, to meet them in person. This followed our correspondence while *Diary* years 1939-1942, entered in the set of three books which Wolfhilde had handcrafted, and the unmatched booklet containing 1943-44 were being translated. Briefly into conversation on the afternoon of our meeting, we learned that Wolfhilde's brother Emanuel, father of the afternoon's hosts, had been at the University of Minnesota the very same year I had been in Indiana, and under the same scholarship program—as had the family's long-time friend, Wolfgang Schleich, who studied journalism at the University of Nevada.

Two additional remarkable things grew out of that afternoon:

1) I stated adamantly to the young von Koenig men, that I had come to know the mind of their aunt so well that I knew, just **knew**, there had to be additional volumes of her dairy; that this woman would not have stopped writing just because things looked so bleak; she would have finished what she started out to do. I urged them to get back down into that basement where their father's papers were boxed and do a really thorough search. During the following week, when they did this, they located a packet of loose sheets, each with one jagged side, which indicated they had been cut out of some kind of binding. In these lies the conclusion to her remarkable story: 1945 through her 21st birthday on 8 November 1946.

2) The following summer of 2011, in Germany anyway to visit family and friends, I contacted Wolfgang Schleich and his wife Christiane and was invited to visit them at their home just outside of Munich. He had traveled to the USA in 1950, along with Emanuel von Koenig, whom he first met at that time aboard the *SS Brasil*; I, at the same time, was on the *SS Argentina*. Neither of us had been aware that there had been two shiploads of German students in the USA on the same program at the same time. We could so easily have been on the same ship, could have met then and known each other all these years. Still, it is a wonder that we met at all, and that we came to work on the same project—seeing Wolfhilde's *Diary* into publication.

Reading Wolfhilde's *Diary*, I realized how much easier it was for me to adjust to postwar life; I did not have to re-do my ideology. Easier for Wolfgang, as well. He lived in Berlin, which, as Germany's capital city, remained open to foreign diplomats and other visitors for a longer time, so that the regime's propaganda was never as concentrated there as it was in Munich.

I admire Wolfhilde for her earnest commitment during all those years, for her willingness to help and make sacrifices for what she perceived to be the greater good. Her energy seems focused on helping people in need, albeit within the Nazi ideology; as far as is evident to me, she did no harm. It was not possible for her, circumscribed as was her environment from any outside influence, to see the evil. I cannot but applaud how she spent all her vacations helping people who had lost their homes; organizing transportation for families and children to safer locations in the countryside where there was less danger from bombings; assisting doctors in hospitals, so nurses could occasionally have a vacation. It is remarkable how she accomplished all of this, all the while attending, as well, to her curricular obligations as a student.

CONSULTANT

Wolfgang Schleich, *b.*1928, Berlin, Prussia, Germany —

As pages of the German transcription came to us from the translators, we read them as best we could. For assessment and consultation, we forwarded them to family friend Wolfgang Schleich.

Wolfgang, three years younger than Wolfhilde von König, grew up in Berlin under the Nazi (*National Sozialist*) regime that dominated Wolfhilde's experiences in Munich. He met Wolfhilde's younger brother Emanuel aboard the *SS Brasil* when both were being conveyed to the United States as Fulbright scholars in 1950. Over the course of their lifelong friendship, Wolfgang briefly came to know Wolfhilde as well.

Wolfgang is a journalist, retired since 1990 from Radio Free Europe, where he worked for almost 35 years as a reporter, editor, traveling correspondent and head of the network's Berlin Bureau. His service with RFE is rooted in his Fulbright year at the University of Nevada where he eagerly participated in activities of the *Crusade for Freedom*, the organization being set up to establish a broadcasting network to provide objective news and information for the peoples behind the Iron Curtain; that is, RFE, later RFE/RL.

His comments—little understood by us until we had done several read-throughs of the *Diary*'s English translation, each time overcoming a bit more of our disbelief—are incisive. His comments follow.

FOREWORD
by Wolfgang Schleich

Initially, the material upset me emotionally in an unexpected way. It took me some time to re-read the diary entries one by one to gain a calmer perspective. Of course, for 60 years or longer I have been aware of the strategies and tactics, the techniques and methods applied and utilized by the Nazi regime to contaminate and poison the minds and souls of people—beginning with children from the age of 10—with its fierce, all-embracing ideology.

Never, before reading *Wolfhilde's Hitler Youth Diary,* have I been confronted with such massive, monstrous evidence as to what the Nazi regime was doing to us—and how they did it. What is presented here in the diary of a girl from 13 through 21 years of age is a textbook example—concrete evidence—of how they did it.

Manny is quoted in spring of 1953, the first year of his resident status in the United States: "We got everything we wanted. We were Hitler's children. We got all the athletic goods and overnight camping trips we wanted; we could study art, architecture, sculpture. We were told all kindness came to us from Hitler. We knew nothing but Hitler and his kindness."[1]

That is, of course, the way it began. Later, I, like Manny, starting at age 15, served as a *Luftwaffenhelfer* (LWH, Air Force Helper) manning anti-aircraft artillery from trenches, he in Munich and I in Berlin. On "D-Day" 6 June 1944, I, then a chap of 16 (and anything but a "teenager" as we have come to know them later), was in a Flak gun emplacement on the Berlin outskirts. We fired our 105 mm artillery pieces like mad at some mighty British bomber formation of several hundred during a night raid and at the US Air Force bombers which were active during the day. The Nazi propaganda so successfully played-down the Allied invasion that I did not, for some time, realize its significance. Nor did I realize the significance and consequences of all that had gone before, by which I mean the thoroughness of our ideological training.

---

[1] Article by Carl Hennemann titled "Job here taught ex-Nazi democracy best." *St. Paul Dispatch* 1953.

These accounts of Wolfhilde's everyday life in Germany during World War II—her teenage views of, and attitudes toward, developments as they occur—demonstrate the functioning of a mind held captive within the National Socialist ideology.

She was only 14 when WW II began in 1939. At the end of the war in 1945 she was 20. During those six years she had undergone no intellectual maturation, despite all the harsh experiences she had endured. Of course, political emancipation had been out of the question; there were no alternatives among which she could have chosen.

The young generation was the vital reservoir out of which the Nazis would build the fundaments for their envisaged "Thousand-Year Reich." Just as the exponents of other totalitarian philosophies have stipulated, their objective was to forge a *neuen Menschen*, a "New Man." These New People would firmly believe in the dogmas and doctrines which were drilled into them day-in and day-out. Such men and women were needed to build the absolutely loyal homogeneous society which would be ready to follow the leaders of the One-and-Only party. In the final account they would be ready to die for the ideals in which they had been conditioned to believe; a totally submissive mass which would ban, persecute and punish any individualistic tendencies. It is essentially George Orwell's *1984* horror scenario. In 1946/47 he knew what he was writing about; it had already been played out in Germany.

Germany was on its way toward such a system when Adolf Hitler came to power in 1933. It should be remembered that he did not "seize" power, as has long been said, but that he was appointed chancellor by *Reichspräsident* von Hindenburg after the post-World-War-One first German republic, the "Weimar Republic," failed for various reasons. Once in this position, he wasted no time to really "seize" all the power he could get—and he got it all.

Considering the grave consequences which the disastrous Big Depression had for Germany—widespread destitution, with millions out of work—Hitler soon garnered massive popular support with his promises to abolish unemployment, put the economy back on its feet, bring prosperity to everyone and restore a proud nation. As many millions of people joined its ranks, the National Socialist German Workers' Party—the NSDAP, the only political force left after all other parties were banned—set about forming a giant network of organizations in all sectors of public life to control all citizens and herd them into the "right" direction.

Under the *Hitler Jugend* (Youth) umbrella, boys aged 10-14 were required to join its junior branch, the *Jungvolk*; girls of that age, the *Jungmädel*. At 14, girls graduated into *Bund deutscher Mädel* (BDM, translated as League of German Girls); 14 year old boys became Hitler Youth, *per se.*

Beginning in 1938, boys and girls could be drafted into the respective organizations, even against the wishes and wills of their parents, and taken by police to the weekly gatherings. These took up two afternoons per week for ideological and physical training. Hiking and marching, pseudo-"war games" (including hand-grenade throwing), and weekend excursions with primitive tents and cooking gear were also parts of the program—as were small-group meetings for singing and indoctrination held in intimate settings, the so-called *Heim-Abende* (Home Evenings, often in some roughly furnished basement room in their parents' private homes). Through all conceivable means the Nazis saturated youth with their world-view.

The flag marching song (*Fahnenlied*) written by *Reichsjugendführer* Baldur von Schirach, leader of the HJ from 1933-1940, signifies a seal of accomplishment for Hitler's goal, stated in 1933 as: "My program for educating youth is hard. Weakness must be hammered away. In my castles of the Teutonic Order, a youth will grow up before which the world will tremble. I want a brutal, domineering, fearless, cruel youth." At the 1934 Nuremberg Rally, Hitler said: "While the older generation could still waver, the younger generation has pledged itself to us and is ours, body and soul!" Every verse of the *Fahnenlied* is followed by this chorus:

> Our banner flutters before us
> Our banner represents the new era
> And our banner leads us to eternity!
> Yes, our banner means more to us than death!

With few exceptions the boys and girls would sing it without ever thinking—a great deal, or at all—about the meaning of the words or the insane concept behind them. The ideology settled in their minds without being consciously noticed; they were envenomed, mentally subverted, warped and corrupted without being aware of it.

Wolfhilde appears to be among those who succumbed completely; her diary entries bear witness. They show that she was not just routinely doing what a BDM girl was supposed to do in the way of participating in the decreed activities; she did it with enthusiastic dedication without ever allowing a critical thought. She takes pride in getting recognition—basically a natural human reaction, put to exaggerated use by the Nazis—and being promoted to leader of a small group. She chooses Hitler or Goering quotes to head the annual volumes of the diary; she uses the official Nazi terminology to condemn various aspects of Allied diplomacy and warfare.

Set in the heart of Munich, the city which saw the birth of the Nazi Party and which Hitler held dearest, Wolfhilde's account mingles domestic life with the most devastating aspects of the war, even as defeat approaches and all fronts retreat into Munich for its final collapse.

Wolfhilde is a loyal disciple of Hitler even in his defeat; she is embarrassed by those of her fellow Bavarians who wave the white flag and cheer entry into Munich of the U.S. Army's Third Division.

All in all, the *Diary* is a highly informative document which should be of special interest to readers who favor the immediacy of the journal form. It is primary source material; authentic history.

PREFACE

by Rosalyn Reeder
b. 1930, Brookings, South Dakota, USA –
m. 1951-1989 to Emanuel Von Koenig

I was a junior at the University of Minnesota in September 1950 when I met Wolfhilde's younger brother Manny. He was new on campus, literally "just off the boat" from Germany.

By December we were sharing confidences. He said to me, "You have no idea what it feels like to have been taught one way all your life and then, suddenly, to be told by the U.S. Occupation Forces, and most of the rest of the world, that everything you believe is wrong."

We married the following March. No longer was he a "foreign student." He became "one of us"—even though his people and mine had been engaged in a war to the finish just six years earlier.

We know that recorded history is not without bias; it is written by the victors. War history is about the "victor's side" and the "other side"; it is about "us" and "them." Sixty years lay between 1951 and the completed translation of Wolfhilde's *Diary* in 2011, during all of which time my family thought of the von König family in Munich as "us." Ludwig and Elise von König shared with my parents the status of being grandparents to the same four sons born by Manny and me. The boys were nephews equally of his sister and of my brother and sister.

Manny became a U.S. citizen and balanced his "other side" in the German Navy by serving in the U.S. Army Reserves. He answered everyone's questions about his past as best he could, in ways that would fit in with our understanding of the history we have written. When, in 2010, I first read his sister's *Diary* entry for 29 April 1945, I was stunned that it said the same thing Manny had said to me in 1950. Wolfhilde's entry reads: "Is everything supposed to be over, everything we believed in and everything that we lived for? Should all the sacrifices have been in vain? I cannot believe it."

My understanding of what he said and what she said differs in this way: I heard his words from someone I already considered to be "one of us." What she wrote, and we read now, are the words of "one of them." She wrote day by day records of what was happening on those exact days. Opinions stated are her exact perceptions at those times, long before we got to know her—when she was part of "the other side."

Reading the *Diary*, we become aware that "back in those days," Manny—the husband and father who was always clearly "one of us"—had been, along with his *Diary* writing sister, "one of them." Wolfhilde's experiences were equally Manny's. They were of the same family, gathering for breakfast and supper around the same table. He had told us some of what she relates, yes—but nothing like this. He told us what we were able to assimilate within our view of history, which was a view of history different from his— because our experiences and his were different from each other.

This *Diary* is from the other side of history. Yet, the lives of Wolfhilde and Emanuel as we knew them, and their lives as revealed in the *Diary*, are not separate narratives. The nephews/sons must reconcile them into one, must understand how "they" are also "we"—because their heritage lives on both sides of World War II history.

ACKNOWLEDGMENTS

We, our mother, our wives—Joelene, Nancy, Lorilyn and Karla—and children—Jonathan, Sandra, Benjamin, Nicholas, Alexander and Elise—gratefully acknowledge contributions to this publication made by people already mentioned in preceding passages, and by:

- Judith Clark Von Koenig, Manny's wife from 25 March 1990 until his death in 2009, who passed on to us our aunt's *Kriegestagebuch* manuscript.

- Christiane Schleich, wife of Wolfgang, for being the ultimate solver of several puzzling passages.

- Susan Hubert, Ph.D., author of *Questions of Power: The Politics of Women's Madness Narratives*, who assured us this work is important and kept us going with her moral support.

MAPS

Several lakes are mentioned in the *Diary* but were not placed on the maps. For those who need to know, their locations follow.

Hintersee, Königsee, Saalachsee and Thumsee are located in the southeast tip of Germany, near Berchtesgaden and Bad Reichenhall. Einsiedl is located on the southwest end of Walchensee. Bad Wiessee is on the west shoreline of Tegernsee.

PRELUDE YEARS 1927-1938

by Emanuel Von Koenig

as recalled in 2005

Family.

I was born in Munich, 16 March 1927, on the family kitchen table at Thierschstrasse 34/5th floor/left. Living with me were my father, mother, 1½ year-older sister and our father's father, whose occupation had been as a wholesale dealer in pots and pans. Quite old and blind, he died in a streetcar accident during that year.

For the first two years of my life, until 5 October 1929, Adolf Hitler lived across the street and down the block from us at Thierschstrasse 41/1st floor. We did not know about this at the time because he wasn't anybody yet.

1976; Thierschstrasse 34 (arrow), east from
intersection with Mariannenstrasse.

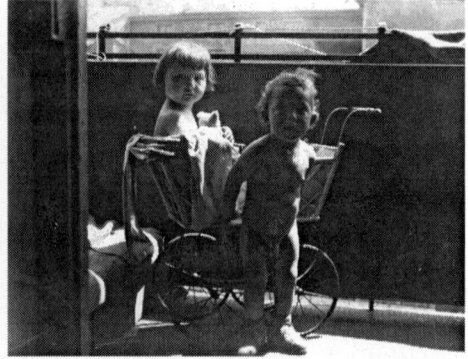

1927; Manny, *Mutti*, Lulu.

Lulu & Manny playing on the kitchen balcony, Thierschstrasse 34. In the background, across the Isar river, the Maximilianeum.

1927; my first Christmas.

1928; my second Christmas.

1929; my third Christmas.

Mother was a native of Belgium, coming from a family of engineers and lawyers. Temperamentally suited for the stage, she should have been an actress.

My father, after serving in the infantry on the East Front in Poland during World War I, became a surveyor working for the State of Bavaria. This made him a Civil Servant. Civil Servants walk a fine line, making sure that nothing ever happens which could affect their reputation—and the security of their jobs. *Vati* was a strict person, lived by the clock, and, in some ways, quite narrow minded.

I do not know how my parents met.

Living Conditions.

We were quite poor. I remember my mother accepting orders to do stitcheries and embroideries to supplement the family income. I also remember my parents sitting down once a week to debate and decide how every penny was to be spent. I remember one incident. We did not have central heating. There was a coal-fired stove in the living room. One day, *Mutti* was burning some papers and, by accident, also burned a 10 Mark Note. This was a catastrophic event. Although poor, we children always had decent clothing and were well fed. Once I started elementary school I learned what poverty really meant. Compared to some of my classmates, we were rich.

When I was still little, *Mutti* would take us to a nearby park and I was allowed to play in the sandbox. A little older, on weekends, our parents would take us on the streetcar to some park where we could run around and play hide and seek.

1931; Lulu & Manny.

1933: *Mutti*, Manny, Lulu.

Mutti.

While still in Belgium, my mother learned to do beautiful work embossing thin copper and we had a number of wooden frames and boxes adorned with her art work. She had to give it up because the arm pressure needed for this type of work started affecting her throat. Her main hobby then became needle work and she was never idle.

1932; Lulu, *Mutti*, Manny.

Vati.

Vati at times made us Christmas presents. One year he made a castle for me and bought some figures to go with it. It was quite nice. For my sister he worked several months to make a large loom for her. When I was still little he made a small pull-wagon for me. Problem was the wheels he made were out of round and not properly centered. During the first use, the people living below us thought their ceiling was coming down. That was the end of that. Wheels came off and it became a storage box.

1933; my sixth Christmas.

Vati excelled at quite a few things; however, there were a few things which did not work out too well. About 1934 or 35 my parents wanted a radio. A finished product was too expensive. So *Vati* bought a kit. As there were no electric solder irons, you heated the slug on the gas burner. The wetting compound was Salmiac. By his constantly leaning over the iron while soldering, the fumes started to color his gray hair and he developed a greenish streak. It looked quite funny. One day the radio was completed. *Vati* plugged it in and started fiddling with the dials. Nothing happened; he became frustrated and his language became quite unacceptable. At this point I need to mention that our electricity system was 110V DC. The doorbell rang, my father answered. It was the neighbor from the first floor who inquired if my father was working on a radio. When answering in the affirmative, my father was informed that the man could hear on his own radio downstairs what my father uttered upstairs. Back to the soldering iron. The radio was eventually made to work and even survived the war.

Another of my father's interests was astrology and he would calculate horoscopes long hand. He also was an artist and made beautiful paintings and charcoal drawings. He was also interested in sulky racing. Not to bet, but to verify that the evaluation system he developed for horses really worked. It did. After the end of the war, a few of us high school buddies went together and placed bets using his system. Most of the time, we had some spending money.

Childhood Summers.

The work routine of my father was that during winter months he would work in his office and supervise the updating of surveys and maps. During the summer months, he would be in the field supervising surveying crews and doing the needed calculations and chart work. Over our school summer vacation time, he would rent a room at a farmhouse and we would be together as a family in the country. It was fun working with animals and there was always a lake or swimming hole near-by. *Mutti* would take us on extended walks and each summer we would get to know a new part of our state. The first night home after vacation was hard because one had to again get used to the squealing and rattling of the street cars passing in the street.

1931; Vati, with his family, and a fellow surveyor in the country.

1932; Lulu, Manny.

1932; in the country.

1932; Lulu, Manny & friend in the
country.

1934: Lulu, *Mutti*, Manny.

1934; Manny on a horse in Mirskofen, about 25 miles due
east of Wolnzach in the Holledau Region.

1934; Lulu, Manny, *Mutti*.

1933, Belgium; Lulu, *Mutti*,
Uncle Leon, Manny.

1933, Belgium; Manny,
Grandmother Jadoul, Lulu.

1935, Belgium; Lulu, *Mutti*, Manny.   **1935, Belgium; Lulu & Manny.**

1935, Belgium. Back row, Grandmother & Grandfather Jadoul. Others, left to right: Aunt Margarete, Manny, *Mutti*, Lulu, unidentified.

My mother had a brother, Leon, and a sister, Margarete, who both lived in the city of Liege in Belgium. My uncle was a high ranking officer in the Belgian army; my aunt was the widow of a very wealthy man. Because of my mother's marriage to a German officer [during the World War I occupation] the siblings had become quite alienated.

My grandmother, also [still] living in Liege, longed to see her grandchildren. Over-ruling any local objections, she financed the trip and we went to Belgium during our 1935 summer vacation. Grandmother, a tall and imposing figure, was delighted to see us. So, too, were Uncle Leon and Aunt Margarete. Of necessity, the siblings reconciled.

My aunt's townhouse in Liege was impressive. It was located on a boulevard along the river Meuse. It had a drive-through entrance, on one wall of which hung a very large Gobelin tapestry opposite a few steps which led up to the foyer. The place was like a museum. A chair used by pope so-and-so, a sofa used by king so-and -so and many more valuable antiques. The walls were covered with valuable paintings.

Connected to my aunt's bedroom was a small alcove with walls of drawers for her jewelry. Behind the house was a large walled-in formal garden. In the center was a round pond with a decorative fountain. She had two servants: a chauffeur who also did work around the house and his wife who did the cooking and cleaning. My aunt also had a top-of-the-line Buick sedan. I assume that by the end of World War II quite a few items in the house had been liberated by the German occupation forces.

Mother took us on walks through various neighborhoods and I perceived the people, although they were speaking a different language, to be nice and polite. They got along with each other and were a functioning society. These impressions stayed with me and were reinforced during our second trip in 1937. The propaganda at home, that Germany is sort of the center of the universe, was no longer that convincing.

On both trips we spent some time at my aunt's country estate which was located near Jemeppe, about an hour's drive from the city. There was quite a large house. Behind it was a large semi-formal garden, beyond that, the farm buildings. A 17 year old farm boy was among the workers there. He and I liked each other and I often went with him when he had to do chores.

Early School Years.

In the fall of 1933 I started going to school. The school was within walking distance from home. There were no school busses and no crossing guards; one simply had to learn to move in traffic. The school building was a three story affair with two wings; one for boys, one for girls.

Since it was located next to a large church, it assumed its name: St. Anna. School started at 8 a.m. and let out at noon. Our teacher was a mild-mannered middle-aged man with white hair and we liked him.

That does not mean however, that at all times we behaved like angels. Punishment, when necessary, was meted out in the form of contact with a bamboo stick about two feet long and about 1¼ inches thick. Two to four hits on the palm of your hand or, if the offense was serious, two to four hits on your

1933; Manny & Lulu off to school.

buttocks. At home I never mentioned any punishment because *Vati* would have supplemented it. As to the bamboo stick, we learned from older students that when rubbed with an onion it would lose its resiliency and become brittle. So on Fridays, somebody always had a piece of onion and hoped for a chance to rub the stick. The following week, when used, it would shatter. This did not upset the teacher, who just gave a small coin to the offender and sent him across the street to a school supply store to get a new one.

During our first year we took many walks and learned the history and the geography of our home town. Our teacher had the ability to make history come alive.

On the way home from school I always was on the lookout to avoid my sister because she was a tattle-tale and would report any prank on my part.

Our apartment was located about halfway between two schools and for my third year, because of overcrowding, I had to go to the other school. The way from home, at Thierschtrasse 34, to school led past the editorial offices of the *Völkischer Beobachter*, the official newspaper of the Nazi party, located at Thierschstrasse 11-17. On quite a few occasions, as I passed, a black Mercedes would stop and Hitler would emerge and enter the building. We sort of developed a nodding acquaintance. I probably did not make that big an impression on him because he did not seem to recognize me when I came with my Hitler Youth group to have tea with him at the *Haus der Kunst*.

1936.

1936; Lulu, Manny.   1936; Lulu & Manny
                                          First Communion.

1937.

1937; Manny.

For the fourth grade I was back at St. Anna's, and in the spring of 1937 I took—and passed—the qualification test for high school admittance. **Endnote (i)**

1938.

While my sister and I were still in the junior *Hitler Jugend,* she in the *Jungmädel* and I in the *Jungvolk,* I distinctly remember two occasions:

Annexation of Austria, the *Anschluss*, in the middle of March 1938, is the first one. German troop formations were moving through Munich on their way to occupy and annex Austria. At a *Jungvolk* meeting that day we were ordered to immediately report any conversation we overheard in which our parents expressed criticism of the Third Reich or of the leadership. Of course I mentioned this to my parents and from that moment on there never was any political or critical comment made in our presence.

Munich Accord, on 29 September 1938, is the other. Our troop was called out to be part of the honor guard. We were selected because we lived close to the place where the occasion took place. It was an old royal palace[1]. We were standing very close to the entrance and could see all the participants arriving and pass us close by: Adolf Hitler, Chamberlain from England, Daladier from France, Mussolini from Italy and many other high ranking officials. It was very interesting and exciting.

---

[1] We have identified the "old royal palace" as *Prinz-Carl-Palais*, located at Franz-Josef-Strauss-Ring 5. Built in 1806, it housed royalty until 1924 when it became the official residence for Bavarian Prime Ministers. Wolfhilde refers to it in her 18 June 1940 entry: "Thousands crowded the streets from Prince Karl Palais to the *Führerbau*." As the Munich Accord was actually signed at the *Führerbau* in the early hours of September 30 (although dated September 29), Manny must have witnessed the beginning of a procession from the *Prinz-Carl-Palais*, in which there is a spacious conference room, to the *Führerbau*, along an established parade route. The *Prinz-Carl-Palais* is, indeed, within a ten-minute walk from his home on Thierschstrasse.

**1938; Manny & Lulu in the uniforms of the
Junior Hitler Youth: the *Jungvolk* and the *Jungmädel*.**

War Diary
1939

**Whatever may come, no one will be able,
ever again,
to overthrow or dismantle
the German Empire, as it stands today!**

Adolf Hitler

Munich, 22 August 1939

A non-aggression and consultation pact is to be contracted between Germany and the Soviet Union. Ribbentrop will fly to Moscow on August 23rd to confer with Molotov and Stalin. This important pact, to be in effect for 10 years, will be signed.

Munich, 24 August 1939

Germany's peace offering to England was rejected. A German airplane with Secretary of State Stuckart aboard was fired upon by the Polish Marine Artillery outside of the Polish aerial territory. In Lodz, 24 ethnic Germans were murdered by Polish troops. Also in other areas of the country ethnic-Germans are being mistreated, abducted and then murdered.

Munich, 26 August 1939

There is mail correspondence between Adolf Hitler and the Prime Minister of France, Daladier, in which the *Führer* explains again that "Danzig and the Polish Corridor must be returned to Germany." Poland mobilizes 19 million soldiers and drops bombs on German homes in Kattowitz. The *Reichsparteitag* [National Party Day rally held annually in Nuremberg] is cancelled.

Munich, 28 August 1939

Vati was recruited into the German Army this morning. We are all surprised, because *Vati* isn't all that young any more. He will first go to Grosskarolinenfeld. Hopefully he can soon return.

Munich, 30 August 1939

I wonder what our *Führer* will announce on September 1st in Parliament. Polish acts of terror against their ethnic-Germans take ever stronger forms. Fearful apprehension is visible on the faces of all the people that I see on the streets, in shops, or that I may pass anywhere else. There is anxiety and worry about the future: "War or Peace."

Munich, 1 September 1939

The order is given. The *Führer* has called his people to arms in order to protect the German country, our Homeland, and to defend it against the enemy. The *Führer* spoke in military uniform. In his great historic speech he said, "The German youth will perform their assigned duties with happy hearts." These words make us proud and confident about the times to come.

Munich, 3 September 1939

England and France declare war on Germany because we will not withdraw our fighting troops from Poland.

Munich, 4 September 1939

"Fill the sandbags" was the drill. First, we had to get the sand from the Isar River. The householders loaned us shovels and pails. The pails, when full, danced wildly and sometimes tumbled off when the wagon drove over a bumpy road. As we worked, we talked about the introduction of food stamps and of the nightly black-out procedures. These are things that we are not used to yet. The *Führer* is at the front. *Ostoberschlesien* [East Upper Silesia] is in German hands.

Munich, 6 September 1939

The first *Heimnachmittag* ["home-afternoon": gathering time for the *Jungmädel,* a Nazi organization for girls aged 10-14] meeting since our vacation. Liesel reported on the advancement of our troops into Poland and exultation filled our hearts. Krakau has fallen; the *Führer's* Frontline has already driven all the way to Graudenz. The Polish government has fled to Lublin. Unbelievable, but the absolute truth! Liesel told of her train station duties and of the refugees from the eastern and the western areas, of all the hardship and misery that she saw. We younger leaders are sorry that we cannot yet perform these duties.

Munich, 8 September 1939

The German press reveals the atrocities committed by Polish marauders near Bromberg. Thousands of innocent German civilians were tortured by the Poles in the most horrific ways and then murdered.

Munich, 11 September 1939

First school day after vacation. The beginning brought some surprises. Our main teacher has been drafted and we have a female substitute. The [weekly] schedule has also changed: school will be held three times in the morning and three times in the afternoon.

Munich, 12 September 1939

The *Führer* is at the Frontline between Lodz and Warsaw. The bulk of the Polish Army has been surrounded at Kutmo. Posen, Thorn, Gnesen and Hohensalza have been occupied. Polish Army by Radon destroyed; 60,000 prisoners.

Munich, 14 September 1939

German troops penetrate Gdingen. The city is handed over without a fight. The *Führer* gives this city on the Baltic Sea the name of *Gotenhafen* ["Harbor of the Goths," an ancient Germanic tribe which had lived in this area]. I am especially pleased by this.

Munich, 16 September 1939
Vati got vacation for the weekend. He visited us in a simple dark gray uniform. He had barely sat down in the bathtub when the bell rang. It was an order. It's getting serious now and *Vati* has to go to the battlefield. Brest-Litowsk has fallen. Invasion of Russian troops into the Polish state area. The first encounter between Russian and German troops.

Munich, 19 September 1939
Führer speech in Danzig: last chance for democracy. Jubilant cheering broke out for Adolf Hitler as he made his entrance into liberated German Danzig.

Munich, 23 September 1939
The campaign in Poland has ended. So far, 450,000 prisoners; 1,200 large weapons taken. Mussolini, in a speech, once again calls on the Western powers to be sensible. Today I handed out food stamps at the Tattenbachstrasse location.

Munich, 25 September 1939
Ribbentrop flies to Moscow. *Reichsminister* Frank was made governor in the occupied Polish area and *Generaloberst* von Rundstedt was named chief of the military administration.

Munich, 28 September 1939
A border and friendship agreement is signed between Germany and the Soviet Union which, by international law, signifies the end of the heretofore Polish States.

Munich, 1 October 1939

Count Ciano in Berlin. The *Führer* welcomes Italy's Foreign Minister to the Reich Chancellery for a several-hours long conversation in the presence of Ribbentrop. Rudolf Hess gives a radio speech on the occasion of conferring Motherhood Medals [given to mothers of four or more children]. The first German troops moved into Warsaw without incident. Infantry General Blatskowitz and Artillery Generals von Kluge and von Reichenau are promoted to *Generalobersten* for their accomplishments in the Polish campaign.

Food stamps for fat (butter, cheese, cooking oil) marmalade, sugar, eggs, and meat. Valid 20 November through 17 December 1939.

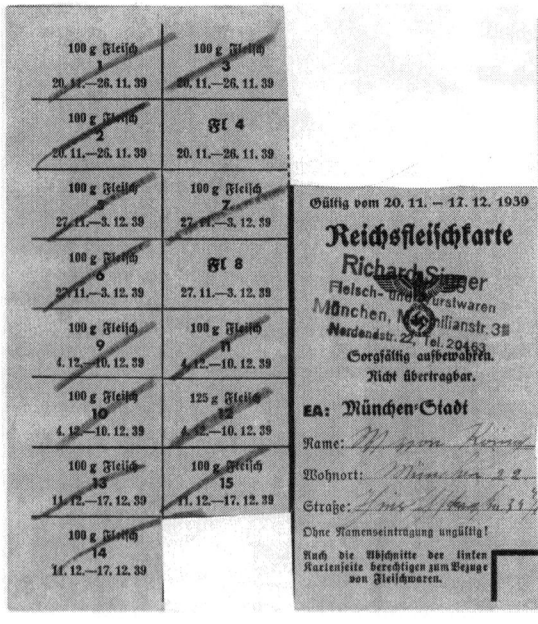

Munich, 5 October 1939
In Warsaw, the *Führer* watches the parade of troops who participated in the battle for the former Polish capital. He thanks the soldiers: "You have fulfilled your tasks in the East with exemplary coordination among the Air Force, Navy and Army. You have fought bravely and courageously. This day concludes a struggle noteworthy for solidarity of spirit among the German troops."

Munich, 6 October 1939
In the *Reichstag* [Parliament], the *Führer* proclaimed a comprehensive and reconstructive peace plan for Europe: no war objectives towards France or England, no further revision claims except for the status of our colonies, weapons reduction, a conference proposal, and the return of Germans to their settlements. In the Polish drive, 10,572 German soldiers died, 30,322 were injured and 3,049 are still missing in action. 694,000 Polish soldiers were taken as prisoners of war.

Munich, 10 October 1939
The *Führer* opens the WHW [*Winterhilfswerk*, Winter Relief Program] 1939-1940 in the Sports Arena.

Munich, 13 October 1939
My wish has finally come true. My first day working at the train station. I got used to it quickly. I had to get train tickets for the refugees from the western areas. Five hours I stood on the job and am very tired. But still, a job like that is very nice and satisfying when one can help exhausted people. A thankful word, along with happy and grateful faces, is enough appreciation for the job done.

Munich, 14 October 1939
In the Bay of Scapa Flow, a German submarine under direction of *Kapitänleutnant* Prien sank the 29,150-ton battleship *Royal Ark* and torpedoed one of the fastest British Naval battleships,

the 32,000-ton *Repulse*.

Munich, 15 October 1939
The first German refugee-settlers from the Baltic area come into Gotenhafen.

Munich, 18 October 1939
The *Führer* greets *Kapitänleutnant* Prien and the crew of the triumphant submarine at the Reich office. Prien receives the *Ritterkreuz* [Knight's Cross]. Berlin residents prepare a jubilant reception for the brave men.

Munich, 20 October 1939
There is a *Jungmädel* leaders' conference in Untergau. Elfriede Horn spoke about the big projects coming up for us: The care for the wounded in the military hospitals, the toy collection for our German children in Poland, train station service, food stamp distribution and other things are our next tasks, which we do with happy hearts.

Munich, 21 October 1939
Friendship agreement between Italy and the Reich: Resettlement of the Germans from South Tyrol. It rained buckets when we were handing out food stamps today; nonetheless, we were able to get it done in two hours.

Munich, 24 October 1939
Ribbentrop's speech in front of Danzig's veteran fighters. England carries the entire blame for the war. Rejecting all German peace offers, Great Britain has been, for years, secretly and methodically preparing for war.

Munich, 25 October 1939
Work at the traffic bureau. Our job was to count out 250 travel stamps for military personnel. Soon our heads were just spinning. We had to do it very quickly because there was a

long line of soldiers constantly pushing forward. My relief came at 4:00 p.m. We picked up Elfriede Horn in Untergau and drove with her to a group inspection. Liesel said goodbye to us. We are sad because Liesel Shick has always been a great comrade.

Munich, 26 October 1939
Our teacher came on a surprise visit. It made us happy that he thought of us. Too quickly he said goodbye again.

Munich, 3 November 1939
Agreement between the German Reich and the Soviet Union: Resettlement of all Germans out of the western areas of the Ukraine and White Russia as well as all Ukrainians; White Russians, Russians, and Ruthenians out of the German occupied former-Polish areas.

Munich, 9 November 1939
Yesterday was my 14th birthday. What all happened on this day? The *Führer* spoke to the Old Guard in the Buergerbraeukeller [marking anniversary of 1923 *Putsch*]. The speech of our beloved *Führer* was aired on all stations. His governmental duties forced him to return to Berlin yet that night so he had to leave the Buergerbraeukeller earlier than anticipated and headed towards the train station where the train was waiting for him. Soon after the *Führer*'s departure there was an explosion in the conference room. Of all those still in the conference room, there were six dead and 64 injured. When I went to bed after the speech, we heard a horrible bang but we couldn't figure out where it came from. The next morning we found out about the horrible assassination attempt on our *Führer*. It was a kind providence for which we will be eternally grateful that our *Führer* was spared. After Munich heard of the attempt, it turned into a swarm of bees. Everywhere you would run into the Old Guardsmen in their

gray uniforms with bandages on their heads and hands. The severely injured are in the Munich hospitals. A 500,000 Mark reward is announced for the capture of the responsible criminals. There was a short but impressive ceremony at the Koenigsplatz. Standing in for the *Führer*, Party Member Rudolf Hess laid wreaths atop the 16 iron caskets of those who had died in the 1923 uprising. It was a colorful spectacle that was presented to the crowd. The sentries who kept the perpetual watch were in field gray uniform. Mixed with this was the brown of the SA, the black of the SS, and the blue of the Hitler Youth and the groups of Wolf Cubs [6-10 year old boys]. We *Jungmädel* stood in formation surrounding the Koenigsplatz. In front of the Temples of Honor, which served as altars for the Party, gathered the old veterans dressed in brown shirts. The Air Force wore blue-gray and the Navy dark blue. Deep doggedness and loathing were written on the faces of these men, indignation toward the perpetrators of the attempted assassination.

Those who died 8 November 1939.

Names of the dead: Wilhelm Kaiser, Franz Putz, Emil Kasperger,
Eugen Schachta, Wilhelm Weber, Leonhardt Reindl,
Maria Henle, Michael Schmeidl.

Munich, 10 November 1939
Still today, the cowardly assault is the subject of conversation among the entire German population, even of the whole neutral world. Tonight at 10:00 p.m. the bodies of the seven dead will be transported to the Feldherrnhalle.

Munich, 11 November 1939
We had no school today so that we could instead report for duty. At 9:00 a.m. we gathered at the University. We *Jungmädel* and our counterparts in the Hitler Youth were to line the procession route from the Feldherrnhalle to the North Cemetery. At 11:00 a.m. the state ceremony in front of the Feldherrnhalle was set to begin. Unexpectedly, the *Führer* arrived to participate. Around 12:15 p.m. the funeral procession approached the North Cemetery, marching to music played by a military band. The first three and the last three caskets were each accompanied by six comrades of the Old Guard. The fourth was surrounded by twelve groups of *Jungmädel*. At the cemetery entrance, the formal delegation said farewell to their fallen comrades. The dead were buried with only their relatives present.

Munich, 14 November 1939
The number of dead rose to eight. Old Party Member Schmeidl died from his injuries. The *Reichskleiderkarte* [clothing rationing] was introduced. This provides that basic clothing needs for all the people will be met.

Munich, 15 November 1939
Vati is home. He has 14 days leave. Shoulder tab and collar are decorated with a silver stripe. He has become a corporal. When *Vati* tells stories, he finds interested listeners in us. He explains some Hussar jokes and talks about life at the West Wall. As part of our *Jungmädel* service, we collected old paper in the afternoon, and also books and magazines for our soldiers in

the military hospitals.

Munich, 16 November 1939
Ships carrying Baltic Germans arrive daily in Danzig. These refugees will go to a large resettlement camp to wait for their new homes in the German East. These Germans left homes and farms in Lithuania, Estonia and Latvia so that they could settle into their proper home, Germany.

Munich, 18 November 1939
On Thursday, in the name of the *Führer* and that of the entire German population, Region Leader Adolf Wagner bid farewell to Michael Schmeidl, who has given his life for the *Führer*.

Munich, 20 November 1939
Distribution of food stamps. It rained buckets but this couldn't dim our joyfulness as we thought of our soldiers in the West and the East. They protect our Fatherland and do not question wind or weather. Duty is duty whether it's in the Homeland or at the Front.

Munich, 21 November 1939
The Munich culprit [in the assassination attempt] has been arrested: Georg Elser. The [assassination] order had been given by the British Secret Service. In addition to Elser, leaders of the British Intelligence Service are in German hands.

Munich, 27 November 1939
Kapitänleutnant Prien, the victor at Scapa Flow, torpedoed and sank a heavy battleship of the London Class east of the Shetlands. Moscow declares that the non-aggressive pact with Finland has expired. Army command: return fire.

Munich, 2 December 1939
Return of the Baltic Germans completed. Now begins resettlement in the reclaimed East German areas.

Munich, 6 December 1939

Mackensen is 90 years old. The *Führer* visits the old Field Marshal. *S.S. Bremen*, the 52,000-ton high speed steam engine turbine ocean liner of the Norddeutscher Lloyd line, returns home. The trip through the British controlled waters took them from New York over Murmansk.

Munich, 13 December 1939

Heavy naval engagement between the German armor-plated battleship *Admiral Graf Spee* and three British cruisers at La Plata Bay. After inflicting severe damage to the stronger opponent, *Graf Spee* enters the Uruguay harbor of Montevideo to repair its damages.

Munich, 16 December 1939

Reich's Street Collection. A huge success. Over half a million beautiful wooden figurines were sold in Munich alone. Not to mention the many old medals, which were also sold rapidly. It was really cold. The wind blew fiercely and there was heavy snowfall, but we pulled it off anyway.

Munich, 17 December 1939

On Saturday afternoons and Sunday mornings, our school has Day of Home Music, during which we girls sing and play instruments. *Vati* is not coming for Christmas. The Fatherland demands this sacrifice and we accept it. Countless others make this sacrifice as well. *Admiral Graf Spee* has been destroyed by its own crew. The *Führer* gave this command after the Uruguayan government denied the port-time which would have been necessary to repair this battleship.

Munich, 18 December 1939

An extraordinary victory for the German Air Force above the German Bay [The Bay of Heligoland]. After a hard-fought battle, fighters of the Schuhmacher Squadron shot down 36 out of 52 English warplanes.

Munich, 20 December 1939
Last *Jungmädel* home afternoon gathering before Christmas. We had a small Christmas party. Christmas tree branches and candles decorated the room. We sang our beautiful old Christmas songs. Our little ones performed "Snow White" and "Goose Girl," both old German fairytales. The childlike sincerity of their performance was a joy to behold. With best wishes for Christmas and the New Year, we said good-bye to each other.

Munich, 23 December 1939
Vati came home unexpectedly. He will stay with us for a while. The Christmas season will now be even better.

Munich, 24 December 1939
Today is Christmas Eve. The morning and the afternoon passed slowly. But around 5:00 p.m. *Mutti* sent us out. I went to my room and wrapped presents for my parents and my brother. Finally, *Mutti* played the song "Silent Night, Holy Night" [on the piano]. Then we began passing out the gifts. First, my brother. He found at his place *Lausbubengeschichten* by Thoma, a book about the Spanish Air Force; *With Hitler in Poland* and the Cosmos Calendar 1939-1940. His main present, a large Maerklin set [model train construction/assembly kits, currently marketed in the U.S. under the trademark Marklin], he had to search for. Then it was my turn. A brown handbag made of calf leather is now my greatest pride. From *Mutti* and Aunt Ida I received two tasteful stationery folders and an apron to embroider. *Vati* gave me *Der Hitlerjunge Quex* [propaganda novel, required reading for all Hitler Youth] and two humorous books for *Jungmädel*. But, there was still something more. Carefully I opened the box. A bracelet made of authentic German gold, of amber! A long-time wish was

now fulfilled. A broche pleased me for its large shiny stones. My brother gave me a picture of the *Führer* in a cherry wood frame. Then I went to my room and lit the candles on the small Christmas tree. My mother was pleased with her stationery folder and a bookmark that I made for her. My brother was happy with his naval-fleet calendar, writing pencils and colored pencils. Next we led *Mutti*, with her eyes covered, over to her gift table. The present from *Vati*: dinner service for six. *Mutti* exuded sheer delight. The candles were snuffed and we returned to the living room. At 12:00 midnight *Mutti* and I went to Mass.

Munich, 25 December 1939

On December 21ˢᵗ the commander of the *Graf Spee*, Captain Langsdorf, followed his battleship to his death. On Thursday he was buried at the German cemetery in Buenos Aires. Many people attended the funeral. The *Führer* spent Christmas with his soldiers in the West. He brought them small gifts and little Christmas trees, but the best gift for the soldiers had to have been the presence of the *Führer*.

Munich, 26 December 1939

Today I went with *Mutti* and Manny to the *Deutsches Theater*. Among the acts was a young girl whose performance on the high wire had impressed me three years ago. She received huge applause. Alternating acts of classics, dance and comedy made a delightful variety show.

Munich, 31 December 1939

New Year's Eve. Last day of the year 1939. At 7:00 p.m. we listened to *Reichsminister* Dr. Goebbels. He discussed the situation with the enemy and decreed the theme for 1940: "Fight and Work." Before his speech we listened to the 25ᵗʰ Armed Forces Request Concert with famous artists of theater, movie and cabaret. Happily we embraced the New Year which will hopefully bring us peace. I will again bring to mind, and write down, the most important events of this first year at war:

War Year   1939   Year of Destiny

The German volunteers of the Condor Legion returned as brave and triumphant soldiers from the Spanish Freedom Battle and paraded in front of the *Führer* in Berlin on June 6th. In the name of the German people, Adolf Hitler thanked the veterans of the Spanish campaign soldiers for their exemplary work.

A wall of steel and cement—the West Wall—was finished in July 1939. The ingenious structure, which contains 22,000 bunkers and which became an impenetrable wall against the enemy, was erected under orders of the *Führer*.

The *Führer* with the Germans in Bruenn: German troops occupied Bohemia and Moravia on March 15th to remove the unbearable conditions for the many different nationalities that lived in this country and to establish the possibility of a permanent new order. Memel became German again. The Memel territory, which had been taken from the Germans 20 years earlier through the Versailles Treaty, was given back by Lithuania on March 23rd and was occupied by troops of the German Army and Navy. The long awaited liberation made possible by the *Führer* had arrived.

A historic moment at the Kremlin: On August 24th the negotiations of Secretary of State von Ribbentrop with Stalin and Molotov concluded a non-aggression pact between Germany and the Soviet Union. It was the hour in which the English policy of encirclement was broken, through a masterpiece of diplomacy.

A memorable day: The *Führer* in Danzig. Shortly before the

end of the Polish campaign, the *Führer* came to Danzig where he was greeted with wild enthusiasm by the people who were finally freed from the despotic Polish government. Danzig once again became what it used to be, a German city. A picture of the 18 day campaign: The strategic layout of the Polish campaign was a master work without historical precedent. It took just eight days for the fate of the enemy to become evident. Within three weeks the Polish troops were either killed or captured.

Watch in the West: During the battle in the East, our Armed Forces protected our western borders against the French and the English. The enemy had to return small perimeter areas they had seized earlier. The enemy did not dare engage the German troops which were protected by the West Wall. The heroic feats of the German U-boats and battleships severely diminished England's naval supremacy and its ability to provision its island nation. In the first three war months, the British loss in naval shipping totaled 800,000 tons. Along with this, they lost their invaluable sense of fleet cohesion.

1940

**For as long as the Germans are willing
to give their lives for their people
and their Fatherland,
that long will we be invincible.**

Hermann Goering

Munich, 4 January 1940
Hermann Goering takes over the entire direction of the war economy.

Munich, 6 January 1940
Food stamp distribution. Icicles hang down from the rooftops; wind whistles in the streets; snowfall is heavy. A cold snap like at the North Pole. This time we receive fewer food stamp folders, which we have to walk a long way to get. But by 11:30 we are finished and go quickly home to a warm room. *Vati* didn't have it any easier today. He had to gather together coats of arms for the main cities of the *Traditionsgau*.[ii] But he, too, quickly accomplished his task.

Munich, 15 January 1940
A long awaited letter arrived. In jovial fashion our teacher thanked us for the package we sent him for Christmas. He might come the day after tomorrow and we are already excited today. Today we visited the exposition *Raubstaat Engeland* [Predatory England] in the new State Gallery on the Koenigsplatz.

Munich, 25 January 1940
After returning from a successful battle at sea, the cruiser *Deutschland* is renamed *Lützow*. Resettlement of the German people from Galicia and Volhynia is completed. Baltic German resettlement was accomplished on January 11.

Munich, 30 January 1940
Seventh anniversary of the founding of the Third Reich. In school, in a modest celebration that we arranged ourselves, the meaning of the day was highlighted. At night, the *Führer* spoke at the *Sportpalast* [Sport Arena]. He caustically called the French and English to account. He mocked them and, in so doing, spoke the absolute truth. Jubilation and roaring applause accompanied his words. After singing the *Deutschlandlied* and the *Horst-Wessel-Lied* we sang the song "We march on England." This is the song for the soldiers and the German people. Its first performance was in an Armed Forces Request Concert. The poet is Hermann Loens; the composer is Herms Niel.

Munich, 3 February 1940
Collecting. Today was Reich Street Collection day [for Winter Relief]. Comical Wilhelm Busch figurines were for sale. We sold figurines we ourselves had made since the others were not enough by far. We made them of cardboard and painted them with watercolors. In no time at all we were sold out.

Munich, 4 February 1940
Youth film hour. We saw the movie *The White Squadron*, an Italian movie which had been honored with a Mussolini Award. An administrator of the Reich Youth Leadership said to the assembled parents, "We show the girls only worthy first-class movies from which they can learn and can gather strength and inspiration." The choir and the orchestra of the radio youth group added a festive feeling to the youth movie hour.

Munich, 5 February 1940
Hurray! We have school vacation days because there is not enough coal to heat the school.

Munich, 7 February 1940
Well known leader of the Alsatian autonomy movement, Voos, who had been imprisoned and sentenced to death by the French, was shot Wednesday morning in Nancy.

Munich, 8 February 1940
Yesterday was the opening ceremony of the leadership conference of the BDM [*Bund deutscher Mädel*, League of German Girls, ages 14-18) and the *Jungmädel* at the University of Munich. The opening speech was made by BDM Untergau leader Elli Wolpert. The leader of Munich's radio youth group explained the song workshop which, besides the physical education and the German ideology schooling, plays a great role in the education of the BDM and the *Jungmädel*. Under his leadership, we quickly learned some songs which he will direct us in singing many times during the leadership conference.

Munich, 9 February 1940
Last night again at the University. The Munich County [*Kreis*] leader spoke to us. He reminded us that we in Munich have a duty towards those in the Reich. He promised that he would do everything in his power to get us a meeting room. Recorder music and our songs rounded out the evening.

Munich, 10 February 1940
This afternoon there was a special session of the JM leaders. Elfriede Horn, the JM Untergau leader, introduced the meeting. Then our Obergau leader Anneliese Steiner spoke. She acknowledged the work that had been completed and spoke of the coming challenges which await us in the "Year of the Trial," as Baldur von Schirach has named it. Music, songs and poetry gave the afternoon at the University a festive air.

Munich, 11 February 1940
Morning activities in the Odeon Concert Hall. Obergau leader
Martha Middendorf spoke to us. She spoke of the tasks and
duties of a leader in these times. She reminded us of the World
War and how the youth of that time squandered opportunities.
We have the duty to fight this evil by preventing it, to educate
the BDM and *Jungmädel* in the German way. The conference
was called so that we could gather enthusiasm and strength for
the challenges that lay ahead. Music and song brought a festive
feature to this otherwise straight forward morning gathering.
Then, we JM leaders marched to the University. Elfriede Horn
said in a short speech that we would now have the most
important part of the conference: political education. Party
Member Stadler spoke earnestly on the theme "Germany-
England." We heartily applauded his address. After a short
midday break, we all met at the University again. Elfriede
Horn gave us an overview of the work accomplished so far.
She added, though, that many things have to be done
differently and better. Our group was praised for having not a
penny in debt, which could not be said of the other groups.
Many questionable issues that concerned us were discussed.
Now that the answers are clear to us, we know we can do our
duty. At 4:00 p.m. we marched to the Odeon for the closing
ceremony. First, Eli Wolpert gave an overview of last year. The
Reich winners in winter sports and the best BDM and JM
groups received the victors' prizes. Martha Middendorf
provided guidelines for the upcoming work. The *Führer* should
be our shining example; as we work, we should always think
of him. The National songs closed the festivities and,
therewith, the conference of the BDM and JM leaders of
Munich.

Munich, 15 February 1940
In these last few days several hundred return-settlers from our
colonies arrived in Berchtesgaden. They had been forcibly

driven from their farms by the English. Now they work in Germany and wait for the time when their Fatherland takes back their colonies. Then they will return to their chosen homeland, Africa. In addition, from Volhynia [in the Ukraine] over 60,000 ethnic-Germans have returned to their German homeland. All those who responded to the *Führer's* request are making huge and heavy sacrifices. But their greatest wish came true: to be able to live and work in Germany. Similarly, thousands of return-settlers are arriving in Innsbruck from South Tyrol and Italy.

Munich, 16 February 1940
General Field Marshal Goering spoke over all German radio stations to the German farmers about the agricultural tasks of the spring farm work and related issues about the population's basic food supply.

Munich, 17 February 1940
At 12:55 a.m. the captain of the commercial ship *Altmark* announced that at 10:00 p.m. in the innermost part of Joessingfjord [Norway], the English battleship *Cossak* had captured and boarded the *Altmark*, overpowering the crew of the ship. During this siege there were German deaths and injuries. At 3:05 a.m. the German captain radioed that the battleship opened wild gun and machinegun fire on the sailors who were on the ice or looking for cover, as well as the ones swimming in the water. On the ship's decks lay four dead and five severely injured. The result of the attack: seven dead, five severely injured, one missing.

Munich, 19 February 1940
The whole world denounced, in dismay and unanimous indignation, the brutal and internationally illegal act of the British assassinators against the sailors of the German ship *Altmark*. On Monday afternoon the victims of this cowardly surprise attack were laid to rest in Norwegian soil.

Munich, 20 February 1940
Yesterday we *Jungmädel*, under the leadership of Elfriede Horn, welcomed the Romanian *Jungmädel* and *Hitler Jugend* leaders who came to attend the winter sport games of the Hitler Youth in Garmish. Two blonde German JM presented a beautiful tulip arrangement to the Romanian JM leader and welcomed her in behalf of the city of Munich.

Munich, 24 February 1940
On the anniversary of the founding day of the NSDAP, the *Führer* spoke to the Old Party Members in Munich. With cutting ridicule, Adolf Hitler critiqued foreign war mongers.

Munich, 1 March 1940
A U boat, under the leadership of Herbert Schulze, returned victorious. Up to now it has destroyed almost 115,000-ton of English ships.   Equally successful, another German U boat under the leadership of Werner Hartman returned to port. This ship, after only its second long distance journey, has already destroyed 90,000-ton.

Munich, 9 March 1940
Secretary of State von Ribbentrop went to Rome for a conference with the *Duce* and Count Ciano.

Munich, 10 March 1940
The *Führer* spoke at the Berlin *Zeughaus* [Armory] for Veterans Day.

Munich, 17 March 1940
In an attack at Scapa Flow, German pilots demolished battleships, cruisers and destroyers of the British fleet. Airports and anti-aircraft stations were also bombed, resulting in the biggest defeat of the British Navy.

Munich, 18 March 1940
On the occasion of the visit of Secretary of State von
Ribbentrop to Rome, a meeting, long in the planning, between
the *Führer* and the *Duce* was arranged. Adolf Hitler and
Mussolini met Monday at noon on the Brenner. *Vati* has been
transferred to Innsbruck for two years. A peace treaty between
Finland and Russia was finalized.

Munich, 20 March 1940
French Premier Daladier has stepped down. His successor is
England's stooge, Paul Reynaud.

Munich, 9 April 1940
The German Army marches into Denmark and Norway. They
were barely ahead of the English by ten hours. Denmark
accepts German protection. Occupation of the country
proceeds without complication. We lost the battleships *Blücher*
and *Karlsruhe* which ran into mines.

Munich, 14 April 1940
The OKW [*Oberkommando der Wehrmacht*, High Command of
the Armed Forces] announces: German battleships under
direction of Commodore Bonte, who secured the landing in
Narvik and the first establishment of troops there, in recent
days of heavy battle supported by German U-boats and
airplanes, deflected repeated invasion attempts of English
naval forces.

Munich, 19 April 1940
Tonight, the night before the *Führer's* birthday, we recruit the
ten year olds into our group of *Jungmädel*. A few days prior,
the BDM took our group of fourteen year olds into their ranks.
I have to give up the *Jungmädel* group of which I had grown so
fond. Now I have younger girls in my group. Today I got my
driver's license. All of Norway and Denmark are in German
hands. The German Air Force destroyed many English ships.

Munich, 20 April 1940
The *Führer's* birthday; *Reichsmarshall* Goering reports on the great success of the metal donations [for recycling, in honor of the *Führer's* birthday].

Munich, 10 May 1940
Beginning of the offensive in the West. German troops march into Belgium and Holland. The English planned to march through Belgium, Holland and Luxemburg to seize the German Ruhr region, but, again, Germany got there before England.

Munich, 13 May 1940
Luettich has fallen. Forward march over the Belgian-French border. Breaking through Holland's fortifications, the *Führer* is at the Front. The Dutch government flees to London.

Munich, 14 May 1940
Surrender of the city Rotterdam. Capitulation of the Dutch Army. Extension of the Maginot Line by Sedan is broken through. Dyle-Stellung reached.

Munich, 16 May 1940
Dyle-Stellung broken through. The one hundred kilometer wide Maginot line north of Longvy is breached. Twelve thousand French taken as prisoners.

Munich, 17 May 1940
Invasion of Brussels. Loewen falls. Belgian government flees to Ostend.

Munich, 18 May 1940
Pursuit on the entire Front. Antwerp, St. Quentin and Le Cateau under German control. West of Antwerp, the Schelde River is crossed. All of Holland is under German control. Seyss-Inquart becomes *Reichskommissar* for the occupied Netherland

areas. Eupen and Malmedy are back in the Reich through the *Führer's* directive.

Munich, 20 May 1940
German troops reach the Somme Battlefield. The encirclement begins. Laon and Rehtel are taken.

Munich, 24 May 1940
Conquest of Loretto-Heights. Three French Armies, Belgian's entire Military Forces and England's Expedition Corps are all finally locked in. Calais surrounded; Bologna, Kortryk and Ghent occupied.

Munich, 28 May 1940
Calais under German control. Airports near Paris bombarded. Unconditional capitulation of the Belgian King and the Belgian Army. Lille, Bruges, Ostend, Armentieres occupied by our troops.

Munich, 30 May 1940
Ypern and the Kemmel stormed. Last English opposition along the coast. Much of the French Flanders Army imprisoned or destroyed.

Munich, 4 June 1940
Fortress of Dunkirk, after heavy fighting, taken over. The Weygand Line is broken through. Strong enemy forces at Somme and Oise smashed.

Munich, 10 June 1940
Italy enters the war. The heroes of Narvik are fully victorious. The English and their allies retreat. The Norwegians capitulate.

Munich, 13 June 1940
The French government flees to Bordeaux. Le Havre is taken.

Munich, 14 June 1940
March into Paris.

Munich, 18 June 1940
The *Führer* and the *Duce* in Munich. They discuss the armistice.
No Munich resident stayed home today. In the morning at 8:00
we went to the train station to stand in line formation among
the beautiful decorations. The poor SS [*Schutz Staffel*, Security
Squadron], earnestly parading back and forth trying to keep
order, had their true plague with all of us. Munich had never
before seen such endless cheering. Was it happiness over the
meeting of the *Führer* with Mussolini? Was it jubilation over
our triumphant troops? Thousands crowded the streets from
Prince Karl Palais to the *Führerbau* [*Führer* Administration
Building] at the Koenigsplatz. The *Führer* and the *Duce* stood
upright in their vehicle. Radiantly they thanked us residents of
Munich for this jubilant welcome. Today I actually only went
home to eat. It was too nice to stand in the first few rows and
to experience all of it. Now it is 10:00 p.m.; the *Führer* and
Mussolini drove off a short while ago. I am truly tired now but
it was so wonderful.

Munich, 21 June 1940
The *Führer* in the forest of Compiègne. Delivery of the
Armistice conditions to the French.

Munich, 22 June 1940
Signing of the Armistice in Compiègne. A memorable region,
this forest of Compiègne. Until now, when we thought of
Compiègne, the shameful Armistice Treaty of 1918 came to
mind. Nevertheless our conditions are just, even if they are
hard.

Munich, 24 June 1940
Over the night from the 24th to the 25th at 1:35 a.m. both sides
entered a cease fire. *Mutti* waked us up beforehand and we

listened to the radio. At 1:35 a.m. the signal sounded "All Clear." The Netherlands Thanksgiving prayer and National Songs closed this historic in-the-dark-of-night broadcast. The fight in the West is over and now the call is to "Bomb England."

Munich, 6 July 1940

After an absence of 10 weeks, the *Führer* returned to Berlin. The joyful cheering of the Berliners knew no bounds. They prepared for the *Führer* a triumphant entry into the Reich's capital city.

Munich, 7 July 1940

Count Ciano, Italy's Foreign Minister, arrived in Berlin. He has meetings with the *Führer*. Then he will travel to the Front and visit the occupied areas in the West.

Munich, 10 July 1940

Today we had to work all day. Munich again stands in the spotlight of events. The *Führer* welcomes Ciano, Teleki and Csaky. In the morning at 7:00 it started. Count Ciano was awaited. We had wonderful seats in the beautifully decorated train station. Reich Foreign Minister von Ribbentrop welcomed the visiting dignitary onto the train platform. When Hungarian Foreign Minister Teleki and Prime Minister Count Csaky arrived in Munich, they were welcomed by Ribbentrop as well. "The *Führer* is in Munich!" This call brought the last *Münchner* out into the streets. We marched ahead of the *Führer* to the Koenigsplatz. One after another the politicians lined up for their turn to have a memorable few words with the *Führer*. Another beautiful day filled with life-enriching experiences comes to a close.

Innsbruck, 13 July 1940

We have now arrived in Innsbruck. Manny [brother, 1½ years younger] and I received vacations eight days earlier than expected. When *Mutti* has made it through her goiter operation, she will follow. The trip was wonderful.

Snowcapped mountains surround the city. The sun has come out. In Rum, a small village outside of Innsbruck, the lady of the house where we will be staying welcomed us. We settled in and then took a walk around the town. The setting sun illuminates the surrounding mountain summits and peaks. For the first time I see the Alps glowing in all their beauty. The Patscherkofl, Habicht, the Zuckerhuetl, and the saw-toothed north chain are plunged into a ghostly red light. In the distance, the glistening towers of the city greet us. The express train hastens through the area. Otherwise, all is still and quiet. The forests that make their way up the mountain are dyed in red. In those areas where the forest opens up, there are quaint, cozy little towns nestled in the mountain cliffs.

Innsbruck, 14 July 1940

Another long day has passed. In the afternoon we visited the district's capital city, Innsbruck. The main and most heavily trafficked thoroughfare is Maria-Theresien Street with the Anna Column. At the end of Herzog-Wilhelm Street is the famous house with the golden roof. We walked through the Hofgarten which is like Munich's English Garden. The city itself has many green areas. Everywhere, from wherever one is, one sees the mountains on which new snow has fallen. Innsbruck's site is uniquely beautiful. No wonder it is given the name "Pearl of the Alps."

Innsbruck, 17 July 1940

Mutti is now in the hospital. This afternoon we went to Hall. There you feel as though you are in a medieval city. Old Solbad Hall [full name of the town] with its narrow alleys, old towers and houses, appeals to every visitor.

Innsbruck, 19 July 1940
In a historic session of the *Grossdeutschen Reichstag* [Parliament of Greater Germany], the *Führer* lauds the heroism of the German soldiers and the accomplishments of the military leadership. Hermann Goering becomes *Reichsmarshall*. The following are promoted to become General Field Marshals: Brauchitsch, Rundstedt, Leeb, Bock, List, Kluge, Witzleben, Reichenau, Milch, Sperrle, Kesselring and Keitel. General Dietel, the victor and hero of Narwick, becomes the first officer of the German Armed Forces to be honored with the *Ritterkreuz*. Adolf Hitler directs one last call to the English for them to come to their senses.

Innsbruck, 23 July 1939
The English bombard open German cities on the coast and in northern Germany. This is their answer to the *Führer*'s call for peace. The English government decided to keep fighting. They will, however, learn how it feels when the Germans come. The dice have been rolled.

Innsbruck, 26 July 1940
Romanian statesmen Prime Minister Gigortu and Foreign Minister Manoilescu are welcomed by the *Führer*.

Innsbruck, 27 July 1940
Bulgarian Prime Minister Filoff and the Bulgarian Foreign Minister Popoff are with the *Führer*.

Innsbruck, 28 July 1940
The *Führer* welcomes Slovakian statesmen Tiso, Tuka and Sano Mach.

Innsbruck, 6 August 1940
Mutti is finally here. She came through the operation well, although she still feels very weak and tired. But with this marvelous mountain air, she will soon get stronger. Every

second day we must go to the clinic in Innsbruck for treatment of the wound that is not closing properly.

Innsbruck, 17 August 1940
Through diplomatic notes to the entire neutral world, the German Reich explains its total blockade of England. Up until now, yesterday was the most successful day in air strikes against England. The British lost 143 airplanes and 21 barrage balloons.

Innsbruck, 28 August 1940
Count Ciano was welcomed by the *Führer* on the Obersalzberg. The Hungarian prime minister and the foreign minister as well as the Romanian foreign minister were asked to come to meetings in Vienna.

Innsbruck, 30 August 1940
Arbitration in Vienna. The Arbitration Treaty of the Axis Powers set new boundaries between Hungary and Romania.

Innsbruck, 1 September 1940
Last night I visited for the last time the home evening meeting of the girls of Rum. Everything that happens is an exciting experience for me. This is where I have learned to know the people of Tyrol. They have to struggle to make the barren earth fruitful. But all love their piece of land and, by extension, their Homeland, "Tyrol." Most of the girls are serious. They think about the time before the return of the *Ostmark* [Austria] into the Reich. With what love they sing the song "Nothing can steal from us the love and belief in our country." They are happy when someone comes from the Reich to tell them about the *Führer* whom they would all like to see and in whom they believed during the hard times.

Innsbruck, 4 September 1940
Tonight we will travel to Munich by way of Garmisch and

Mittenwald. It is sure to be wonderful. This great weather is making it hard for us to leave this glorious city in its one-of-a-kind mountain world.

Munich, 5 September 1940
We have been back in Munich since last night. The trip was truly wonderful. Last night, the *Führer* opened the second wartime WHW [*Winterhilfswerk*, Winter Relief Work] in the Berlin Sport Arena and holds British air piracy responsible [for the need].

Munich, 6 September 1940
We have become accustomed to being back in Munich again. *Mutti's* incision on her throat is still not closed. So I went with *Mutti* to the Nymphenburg Hospital. This clinic lies in a beautiful setting and is beautifully furnished. In Romania the constitution was suspended. Antonescu holds all the governmental powers. King Carol resigned in favor of his son Michael. The way is now clear for a militarized Romania, as Codreanus [who died in prison in 1938] meant for it to be.

Munich, 17 September 1940
The *Führer* welcomes Spanish Secretary of the Interior Serrano Suñer.

Munich, 18 September 1940
Reich Foreign Minister von Ribbentrop travels to Rome for consultation with the *Duce* and Count Ciano.

Munich, 20 September 1940
On the occasion of his 40th victorious air battle, Major Moelders is received by the *Führer* and honored with the *Eichenlaub zum Ritterkreuz* [Knight's Cross with Oak Leaves].

Munich, 24 September 1940
The *Eichenlaub zum Ritterkreuz* is awarded to Major Galland for

his 40th air strike victory. To date, Prien has sunk 151,400-ton.

Munich, 27 September 1940
Signing of the Tripartite Pact. State ceremony in the Reich Chancellery: Signing of the Tripartite Pact Germany-Italy-Japan.

Munich, 4 October 1940
The *Führer* and Mussolini meet on the Brenner in the presence of the Foreign Minister and General Field Marshal Keitel.

Munich, 5 October 1940
Captain Wick achieves his 41st air strike win and is given the *Eichenlaub*. For this occasion he was received by the *Führer* on the Obersalzberg.   He was promoted to Major by the *Reichsmarshall* and entrusted with the leadership of the Richthofen Fighter Squadron.

Munich, 20 October 1940
Kapitänleutnant Prien also receives the *Eichenlaub zum Ritterkreuz* for sinking 200,000-ton of enemy shipping.

Munich, 24 October 1940
The *Führer* meets with General Franco at the French Spanish border. The day before, he welcomed French Vice President Laval. Lieutenant Colonel Moelders reaches his 50th air strike victory.

Munich, 25 October 1940
Marshal Petain is welcomed onto French soil by the *Führer*.

Munich, 28 October 1940
Meeting of the *Führer* and the *Duce* in Florence. Italy demands from Greece guarantee of neutrality and concession of their bases. Greece rejects the proposal. Thereupon, at dawn, Italian troops take up battle from Albania.

Munich, 3 November 1940
Kapitänleutnant Kretschmar tallies a total of 217,198-ton sunk and receives the *Eichenlaub zum Ritterkreuz.*

Munich, 6 November 1940
Today I want to enter all my thoughts and experiences of the past few days into this little book. Today we had a wonderful afternoon group meeting. Elfriede Horn said good-bye to Traudel Kollman and Lisl Blaha. Christa Strobelt and I took their places. Then Elfriede spoke of the tasks coming up for our *Jungmädel* group. All the girls were enthused. Two lovely songs, which we quickly learned, closed the festive hour. Afterwards we had a leadership meeting, where we talked about our work. We made big plans, which we have every intention of following through.

Munich, 8 November 1940
Today is my 15th birthday. Books, a pretty necklace and ethnic-dress cards, as well as an ethnic-dress album, were the beautiful gifts. Petra was here this afternoon. Inge and Hannelore came for a short chat. *Vati* was able to make a surprise visit at 9:00 p.m. He had barely seated himself when the sirens went off. So there! The Tommies wanted to ruin our 9th of November [annual *Putsch* commemoration]. From our places in the cellar we could hear the shooting of the flak and the impact of the bombs. Then *Vati* announced that the Old City is in flames. The beautiful old City Hall and a number of business buildings were burning. The alarm lasted for over three hours. A nice finale for my birthday party! Something always happens on this day. Last year the vicious assassination attempt; this year the air strike.

Munich, 9 November 1940
Whew, today it is cold. The roofs are hoary with frost. Warmly dressed, we marched to the Koenigsplatz. Rudolf Hess came at

1:00 p.m. and placed wreaths on the caskets. It was a simple but impressive ceremony. On the way home we saw destruction caused by the attack. The *Bauerngirgl* [a pub near the East Cemetery] and a number of other business places were damaged. Addressing the Old Guard, the *Führer* gave a splendid speech which met with his warriors' hearty approval. Adolf Hitler had already spoken in the afternoon so the plan of the English was not fulfilled. Surely they wanted to interrupt his speech but, as happens so often, their planning was off.

Munich, 12 November 1940
Chairman of the Council of the People's Commissars Molotov arrived in Berlin where he has important and significant meetings with the *Führer*. Neville Chamberlain died.

Munich, 17 November 1940
Today we had a youth film hour. The wonderful, impressive film *Jud Süss* was shown. This film, that even received hefty applause in Italy, was simply fabulous. Ferdinand Marian, Werner Krauss and Kristina Soederbaum as principal actors turned this film into a memorable experience.

Munich, 18 November 1940
Italian Foreign Minister Count Ciano, who arrived Monday morning in Salzburg, met the *Führer* for a lengthy meeting in the afternoon. Adolf Hitler also welcomed Spanish Foreign Minister Serrano Suñer.

Munich, 19 November 1940
Reich Foreign Minister von Ribbentrop and Count Ciano traveled from Salzburg to Vienna, where they were welcomed by Reich Representative von Shirach. In conjunction with a private visit to Germany, King Boris of Bulgaria visited with the *Führer*.

Munich, 20 November 1940
The *Führer*, Ribbentrop, Ciano, Teleki and Csaky in Vienna. Hungary joins the Tripartite Pact which was signed on September 27th.

Munich, 23 November 1940
Romanian President Antonescu and Foreign Minister Prince Sturdza in Berlin. Romania joins the Tripartite Pact.

Munich, 24 November 1940
Dr. Tuka, Slovakia's Prime Minister, is in Berlin. He also signs the Tripartite Pact.

Munich, 30 November 1940
Finally everything is done! The sigh is due to the completed workshop. We put all of the beautiful things on exhibit. Doll houses, fabric-stuffed and wooden animals, games, building boxes — all that a child's heart could desire. Hopefully they will bring Christmas cheer to the many German children who have returned from South Tirol, Volhynia and Romania. That is then the best thank you for all the effort and work.

Munich, 1 December 1940
First Sunday in Advent. Fiftieth Armed Forces Request Concert. The highest ranking generals, Dr. Goebbels, and the diplomatic corps were present. Outstanding artists such as Marikka Roeck, Rosita Serrano, Zarah Leander, Italian and Japanese artists participated. Heinz Goedeke, the creator and director of the Request Concert received the *Verdienstkreuz* [Service Medal] for his professional contribution.

Munich, 4 December 1940
Commander of the Richthofen Squadron Major Wick did not return from his last flight over enemy lines. Major Wick had become one of our most successful fighter pilots. His plane most likely crashed during an air battle with the English.

Losing him is very painful for us.

Munich, 10 December 1940

Air raid protection course. These were pleasant and informative hours. We learned ways to protect ourselves as we defend our Homeland. At 12:00 the *Führer* spoke to the armament workers. He spoke thanking them and the entire German population for all the work they have done.

Munich, 14 December 1940

Whew, it's cold out today, and it was still dark when Hannelore and I left with our badges and tin boxes. But wow, how quickly we sold our little figurines that go so well with the Christmas tree. It was also high time; we are already totally blue from the cold. But elated and with happy hearts, we got the job done.

Munich, 16 December 1940

Yesterday we went with *Fräulein* Kleber to the theater. *Die Nibelungen*, their lives and deaths, were made real on stage before our very eyes. Good performances by the actors made the Hebbel play a great experience for us.

Munich, 20 December 1940

Finally vacation! My report card was good. Then one can get excited about vacation. It's almost Christmas; I still have to work hard; so many stars I still have to finish. Little gnomes and angels are still waiting to get done. *Eichenlaub* for U-boat commander *Kapitänleutnant* Schepke, who sank 40 ships with 288,975-ton.

Munich, 22 December 1940

Tonight there was an air raid alarm. Thank God no damage occurred.

Munich, 24 December 1940
Christmas, the holiday for all Germans, is finally here again. The gift table was arranged so beautifully. A beautiful winter-dirndl with apron, a small umbrella, books, a calendar, ink pen, an easel for a picture, bracelet, a picture book of traditional ethnic attire, and many cards of the *Führer* and of places where great events have taken place. Not to mention the presence of sweets, even though there is a war going on. *Mutti* was happy to receive a coffee warmer, cake server, glass service and stationery. *Vati* got schnapps, neckties and socks. Manny was happy with his *Märklin* box, ship-building kit, books, ink pen and a lot of sweets.

Munich, 25 December 1940
The *Führer* spends his Christmas Day with the troops at the Front. He visits them in their dug-outs and in their quarters at air bases and anti-aircraft sites. Everywhere he goes he brings joy with him and gives every man a gift. For these soldiers, however, the greatest gift is to be in the presence of the *Führer*.

Munich, 27 December 1940
This morning I received a letter from the Front. The soldier, who was a random recipient, thanked us for the Christmas package we had sent him. This bridged the gap between Homeland and the Front. In the afternoon, Baerbel, Petra and Luise came to our yearly get-together. There was a lot to laugh about, especially during our *Ulkstaffel* [joke relay].

Munich, 31 December 1940
We stand at the turning of the year; for the second year in a row, at war. We have achieved great victories. We have conquered Denmark, Norway, Holland, Belgium and France. A year full of hopes and wishes is about to end. May next year be the last year at war and may England, our mortal enemy, be stomped to the ground.

1941

Any weakling can handle victory; ill-fated reversals of fate can only be endured by the strong.

Adolf Hitler

Munich, 1 January 1941
The *Führer* gives the order of the day to his military and a New Year proclamation to the German citizens.

Munich, 18 January 1941
At the German Consulate in San Francisco, a German flag was ripped apart by members of the US Marines, to the cheers of an approving crowd.

Munich, 19 January 1941
Yesterday I was at Schiller's *Wilhelm Tell*. This play, which brings us closer to Schiller's spirit, was greeted by us with great applause. The evening served as a festive prelude to the Hitler Youth theater series.

Munich, 21 January 1941
The *Führer* and the *Duce* have an intense conversation about the situation.

Munich, 27 January 1941
The Region of Silesia gets split into Regions Lower Silesia and Upper Silesia. Region Leader for Upper Silesia is Fritz Bracht and for Lower Silesia, Karl Hanke.

Munich, 29 January 1941
Reich Attorney General Dr. Guertner died of a heart attack.

Munich, 30 January 1941
Important speech by the *Führer* in the Berliner Sportpalast as he calls to account the Jewish-Anglo-Saxon world conspiracy.

Munich, 6 February 1941
Captain Oesau receives the *Eichenlaub zum Ritterkreuz des Eisernen Kreuzes* [Knight's Cross with Oak Leaves of the Iron Cross].

Munich, 14 February 1941
The *Führer* welcomes Yugoslavian Prime Minister Cvetkovic and Foreign Minister Cincar Markovic at the Berghof for a long conference.

Munich, 15 February 1941
Vati finally returns from Innsbruck. But that also means he will have to leave again soon. One of the oldest battle comrades of the *Führer*, SA *Obergruppenführer* Ambassador Hermann Kriebel, dies in Munich. The *Führer* orders a state funeral.

Munich, 24 February 1941
Today the *Führer* spoke at the Party's anniversary in the Hofbraeuhaus in Munich. He announced the sinking of 217,000 -ton of British shipping. This news elicited storms of rapturous applause.

Munich, 26 February 1941
Today we started our health care course. We will all learn what we have to know for first aid procedures. It is almost spring, when accidents in the camp and in sport activities increase. There we have to be able to give immediate and appropriate care because there is not always a doctor around.

Munich, 1 March 1941
In a state ceremony in Vienna, in which the *Führer* participated, Bulgaria enters the Tripartite Pact.

Munich, 3 March 1941
To ward against British troops amassing in southeastern Europe, and with approval from Bulgaria, German troops began to invade Bulgaria on March 2nd. Today I received the news that Baerbel Luyken's mother died after a short illness. Baerbel has gone with her father to their home in Niederhein, where her mother will have her final resting place.

Munich, 6 March 1941
A while ago, there was an appeal to the citizens asking us to take into our homes a child displaced by the air raids. We decided to take one and awaited her daily. Liselotte, our foster child, came today. She arrived pale and shy. Homesickness for her mother disappeared when she saw all of the toys that I unpacked. Soon she will trust us and will settle in.

Munich, 12 March 1941
The *Führer* spoke in Linz at the third anniversary of the reunification with the Reich. Dr. Goebbels honored the same event by speaking before thousands of Viennese. Liselotte Kraschinski is now going to school. She is a little wild one, but one has to love her anyway. She is happiest when she can go for a walk with Aunt Lissy [*Mutti*] and the doll carriage.

Munich, 15 March 1941
Squadrons of our Air Force attack the English cities daily. During the nights, highly successful bombing attacks are made on the harbors of Liverpool, Glasgow and Hull—destroying armament works, shipyards and airports.

Munich, 16 March 1941
Again this year on Memorial Day, the *Führer* spoke in the

Berlin Armory. The *Führer* presented General Dietl the Narvik Shield.

Munich, 21 March 1941
The *Führer* welcomed Hungarian Foreign Minister von Bardossy to the *Führer* Headquarters in Munich. *Kapitänleutnant* Prien and Kretschmer were promoted to *Korvettenkapitänen*.

Munich, 22 March 1941
Lieutenant General Rommel is awarded the Knight's Cross Oak Leaves of the Iron Cross. After his great successes in the West, Rommel takes his armored divisions into Africa.

Munich, 25 March 1941
Yugoslavia joins the Tripartite Pact. Krista Strobelt said goodbye today. Together with Elfriede Horn, she handed over the *Jungmädel* group to Erika Behr. I now have the group of seventeen year olds.

Munich, 26 March 1941
Japanese Foreign Minister Marsurka arrived in Berlin. His entrance into the Reich's capital city was jubilantly cheered by Berliners. The *Führer* welcomed Masurka into the Reich's Chancellery for a lengthy meeting. A number of different receptions and visits with highly placed leaders and ministers rounded out the Japanese state visit. From Berlin the Japanese Foreign Minister will go to Rome where he will have similar meetings with the *Duce*.

Munich, 28 March 1941
Members of the Cvetkovic government were arrested in Yugoslavia. Crown Prince Peter was proclaimed King. Riots against the Germans are growing. Prince Regent Paul, a friend to Germany, also had to flee. The USA promised to help Yugoslavia.

Munich, 29 March 1941

Today I had to say farewell to friends with whom I have been together for the last five years. Bertl Westmaier goes to work in an office as an accountant. Baerbel Luyken, who is very close to me, moves the farthest away. She will study on scholarship for a year in the Rhine province so that after her studies she can take over her father's business. She is excited at the prospect and sees a clear future. I also had to separate from Petra. She has been given leave of absence for the entire next trimester to go to Vienna for rehabilitation. May the treatment finally help so she can use both of her hands again. So for the next trimester I will be alone. Lore Bartel and Isolde will see me through. I am very thankful to them for that. Japanese Foreign Minister Matsuoka begins his trip to Rome.

Munich, 1 April 1941

The rioting in Yugoslavia against anything German is on the rise. Roosevelt provokes the situation by sending a congratulatory letter to the now King Peter. As the most outstanding soldier of the regular Army, Private Brinkforth receives the Knight's Cross. Brinkforth is the son of a miner in the Rhineland. He taught himself the craft of baking.

Munich, 4 April 1941

Hungary's Prime Minister Teleki died. Bardossy is now trusted with the office of Prime Minister. The *Führer* welcomes Foreign Minister Matsuoka during his second visit in Berlin. Today I took over a group of ten year olds who will become members of our group on April 20th. To lead them and to make of them *Jungmädeln* is the best job of all. I am glad and happy that I got this job. Today, with palpitating hearts, we awaited the BDM doctor who would be giving us the GD [*Gesundheitsdienst*, Health Service] test. But we quickly developed some confidence in ourselves and everything went well. Even those of us who are considered problematic passed. A load fell off our shoulders when we had our report cards in hand.

Munich, 6 April 1941
After Yugoslavia's Armed Forces achieved the status of "Extreme Readiness" and had been greeted by London as allies, the German Armed Forces moved to protect the interests of the Reich in southeast Europe. German troops crossed the Yugoslavian and Greek borders. Fort Belgrade was bombarded three times.

Munich, 13 April 1941
For a week now there has been fighting in the southeast with great success for the German and Italian troops. Saloniki, Nisch, Ueskueb, Marburg and Belgrade fell. Croatia is declared an independent state. Hungary also marches against Yugoslavia.

Munich, 18 April 1941
Germany and Italy acknowledge Croatia as an independent state. In the occupied areas of Untersteiermark, Kaernten and the Krim, chiefs for civil administration are installed. The entire Yugoslavian Army laid down its arms in surrender. The Reich's war flag waves over Olympia.

Munich, 20 April 1941
It is the *Führer*'s birthday. The thoughts of the German people rush to him in his headquarters. Dr. Goebbels speaks from the heart when he says, "Love and admiration for him inspire our struggle and our efforts toward victory."

Munich, 24 April 1941
The Epirus and Macedonian Army of Greece surrendered unconditionally. The widely expanded Thermopylae Pass was captured. The submarines of *Korevettenkäpitan* Kretschmer and *Käpitanleutnant* Schepke did not return from enemy raids. Kretschmer has been captured.

Munich, 26 April 1941
The *Führer* pays a visit to liberated Marburg. The *Führer* drove through the city while being cheered on by the liberated people of Untersteiermark.

Munich, 27 April 1941
Athens is under German rule. Paratroopers took the Isthmus of Corinth. Then the 94th unit of Hitler's Bodyguard forced its way across the Gulf of Patras and penetrated into the Peloponnese. The *Führer* visits Klagenfurt.

Munich, 1 May 1941
Amann, Ohnesorge and Messerschmitt were honored as Pioneers of Work.

Munich, 4 May 1941
Reichstag session. The *Führer* settles with Churchill. He lays out the results of the Balkans expedition. He tells of the enemies' losses. German losses are very small.

Munich, 17 May 1941
Croatia offers the crown to a Savoy Prince.

Munich, 22 May 1941
There was no school this morning: Martha Middendorf, our Obergau leader, got married today. We were the guard of honor in the alleys all the way to the culture ministry conference room. Region Leader Adolf Wagner awaited the young bride and her groom, Area Leader Thorn Staekel. The radio broadcast band and actors gave the wedding a festive setting.

Munich, 26 May 1941
Guenther Prien did not return from an enemy attack made on May 23rd. We are out of school for 14 days since a scarlet fever epidemic makes school functioning impossible. We said to

ourselves, "We will register for factory service." Everyone was so excited about this plan. Irmi Ostermann put our names on the list and made sure that we filled in every line on the applications.

Munich, 27 May 1941
At exactly 6:30 a.m. we stood confidently in front of the factory doors. After a few mix-ups at the beginning, we were sincerely welcomed by the factory leaders. Next we were walked through the entire factory. Some decided to work in the confectioner's shop and the bakery. They have to be at work by 5:00 a.m. Others were placed in the warehouse, dispatch, sausage and produce departments. Along with some other comrades, I got into the lemonade department. We put on long rubber aprons and wooden shoes. From this moment on, we learned what it means to stand at one machine all day long and to always make the same hand movement. My first job was to close the bottles. One had to be fast because the next machine was already waiting. Slap by slap she pasted the labels on the bottles. Then I relieved the worker from her machine. Now I had to bend down, get the bottle, place it into the machine, take the finished ones out and put them in the carry baskets. Always fast, fast. Soon my back was hurting from the unfamiliar stooping, but I had to keep going fast. The machine does not stop. The women workers joked with us so that time would not go by quite as slowly. Practice makes perfect, we told ourselves, and sure enough, that thought made it go much better. A half hour for lunch and then we continued working. The others did not envy us in our cellar, but everywhere the young girl leaders and co-workers made friends. They were so happy that there were people to relieve them from their work, which gave them a paid holiday, and who did not even expect a thank you for it. An acknowledging look, the hand shake as the workers departed, was enough thanks for us. By the time we finished the job in late afternoon, we had taken over 6,000

bottles of lemonade to the warehouse. Washing, rinsing, filling and closing of 6,000 bottles in nine hours. I was wiped out, but we all told ourselves that the feeling of satisfaction we gained at having made it through was worth everything. When I got home, there was a huge surprise. Liselotte's mother was there to pick up her child. She could not handle the separation any longer. And so our little guest, who had caused such commotion in our house but, still, had won us over, departed. After a long enemy battle, the German battleship *Bismarck* sank. On May 24th it had sunk the British battleship *Hood*.

Munich, 28 May 1941

I just got home. Now I am sitting in my comfortable room rethinking the day. The bandages on my fingers are making it hard to write, but I can do it. We found the lemonade department closed when we entered the factory at 7:00 a.m. today. Our work leader told us that today we would go to the bottle rinsing department. He sent us to the department's manager. She was happy to get the help. First we sorted out the wine bottles and brought them to the shed. Then a worker entrusted me with her machine and I learned the operation of bottle rinsing. The older worker watched and smiled at my first attempts. But soon I had figured out the manipulation. Happily we worked together. The dirty bottles lay in huge containers of hot water. "Ouch," I yelled. Immediately they all came to my side. "That happens fairly often. Let me bandage you up," my co-worker Mrs. Huber comforted me. Soon I could not stretch my hands anymore. But the dirty water could not penetrate through the bandages. The others watched me curiously as they sorted the bottles. I soon learned to like my job. It was so nice and quiet; only the machine went tack-tack. When the clock pointed at 4:30 p.m., though, I did let out a sigh of relief. Quickly I took off the heavy wooden shoes and the rubber apron. Outside the sun was shining so nice and warm and we hadn't noticed any of it in the cellar.

Munich, 31 May 1941
Today is Saturday. At 11:30 a.m. we were already done with our work. One day goes by like any other. One time lemonade, one time dishwashing. We learned to appreciate real work and know now what it means to do the same motion day after day. How hard it is for people to earn their living. Therefore, we are happy that we can relieve 40 workers and mothers. Especially during their children's vacations, they are doubly appreciative. We have to pull ourselves together in order to fully and completely do the job of skilled workers.

Munich, 2 June 1941
The *Führer* and the *Duce* meet on the Brenner. Crete is free from the enemy. This island was conquered through fierce fighting of our paratroopers against England. Tomorrow my job at the factory begins again.

Munich, 6 June 1941
Our labor will end soon. Tomorrow we will stand at our machines for the last time. Today we experienced special joy. Anneliese Steinert, our Region Leader, and Irmi Ostermann visited us. They conversed with each one of us. They allowed us to show them our work and spoke with our co-workers. Afterward, they were as thrilled with her as we always are. Coincidentally, I was working with a co-worker at the dishwasher when our press photographer came and took our picture. Perhaps something will come of it. The factory organized a farewell get-together with coffee and cake after work. The business manager thanked us for our work and told us that he had not thought we could do it. That we succeeded filled us with pride. Of what importance was our work compared to that of the soldiers? Croatian State Leader Pavelisch is with the *Führer*.

Munich, 7 June 1941

Today was our last work day. We cleaned the floors, containers and the machines until they were bright and shining. But soon all this was finished. For the last time, we took off our wooden shoes and pulled off our rubber aprons. Before that, Hilde Dziwers surprised us with her visit. She was our first Obergau Leader and she will forever have ties with us. Sincerely we said farewell to the workers.

Munich, 9 June 1941

School began again today. In the evening, the theater group staged the play *The Bartered Bride* in the State Theater. First rate casting made this play a wonderful experience.

Munich, 14 June 1941

Today nothing could hold us in school. Soon we got permission to go. We had to go to the welcome of General Antonescu. The *Führer* welcomed the Rumanian Chief of State in the *Führerbau*.

Munich, 15 June 1941

Reich Foreign Minister von Ribbentrop traveled yesterday to a meeting in Venice. In Venice, Croatia joined the Tripartite Pact.

Munich, 21 June 1941

A friendship pact was reached between Germans and the Turks in Ankara on June 18. For his great accomplishments, Lieutenant Colonel Adolf Galland was awarded the *Eichenlaub mit Schwertern zum Ritterkreuz des Eisernen Kreuzes*.

Munich, 22 June 1941

Greater Germany's Armed Forces move against the Soviet Union in the East. Moscow admits to conspiracy with London. Even Italy enters into the war against the Bolshevists. General Antonescu calls on the Romanians to fight. A letter from the Foreign Office proves the planned treason of the Soviet Union against the German Reich. The *Führer* issues a command to the Armed Forces and a proclamation to the German people.

Munich, 30 June 1941
Even Finland defends itself against the Bolshevists' attack. Lemberg and Libau were taken. To date over 4,100 aircraft and 2,200 tanks have been destroyed. Theater group: *Maria Stuart*. The presentation of the title role by Angela Saloker was riveting and will not let us forget this play. She found a worthy opponent in Anna Kersten. Great applause and beautiful flowers thanked the two actresses for their performances which brought us completely into Schiller's world.

Munich, 7 July 1941
Capture of Riga and Wintau. The Dnieper River was reached east of Minsk. Kolomea and Stanislaos taken. The German-Romanian attack in Bessarabia begins. Chernowitz taken.

Munich, 10 July 1941
The double battle for Bialystok and Minsk locked in. On the Finish Front, Salla taken. *Eichenlaub* honoree Captain Balthasar found a hero's death at the Channel. Witebsk taken. The Stalin Line broken through in all decisive positions.

Munich, 13 July 1941
Roosevelt gives the American fleet orders to fire.

Munich, 16 July 1941
Today was the last school day. Saying goodbye was not so easy this time. After vacation our classmates, who have come to know each other so well, will not come together again. Some have opted for the academic route while others have chosen the path to homemaking. Lieutenant Colonel Werner Moelders attained his 101st air strike victory. Counting the 14 air strike victories over Spain, he is at 115. He is the best and keenest air

pilot in the world. The *Führer* awards him the newly established and highest German medal for bravery: *Eichenlaub mit Schwerten und Brillianten* [Oak Leaves with Swords and Diamonds]. All the people share in his victory. He still is the modest and always funny comrade. He is loved and honored by his squadron, as well as by all of the German people.

Munich, 17 July 1941
Today we go again to Waging.

Waging, 19 July 1941
We have already, for the last two days, been in our quiet Waging. But it is not as quiet as it was the last time we were here. The place is now densely occupied by northern Germans. Most are women from the dangerous areas who, with their children, need rest in order to recover. Smolensk taken.

Waging, 9 August 1941
We have finished three great encirclements: of Smolensk, Uman in the Ukraine, and Roslavl. The losses of the enemies were huge: over 450,000 prisoners taken, 3,750 tanks destroyed and 4,900 guns captured or destroyed.

Waging, 20 August 1941
Time flashes by. Every day brings special messages of our victories in the East. The administration of the Lemberg areas has been subordinated to the general government. Nikolajew, Nowgoroth and Narva were taken. The battle near Gommel has come to an end. The enemy had huge losses there as well.

Waging, 28 August 1941
The *Duce* has been at the East Front since August 25th, where he is having discussions with the *Führer* and staff Generals. He is disgusted with the poverty and misery in this eastern area. Tomorrow we will go home again. We would have stayed longer but the weather has been rainy and cold for weeks. I

really long to be home, where I have my work and where I can pursue my hobbies.

Munich, 29 August 1941

Tonight we arrived back in our Munich. The trip went fairly well. The weather was also pleasant. The apartment seems so strange to us. But this feeling will soon go away. Over the radio we hear that *Eichenlaub* honoree Captain Joppien died. He did not return after his 70th air battle victory. Who does not know his always cheerful face. His father is a miner in the Ruhr.

Munich, 1 September 1941

Two years of war. What have they brought us? The Polish battle of 18 days; Norway and Denmark; the invasion of Holland, Belgium and France; defeat of the enemy in Yugoslavia and Greece and now the campaign for destruction of the Bolshevists. A unique triumphal march of the German Armed Forces. What will the third year of war bring us?

Munich, 8 September 1941

The most important strategic point at Ladoga Lake was conquered. Leningrad is locked out from all land connections. The British air raid on Berlin broke down under German defense. Twenty British planes were shot down.

Munich, 15 September 1941

Today a state ceremony was held to honor *Generaloberst* Ritter von Schobert who died in the southern sector of the East Front on September 12th. A mine, over which he drove his aircraft, ended his life and that of his adjutant. During the same hour as the memorial in Munich, his body was being buried in the East.

Munich, 16 September 1941

After another extension of the vacation period, school started today. Those of us who had chosen the academic route were united into one class. After some evident confusion we did not get Professor Basserman. Instead we have Professor Joseph Zweckstaetter as class teacher. There are several new teachers. Latin and chemistry have been added as new courses. Sadly, I am now separated from Petra, Erika Mueller and Lore Bartel. Inge Rahn is now in my class again. We have known each other since first grade. I am glad that she is here because she is a great classmate.

Munich, 21 September 1941
Kiev is now taken over, as well as Poltona. Oesel Island has been completely occupied. The British try again and again to penetrate into the Reich. They have lost 78 aircraft in the last few days.

Munich, 27 September 1941
Region Roll Call at Circus Krone. A main party leader gives an accountability report. After that, Region Leader Wagner speaks. He gives the mandates for the coming year. After formations in an impressive rally, Gerhild Nibitsch, the new Main Group Leader from the North, was introduced. We are very saddened that Irmi Osterman gave up her leadership position. She had worked and lived together with us so well.

Munich, 30 September 1941
This afternoon Irmi Ostermann trained Gerhild Nibitsch in her job. Even Irmi, herself, finds it hard to leave our group, but we have one consolation, West is not far from North. Even with Gerhild we will work hard so we can claim our place as the best group. But today we had something else planned. It is Region Leader Wagner's birthday. We marched along Prinzregenten Street and Schaefel Street to Kaulbach Street. We sang our best songs. Smiling gratefully, he walked the length of our rows as we stood in review. The march through Munich,

as the day waned, was wonderful. The silhouette of the Feldherrnhalle seemed black against the reddish evening sky. This march strengthened all of us for the coming work and intensified our sense of community. In the Hofgarten we sang together the song "Good Night Comrades" before we parted. Thus, a beautiful afternoon came to its close.

Munich, 3 October 1941
The *Führer* opens the KWHW [*Kriegswinterhilfswerk*, War Winter Relief Work] in the Sportpalast in Berlin. The KWHW 1940-1941 brought in 916,214,000 Mark.

Munich, 5 October 1941
As of today our 10 year old girls become real *Jungmädel*. They are now allowed to wear a knotted neckerchief. This makes them very proud. They are even more excited over the coming jobs because now they count just as much as the older girls. After the initiation ceremony in the Student House we saw the movie *The Path to the Führer*.

Munich, 12 October 1941
At the Luitpold Cinema Theater opening of the winter movie season for youth, we saw the recipient of the first Film of the Nation award, *Ohm Krüger,* with Emil Jannings in the title role. Romanian troops marched into Odessa.

Munich, 21 October 1941
During the night there was an air raid alarm. The Baltic area is completely free of the enemy now that Dagoe Island has been occupied.

Munich, 24 October 1941
Charkov is in German hands. Access to the Krim peninsula has been achieved.

Munich, 8 November 1941

It is now 12:30 in the morning. They just gave an all-clear and we are celebrating my 16th birthday. Books, cards, a tile picture and flowers were the nice gifts. Today is the day I have my first dance lesson, but I can only write about that later. Petra was there the entire afternoon. The first dance lesson at Valenci's was nice and entertaining. We felt like recruits who are just learning to walk. The time went by much too fast and we cannot wait until our next lesson. In the evening the *Führer* spoke to his Old Guard at the Loewenbraeukeller in Munich. He observed that, for the first time, Europe fights unanimously united in joint recognition that the world enemy is Bolshevism.

Munich, 9 November 1941

Today I had to be at the Theresienhof at 8:30 a.m. Inge Rahn and I were promoted and confirmed as group leaders. In an unforgettable ceremony, 93 leaders, we two among them, received our green strings. Then, at the Koenigsplatz, came the annual demonstration honoring the victims of 9 November 1923.

Munich, 17 November 1941

Alfred Rosenberg was named *Reichsminister* of the occupied eastern areas. The harbor town Kertsch on the Krim was taken. The German people suffered a hard blow when they were told of the death of *Generaloberst* Ernst Udet. While testing a new weapon his plane went down in flames. The great World War pilot and Chief of Aircraft Procurement and Supply of the new, young Air Force met a hero's death. The *Führer* ordered a state funeral. In Udet's honor the Third squadron will now bear his name.

Munich, 22 November 1941

With the *Führer* present, a state funeral for *Generaloberst* Udet was held. *Reichsmarschall* Goering spoke in clear words of the life and death of this man who was his friend. In the Invaliden Cemetery he finds his final resting place next to his comrade Manfred von Richthofen. We barely recovered from the death of Udet when we all got a second terrible blow. Colonel Werner Moelders died during a flight in a plane that he was not piloting himself. Werner Moelders, the youngest Colonel in the entire German Armed Forces, the only bearer of the

greatest Medal of Bravery, should no longer be with us? The undefeated hero of 115 air battles! It is inconceivable. The best fighter pilot in the world and the best comrade to all his subordinates is gone. The *Führer* ordered a state funeral. His squadron, that he led from victory to victory, will now carry on his name. Our friendly nations share our pain, especially Spain where he was the best fighter pilot of the Legion Condor in the Spanish Civil War.

Munich, 27 November 1941

During a state ceremony in the Reich Chancellery, the Anti-Comintern Pact was extended for another five years. Bulgaria, China, Denmark, Finland, Croatia, Romania and Slovakia all join this pact. In a special audience, the *Führer* receives the statesmen of the countries that had just joined the Anti-Comintern Pact, after which they returned to their own countries. Dr. Rainer was named Region Leader in Kaernten and Dr. Schall, Region Leader of Salzburg.

Munich, 28 November 1941
Representatives of both the foreign and interior ministries stood with the *Führer* at the state ceremony for Werner Moelders. *Reichsmarschall* Goering expressed sorrow for the tragic loss of this German hero, its best fighter pilot, who so tragically lost his life. The entire country mourns his death along with his mother, siblings and young wife. Thousands of Berliners lined the streets on which the funeral procession was parading to the Invaliden Cemetery. In this cemetery which has taken in so many German soldiers, Werner Moelders will now find his resting place. He lies embedded next to Manfred von Richthofen and *Generaloberst* Udet.

Possessions die, clans die, you die even as they.
But one thing I know that lives forever, the
praiseworthy deeds of the dead.

Munich, 5 December 1941
Hungarian Prime Minister von Bardossy announces that England has declared war against Hungary. On the same day England declared war on Finland and Romania.

Munich, 8 December 1941
Japanese Headquarters announces — on the same day as the naval battle in Hawaii — that they are at war against England and the USA. Japanese troops land in the Philippines and begin their attack against Singapore on the Malayan Peninsula. The battleships *Prince of Wales* and *Repulse* were sunk off the east Malayan coast by Japanese navy pilots.

Munich, 11 December 1941
Führer speech in the German *Reichstag* [Parliament]. The *Führer* announces that Germany is at war with the United States. He made known that the total number of imprisoned Bolshevists as of December 1st is 3,806,865; the number of captured or destroyed tanks is 21,931; of guns and cannons 32,541; and

aircraft 17,322. From 22 June 22nd to December 1st in this heroic war, the German Armed Forces has lost 162,314 dead, 571,767 injured and 33,334 missing. The *Duce* announced at the Piazza Venezia in Rome that Italy is also on the side of the Germans and that Japan has entered with them into the war against the USA.

Munich, 14 December 1941
Bulgaria, Croatia, Slovakia, Romania and Hungary proclaimed a state of war with the USA. Having taken this step Bulgaria, Croatia and Slovakia also proclaimed their entrance into the war against England. This afternoon was our concert in the Odeon Concert Hall. The whole house was sold out. We all had put forth a lot of effort preparing for this occasion. In the first part, we performed songs from the *Creation* [by Haydn]. We received great applause, but the acknowledging smile from "Brummer" was worth even more to us. Songs, orchestra compositions and solo performances were mixed in a colorful presentation. All listeners were in awe when we sang "The heavens declare the glory of God" [*Ehre Gottes aus der Natur*, Beethoven] accompanied by wind instruments of the State Opera. Dr. Brunner took many curtain calls and bouquets were abundant.

Munich, 18 December 1941
The Navy Department of the Imperial Japanese Headquarters announces the results of the huge sea battle near Hawaii: Five USA battleships and two heavy cruisers were sunk. Three battleships were so damaged that repairs were impossible and another battleship was seriously damaged. American airplane losses were set at 450.

Munich, 21 December 1941
The *Führer* himself now takes over sole High Command of the Armed Forces and of the SS. Field Marshal von Witzleben

resigned from his post for health reasons. The *Führer* issued a proclamation to the soldiers of his Army and the SS.

Munich, 22 December 1941

A German submarine commanded by *Kapitänleutnant* Byalik, sank an English aircraft carrier in the Atlantic.

Munich, 24 December 1941

Christmas. Today we are celebrating the third wartime Christmas. It must be as quiet in many homes as it is here in ours. Our thoughts are often at the East Front which changed from a war of aggression to a defensive war. It is now bitter cold there and the soldiers are making great sacrifices. When we think of them, we do not notice that the gift table is not as full as it was during peacetime or over the last two years of war. Today, nonetheless, the flickering of the Christmas candles fills us with joy. We feel like we are children again. The blue candle on the tree is for the Germans living abroad; above all, for our soldiers in the distant fronts East, West and South; also for those at the North Pole. Manny received a savings account book with something in it instead of presents that cannot be acquired right now. My deepest wish was granted. I received an album with pictures of those to whom the *Eichenlaub* has been awarded, honored Region leaders and pictures of the invasion into France. An embroidered Dirndl apron, a nice letter opener, books, a candleholder and sweets made me happy as well. *Vati* got a shirt, neckties and cigarettes. *Mutti* was happy with a picture painted by *Vati*, a porcelain snake charmer and books that were written in the language of her childhood homeland [Belgium]. Then I disappeared into my room where even today, in spite of current conditions, there is a small Christmas tree, and I lit the candles. Manny treasures the briefcase that I finished up for him because he can make good use of it. *Mutti* complained that I had made too much work for myself with the old German stitching on the cushion cover; nonetheless, she liked it very much. She was thrilled over the plywood cutout of a couple wearing traditional dress. Too bad I could not have gotten more of them. Manny gave her flowers, after his hand-made gift did not work out. I think now about the many Munich children who are all holding a gift in their hands, which we *Jungmädel* [Young Girls, aged 10-14] and *Pimpfe* [Wolf Cubs, boys aged 6-10] put together during evening group meetings. Those were exciting weeks for us. It became a real competition. Our group put together one train after another, in addition to crafting toy cradles and kitchens. What pushing and shoving in our workshop, but there was even more in the Christmas market where we sold them. Anything a child's heart might want, a mother could buy from us and the proceeds would go to the WHW [Winter Relief]. We were so proud when the radio announced during the news: "Obergau Hochland has displayed wonderful hand crafted work in the Munich Christmas market. This alleviated the shortage of toys and, in addition, enabled the contribution of over 50,000 Mark [money] to the WHW." But the happiness of our children is our best reward. "It is better to give than to receive."

Munich, 26 December 1941
A German cruiser was sunk in the Spanish territorial waters by a British bomber, which then opened fire on the rescue boats. Again, a cowardly attack against the defenseless.

Munich, 29 December 1941
Today I got a big surprise. After relentless ringing of the doorbell, I opened the front door. Who should be standing there but Baerbel Luyken! Big, strong and tanned. She has grown up and is no longer the thin young girl from our school days. She likes her job. Radiantly, she announced that she is getting closer and closer to her goal of becoming master of her own property. We enjoyed a pleasant hour of catching up.

Yesterday the English attempted a surprise attack on Norway, but the attempt was unsuccessful; a destroyer was sunk. On the East Front many Soviet attacks were repulsed.

Munich, 31 December 1941
New Year's Eve 1941. I reflect on this past year. Rich in victories and in wars. In the spring the war on the Balkans. Crete fell. In North Africa we re-conquered the area. Then the big decisive battle in the East. England's naval power was severely diminished. Since December 8th we are at war with the United States. Difficult struggles and huge sacrifices are borne by the German people. Many of our best will not see the turning of the year. Guenther Prien and Scheppke did not return. Kretschmer became a prisoner of war. *Generaloberst* Udet and Werner Moelders died fulfilling their military duties. Over and above all of the sacrifices stands the will to victory. May the coming year at war bring us final victory! It will not fall in our laps. We will have to work, but one day the bells of peace will ring.

> For those who want to live nowadays,
> A brave heart they must have.

1942

**We stand behind our soldiers,
as they protect us.**

Adolf Hitler

Munich, 2 January 1942
Manila, the capital of the Philippines, was taken by the Japanese.

Munich, 5 January 1942
The collection of wool has now ended. Over 67 million fur or wool items were donated. Also 1 million skis. The Homeland responded to the needs at the Front quickly and effectively. Day after day we labored in our sewing rooms working on many beautiful things, which only needed a few repairs. Hundreds of snow shirts, snow hats and backpack covers were sewn. Our work group is one of the best.

Munich, 17 January 1942
Generalfeldmarschall von Reichenau died unexpectantly. Today we were in the Volkstheater: *The Lost Heart*. It was only a fairytale but with the great performance of the actors we enjoyed it immensely.

Munich, 23 January 1942
Coal vacation [due to shortage of coal]. For the time being we go to school only Monday, Wednesday and Friday for four hours each day in the afternoon.

Munich, 28 January 1942
The *Führer* honored Colonel Gallant as the second officer to receive the *Eichenlaub mit Schwertern und Brillianten.* Colonel Gallant, successor to Moelders, is named inspector of the paratroopers.

Munich, 29 January 1942
On the 28th of January, Sollum, after heroic resistance, surrendered. Yasi was occupied by German-Italian troops.

Munich, 30 January 1942
On occasion of the ninth anniversary of the seizure of power, the *Führer* gave an exciting speech in the Sportpalast.

Munich, 5 February 1942
Reichsmarschall Hermann Goering returned from his trip to Italy where he had been welcomed by the King and Kaiser and by the *Duce.* Today we visited the exhibition "From Musketeer to Field Marshal." *Reichsminister* Todt had a fatal accident. In a state funeral the *Führer* eulogized at length Dr. Todt's accomplishments. The *Führer* honored him, posthumously, as the first recipient of a medal newly established to be the highest order which can be bestowed by the German people. Professor Albert Speer was named his successor.

Munich, 15 February 1942
Singapore taken by the Japanese. The youth film hour: *Enemies,* a movie about the struggle of the German people before 1 September 1939. The war brought them liberty.

Munich, 23 February 1942
The theater series presented *The Funny Vagabonds.* The performance of the actors made good a play we otherwise did not like. Pity, that the main actor suddenly became ill and someone else took over his role.

Munich, 24 February 1942
Bolshevist assassination attempt against Ambassador von Papen in Ankara.

Munich, 10 March 1942
Group competition. Everything came together perfectly. The gymnastics, singing and the drills were good. Hilde was certainly pleased by the handicrafts. The highlight was our original fairytale creation, performed without a hitch. Like all of the other groups, we really worked hard to present something which would mark us as the best. Cross your fingers and hope.

Munich, 15 March 1942
Führer speech for Memorial Day.

Munich, 18 March 1942
Theater series: We saw Schiller's first drama, *The Robbers*. Today, as ever, people were elated by the story. The closer we got to the end, the more exhilarated we became. We saw Reich Consultant Ruediger amongst the guests of honor.

Munich, 19 March 1942
The Obergau transfer. Transfer of leadership of the Obergau [name of the Region] took place today in the presence of Reich Youth Leader Arthur Amman and Region Leader Adolf Wagner. Martha Stoeckel transferred her Region in order to be able to dedicate herself to homemaker duties. Among the guests, also, was Area Leader Stoekl. We are all sorry that Martha is leaving because she was always a good leader for us and had captured our hearts. This is not a reason for us to close our hearts and minds to the new Obergau Leader, Edith Ludwig. The Reich Youth Leader said in his speech that she comes from the Westmark and that she is very competent. He bestowed the Hitler Youth Gold Medal on Martha, who had

been especially influential during the development of the BDM [*Bund deutscher Mädel*, League of German Girls] organization. The Region Leader found fond words of farewell for Martha and greetings of welcome to the new Region for Edith Ludwig.

Munich, 22 March 1942
The commitment of the youth took place at Circus Krone and in the Hofbraeuhaus this morning. Most of them are entering the job market and are now pledged to the *Führer*. In the afternoon we performed the second concert for the KWHW [War Winter Relief]. This time, also, it was a great success. Enthusiastically we sang our songs. Dr. Brunner got great applause.

Munich, 31 March 1942
Lieutenant Captain Engelbert Endruss, bearer of the *Eichenlaub zum Ritterkreuz*, did not return from his last deployment. An excellent submarine commander, he stayed with his brave men and fell at the hands of the enemy.

Munich, 1 April 1942
Another trimester has ended. Last Saturday the school said farewell to the graduating class. After the "March and Choir of the Priests" from *The Magic Flute,* a graduate expressed her thanks to the teachers and parents for providing her with the opportunity for such a great education. After working for the war effort, these graduates will enter into careers. Then we sang "Arioso" by Handel, the song requested by the graduates. Still two more years for us, we thought, and then it will be the hour when others will sing that song for us. But this nostalgic thought is fleeting; sadness does not stay with us. We passed the time by telling jokes. What luck, we all thought, when someone from the fifth grade invited us to a theater play! They performed *A Broken Jug* by Kleist. Adam, the self-important village judge often provoked us to laughter. The clerk

performed his difficult role very well. The court counselor, the two maidens, the lady-farmer and her daughter Eva, Eva's fiancé and his cousin all performed well. They played their parts with authenticity. Great applause was earned by the young actresses.

Munich, 16 April 1942
Today was the beginning of the school year. It brought some changes in school hours, curriculum and faculty. We are feeling the war, especially since only the older teachers and the female teachers are providing the instruction. They also have to teach in other schools. I am excited about tonight. The Hitler Youth theater series will present *Protection*.

Munich, 17 April 1942
Yesterday I saw *Protection* by Gustaf Davis. That we were all excited about this comedy was evident by the ever increasing applause. Especially Wustel Witt with his Bavarian idioms brought us to tearful laughter. He was even presented a beautiful bouquet of flowers by one of the Hitler Youth. I had to pass on my group of 10 year olds, who had always brought me so much happiness. I now lead a group of 14 year olds and we are starting now to craft children's toys for Christmas. We have to work ever harder to make sure that the toy-sellers' booths will be fully stocked.

Munich, 19 April 1942
Every year we enroll the 10 year olds on the day before the *Führer*'s birthday. Last year I became their leader. This year Hannelore Schmitt took over their leadership. Parents and teachers of the boys and girls were together in the festively decorated hall. After the introduction through a handshake, the boys and girls were initiated. The song for the youth and those for the nation finished the commitment ceremonials. Thereafter, we leaders went to the Feldherrnhalle to be part of

the big festivity. All National Socialist Party formations and groups of the Armed Forces and *Waffen* [weaponized, arms-bearing] *SS* [*Schutzstaffel*; Security Police, Blackshirts] were assembled. We merged ourselves with the *Jungmädel* and managed to find good places. After the entry of the flags, Ritter von Ebb and Ludwig Siebert spoke from their hearts when they said: "God save our *Führer* for a long time yet to come." He is the one we have, above all, who unites all the peoples' strength within himself. He is our model and guide. In the evening, the Party arranged festivities in Berlin for the *Führer's* birthday, of which the most important part was Dr. Goebbel's speech. In a touching way he made himself the interpreter for all Germans within and outside of Greater Germany. He found words that touched our hearts, ending with: "With gratitude and loyalty we send the *Führer* our greetings." Like an unbreakable bond, Homeland and Front feel intertwined in these hours. On the eve of his birthday all Germans in the world unite as one in the fervent wish, confirmed anew, that "He will always be for us what he has been and is: Our Hitler."

Munich, 20 April 1942
Today all Germans celebrate the *Führer's* birthday. All homes are richly decorated with flag themed bunting. At school we were assembled in the auditorium to hear a birthday radio transmission from Braunau. After that the classes observed a memorial hour, while two students went to the school court yard for the raising of the flag. After the primary school principal's speech and the national anthem, we sang other national songs.

Munich, 25 April 1942
I just wrote to Colonel General Rommel and asked him for his autograph. I hope to receive an answer soon.

Munich, 26 April 1942
The *Führer* addressed Parliament [the *Reichstag*].

Munich, 28 April 1942
Ring Roll Call: Our Untergau Leader Gerhild Ribitsch informed us that we are the best group of the JM unit. This filled us all with great joy. It is the best reward for our work. But now we cannot rest on our laurels; rather, we must now show that we always, in every sphere, do our duty.

Munich, 29 April 1942
Meeting of the *Führer* and the *Duce* in Salzburg.

Munich, 1 May 1942
On this National Holiday, Volkswagen designer, Prof. Dr. Porsche; airplane designer, Prof. Heinkel; and Reich Minister of Economic Affairs Walther Funk, who also served as Reich Bank President, were honored as "Pioneers of Labor."

Munich, 2 May 1942
I have just returned home, very tired. But it was still a nice day. This morning at 9:00 we presented ourselves at Schoenwaertheim, rehearsed our songs again and then marched to the reserve clinic in the Schwabing Hospital. Here the nurse sergeant welcomed us and we went to the ward. At first only a few soldiers came. The nurse opened the door for the bedridden. At first they were very shy, but when we asked them to join us in singing they did so joyfully. At the end, every soldier got a bouquet of flowers. We did this from ward to ward. In the meantime word had gotten around and everyone everywhere was expecting us. Even though there was a snow storm outside, we brought a bit of spring into the quiet rooms. When we left the hospital we marched to the North Cemetery. There we met up with other *Jungmädel*, who envied us. At the Alten Heide they were already waiting for

us. The children ran towards us and joined us in singing the springtime songs. Even then our day's work was not over. Another military hospital still had to be visited. At 2:00 p.m. we arrived at the Antonien Hospital. Here, also, we ushered spring in with our songs and flowers and brought the soldiers a bit of joy. In the end, that is what it's all about.

Munich, 10 May 1942
Weekend lecture. In the movie theater Surla we had our weekend lecture. At the beginning, Erika Baumholz gave the lecture about Frederick the Great, who reminds us of the *Führer* in many ways. Then we learned the obligatory songs of the month. Organizational matters and our upcoming assignments were discussed. Then we marched to the student building. The regional leader and Anneliese Mueller spoke to us. Anneliese gave the final report of the past winter and announced the new directives. Regional Leader Lederer thanked us for our accomplishments. He also gave us directives for the summer tasks. This summer at war will not be easy but so far we have always managed. What we do contributes only a small fraction towards victory but these are things that have to be done and we are happy to be useful.

Munich, 15 May 1942
Region Leader Karl Roever, of Region Weser-Ems, has died. The *Führer* appointed the acting Region Leader of Region Mark Brandenburg, Paul Wegener, as his successor.

Munich, 16 May 1942
City and harbor of Kartsch in German hands. Mothers Day singing. In honor of Mothers Day, we sang this afternoon at a women's clinic. Our songs were presented very softly as we were not permitted to be loud. We brought flowers to the young mothers, who were very happy to have us visit. The babies had been brought to their mothers by nurses. When we

sang the song "When a mother rocks her baby," all were very quiet and dreamily smiled at their children. We continued all through the silent house. In one ward our songs awakened the smallest infants who lay in their bright beds. Which leader would not have enjoyed doing this? We brought pleasure to these mothers with our flowers and songs.

> Lay down your heroes of stone,
> Build a tomb for every one,
> None [of them] forget their mothers,
> They who died a hundred times.
> [Hans Baumann, the Hitler Youth poet]

Munich, 17 May 1942

Mothers Day. This morning we honored the mothers of our group. We *Jungmädel* called for and escorted the mothers who were going to receive the Cross of Honor. How elated they were. The hall was decorated festively with flowers and garlands. After a few orchestra pieces and a poem written and recited by Karl Steinacker, we sang the song "Now Spring will greet us." After the speech of the regional group leader, the mothers received the Cross of Honor, along with a certificate of authenticity. The Women's Society gave them beautiful bouquets of tulips. The orchestra, a singer and a short play added festive touches to the celebration.

> Mothers, you are all the fire;
> you set all the stars in the sky.
> [Hans Baumann]

Munich, 27 May 1942

In Prague, an assassination attempt was made on Reinhard Heydrich, who was both Chief of the SS [Security Police] and Deputy Chief of the Gestapo. He was severely wounded.

Munich, 30 May 1942

Today the Sport Festival took place. Our *Jungmädel* had trained and looked forward to it for a long time. Their goal was to win medals. The results were good; Petrus [folkloric deity of weather] did not put a damper on it. Once a year we go public with our sports and thereby fulfill our *Führer*'s wish.

Munich, 4 June 1942
The *Führer* delivers to Marshal Mannerheim, Commander-in-Chief of Finland, best wishes from the German civilians and the military on the occasion of his 75th birthday.

Munich, 9 June 1942
State ceremony in the new Reich Chancellery for *SS Obergruppenführer* Heydrich, who died on June 4th. After a eulogizing speech from *Reichsführer SS* Himmler, the *Führer* bestowed on the deceased Deputy Chief of the Security Police the ultimate distinction by making him the second German ever to receive the highest ranking German medal. We are now the best group in the northern association. Full of pride we review our accomplishments. Today, after we were judged by Gerhild Ribbich and Hilde Bechtel, *Mädel* Leader Karla May came. She looked at our handicrafts, listened to our songs and taught us some new things. I think we did not do too badly.

Munich, 15 June 1942
A lecture evening in the German Museum. A co-worker in the Innsbruck National Costumes Information Center gave us leaders a lecture about the correct way to wear the Dirndl, or national costume. We were eager to hear because we finally learned the meaning of wearing of the national costumes. Also, we city girls have a duty when we wear a Dirndl. It ought to be authentic and natural. Not overdone and kitchy. The speaker reported about their work designing new costumes from old models to encourage bringing back the old costumes to the countryside.

Munich, 21 June 1942

State funeral for the Corps leader of the NSKK [*Nationalsozialistische Kraftfahrkorps*, German organization established as a separate formation of the brown-shirted Stormtroopers in about 1929. It was the Motor Transportation Formation of the NSDAP and grew from the various Stormtrooper transportation battalions of the 1920s], Adolf Huehnlein. We were all shocked when we received the message about the death of Hitler's old comrade. He succumbed to his many years of disease. He lies in state in the Senate Hall in the Brown House. The funeral itself was held in the Kuppelsaal of the Army Museum. Before I went to this state ceremony I had a wonderful experience. *Vati* and I were walking together down Maximilian Street when a motorcade approached us. "This can only be the *Führer*," and sure enough, it was him. Serious and full of grief he sits, so often has he had to fortify himself for such a procession through a city giving final escort to one of his loyalists. I am excited and happy that I was allowed to see the *Führer* so close up because each time it is a thrilling experience. Dr. Goebbels gave the farewell with warm and heartfelt words. He described the life of this old fighter, who, even with all his sufferings, fulfilled all his duties for the *Führer* and the Fatherland. Even though he is gone, he will never be forgotten. Inge Rahn and I think back to that Sunday morning when we handed out the food ration cards with him. The *Führer* conferred on his old co-worker, posthumously, the highest German Medal.

Munich, 23 June 1942

Great happiness and jubilation fills the entire German people because Tobruk, the largest desert fortress in Africa, has fallen. Colonel General Rommel, the commander of the German and Italian military forces achieved his greatest victory. Tobruk, the long and bitterly contested desert stronghold, fell. Only through tenacity, courage and endurance of the German soldiers was this unique victory made possible. The *Führer* promoted the Colonel General to General Field Marshal in recognition of his accomplishments. I am proud that I have his autograph and wish, like all Germans, that soldiers' good fortune will be with him now and forever.

Munich, 25 June 1942
Capuzzo, Sollum, Halfaya taken.

Munich, 27 June 1942
The *Führer* ordered Giesler, leader of the south Westphalia Region, to lead the Munich Upper Bavaria Region, replacing the sick leader Adolf Wagner.

Munich, 29 June 1942
Today it was quiet and depressed in the classroom. We simply cannot imagine that our comrade Hildegard Lechner passed away. It hit us all so suddenly; it is unbelievable. We keep thinking that her seat will be occupied tomorrow, her bright laughter will be heard, her face will show up in our group. It will never again be. A malicious illness sought a new victim and our Garri was not resistant to it. We share the sadness of the parents, especially the mother who had just lost her own mother eight days ago. Our class leader remembered the dead with warm complimentary words that came from the bottom of his heart and that recalled Garri's entire being. She will always be in our hearts, especially the older ones of us from the fifth grade, who will never forget her. The teachers also mourn her. Everyone knew Garri, who made the school parties so much nicer with her piano playing and who, just last year, played the xylophone in front of an enthusiastic audience and earned great applause. A gaping hole was formed. Parents lost their only daughter. We lost a wonderful comrade.

Munich, 30 June 1942
Today, for better or worse, we took a walk through the Nymphenburg Castle Park. In the afternoon the entire class assembled in front of the North Cemetery in Schwabing. We simply could not comprehend that Garri is resting under the heap of flowers in the coffin and will never again walk among us. Within a few minutes her mother came to stand with us. We understood her great pain. For the father, his darling is gone. The father spoke graveside words of praise and commemoration. We cannot forget our courageous Garri. Shortly before her death, she knew what lay ahead for her. She wrote her parents and her brother a letter in which she said: "Do not be saddened by my death. I now live in God's will." She challenged her brother to be strong, to be a support for their parents. We fulfill her wish, which she expressed in her letter: "Pray for me." After the long funeral we did not express our condolences to her parents. Being confronted with us — the children of parents who had not lost a beloved little one — would only have intensified their grief. Quietly and in separate groups, we left the cemetery where our Garri rests in her final slumber. Some day we will see each other again, as she said in the farewell letter.

Munich, 1 July 1942
This morning we went to Straubing for the church memorial service. Once there we took a walk, since the train got us to our destination way too early. The service started at 9:00 a.m. We all took seats behind the family. After the service the class leader expressed the class's condolences and spoke earnestly with the parents. Then they invited us into their big, beautiful garden because our return train would be leaving very late. So we saw Garri's home, the small place in her garden where she used to do her homework, her bunnies and the little ones that came over to smell us. Struppi, her dog, barked at us. He misses his mistress very much. Her mother thanked us for our

coming. She is very strong; she accepts God's will and this will give her some comfort. Also, father and son struggle to overcome their great pain.

Munich, 2 July 1942
After a bitter 25 hour long heavy battle, Sevastopol, up until now the strongest land and sea fortification in the world, was defeated. The *Führer* promoted von Manstein to General Field Marshal.

Munich, 6 July 1942
Just three more days of school and then into school vacation. We in the sixth grade get three weeks of vacation and then go on deployment from the beginning of August to the middle of November. I got school vacation two days early so that I can take the GD [*Gesundheitsdienst*, Health Service] course in Bad Wiessee. It is really very nice there and, more important, we surely will learn a lot during this assignment.

Munich, 7 July 1942
Today is my last day at work. Where will I be until November? I hope I can be in a *Kinderlandverschickung* (iii) [evacuation camp for children from bomb-threatened areas] camp as a *Gesundheitsdienst-Mädel* [Health Service Girl]. Cross fingers and hope.

Munich, 9 July 1942
School vacation. What a happy thought. Finally the time has come. I will not be walking through the school doors again for a long time, but I will be stationed somewhere doing my wartime duties. Tomorrow I am going to Bad Wiessee. I am already excited about it.

Bad Wiessee, 10 July 1942
We arrived at Bad Wiessee after a hot and uneventful journey. At the house we were greeted by the camp leader and assigned

to our quarters. To our disappointment, Hilde and I are not together in the same room. But the comrade from Ingolstadt is very nice and has the same goals and wishes as we do. The house and the rooms are exceedingly comfortable. One can really feel at home here. The camp leader and the other girls are very nice and the dorm parents take good care of us.

Bad Wiessee, 11 July 1942

Last night there were strong thunderstorms. Even now it is cool and rainy. After breakfast we had our first class in anatomy, led by a medical student. One is always learning something new. Hilde Wolf and I went for a walk during our time off. We nosed around in the surrounding area. Tonight we will all go together to the theater. Hopefully we will be able to laugh a lot.

Bad Wiessee, 12 July 1942

After time off the day before, we had class again yesterday where we reviewed what we had learned and expanded on it. After dinner we were off again; it was raining once again, but that could not stop us. The piece itself, *The Three Village Saints*, was very nice and entertaining. Since today is Sunday, we were allowed to sleep until 7:30. Morning sports, flag and breakfast. Then the garden lured us to come there for singing. Margret explained the importance of the Health Service within the Hitler Youth. After lunch we boated to Tegernsee to climb from there up the Neureuth Mountain. We had no complaints about the pathway, but even if we had it would not have mattered because the surroundings were so beautiful. It was only a little cool and windy. After a coffee break we began our descent. Climbing down gave us a "cramp in the knee" which went away soon. After a stormy crossing we arrived at the harbor from which we had departed, where a good dinner awaited us. Now we are reading or writing in the living room and soon we will go to sleep.

Bad Wiessee, 13 July 1942
After morning sport, flag and breakfast, we sang. Then we studied our GD books until the medical student came. She spoke with us about personal hygiene. After the general lecture, we were allowed to ask questions that she then answered for us. After our midday rest period we got company: the area doctor, Dr. Feser came. He spoke about health care leadership in the Third Reich, the preventative programs for maintaining a healthy population. He told us of the possibility of our receiving practical training in the adult ward at Tegernsee. This was the part of his speech we liked the most. After a coffee break, the anatomy class continued. Hopefully, we will all pass the exam. After dinner we fulfilled Frau Dill's wish: we shucked peas. At the beginning, we were appalled at the amount. But soon the mountain disappeared. Of course, we did not do this quietly. We talked a whole lot but this didn't seem to bother anyone. Our good housemother picked up on our hint. After we were finished, and after the flag was lowered, she brought us a plateful of sandwiches, which we ate with pleasure.

Bad Wiessee, 14 July 1942
Today I was girl on call. After the singing that we do every morning, we practiced bandaging; here also the principle was true: "Practice makes perfect." The different ways of bandaging require skill and patience. The moment of surprise came after the meal, as it did every day: handing out of the mail. There was even something for me this time: *Mutti* had sent me my tennis shoes in which she had hidden sweets. After our shortened lunch break, we had class with Dr. Froeden, a doctor in Tegernsee. We learned the first measures to take for the different types of injuries and the skills of nursing the sick. After coffee, we practiced lifesaving, but still on dry land. At night we went swimming. It is wonderful to swim out into the vastness of the lake. Out of the water, we dressed quickly

because the air made us feel colder. Once we got back to school, we had to go to bed right away. A nocturnal spook wandered about during the night. With clappers, bells, various disguises and singing, he haunted the premises.

Bad Wiessee, 15 July 1942

After breakfast we studied our text books and practiced bandaging. Then we went swimming again with Gerulda. In the afternoon, a medical student taught us nutrition and her young colleague instructed us further in anatomy. After dinner, Gerulda continued to teach lifeguard skills. Soon we all went to bed because the others were somewhat tired from all the sport activity. Tonight, also, there was a ghost. Poor Hilde sacrificed herself and lay under Margret's bed. It had to have been very uncomfortable there. Even if the spook was not very convincing, the whole thing was still fun.

Bad Wiessee, 16 July 1942

Due to bad weather we did not have morning sport. After breakfast we went to Tegernsee in streaming rain to the enlarged Medical Center. There, Margret demonstrated changing bedding for the ill, bandaging and other handling movements that we have to know as GD girls in service. Thank God the weather cleared up for our ride home. After the meal, a student gave a lecture about medicinal herbs. We already know most of these medicinal herbs from the collection of them we have in our groups. We know how healthful it is to drink German tea and thereby to help our economy so that foreign tea will not have to be imported. Medicinal herbs and herbal bags also work at helping you heal. After the coffee break, the others went to the sport area to take the final tests for their badges. Hilde Schmitt and I took the boat to Tegernsee to pick up her glasses. The crossing over was beautiful, especially since it was warm. After dinner, we learned lifeguard skills at the lake. The swimmers returned home dead tired and hungry.

Bad Wiessee, 17 July 1942
The biggest and most important city of the Donez industrial area, Voroshilovgrad, was taken by storm by the German infantry. After breakfast, we studied until the arrival of Gerhilde, who went with us to swim in the lake. Some earned their Level II swimming certificates and, after that, swam across the lake to the town of Tegernsee. Hilde earned her basic certificate for DLRG [*Deutsche Lebens-Rettungs-Gesellschaft*, lifeguard] before a thunderstorm drove us home. When the sun came out again, we sat on the front entrance steps and Gerhilde gave us the written exam for the basic certificate. After the famous Bavarian Friday meal—yeast dumplings and fruit compote—we had first aid class with Dr. Froeden. He instilled a real fear of exams in us. After a coffee break, we had free time, during which most studied since we were all determined to graduate with good grades, even if just not to embarrass Margret. After dinner my newspaper article was due. The prospect of a free evening was joyfully accepted. Most went to the movie theater, but Rose, Hilde Wolf, Hilde Schmitt and I stayed here. It was a wonderful time, as we told each other stories of our lives and we grew closer to each other on this night. When a thunderstorm broke out, we went to our rooms.

Bad Wiessee, 18 July 1942
After our morning routine of singing, we practiced bandaging, carrying stretchers, how to place splints and some other things we GD girls have to know. After the noon rest period, Hilde Schmitt and I went to Wiessee where we visited the beautifully appointed Berta Schwartz Home, which offers many mothers and their children weeks of recovery and relaxation. Gunhild came and reviewed anatomy, bandaging and nursing. She wished us luck for the exam. Well, I am nervous about it.

During the evening get-together we heard of the lives of two famous doctors: Paracelsus and Semmelweis, the savior of mothers. We now know how these doctors had to fight to implement their thoughts and methods. They had to fight against quacks. Country doctors of today have to fight against this as well, since many farmers would still rather go to a sheepherder. We GD girls still have this problem with some of our girls. But difficulties exist so that they may be overcome. After so much reflection, we decided to take an evening walk. The sun was just setting; all was quiet, only the cow bells on the Alm could be heard. It was a beautiful night in our Bavarian countryside.

Bad Wiessee, 19 July 1942
We had an especially long singing session after breakfast, followed by outdoor games. After lunch we were expecting the upper region doctor, Dr. Gisela Burgdorf. She spoke of the duties of the BDM doctor as a health educator. Every girl should have complete knowledge of her body. It must all be clear and simple to her. The GD girls can help in this educational process. She continued to teach us correct healthcare strategies, which are so obvious and logical but are not always followed through. I was sorry that she had to leave again so soon. While the others went to the field to play Voelkerball and to work off some energy, Irmgard and I thought about what entries we would make in the guest book. After dinner we had a fun evening. We laughed a lot during every single game. This awful rain cannot shake us.

Bad Wiessee, 20 July 1942
Today was an exciting day. All morning we studied earnestly. Time went by so quickly. When lunch was ready we fortified ourselves well, because if the brain is supposed to work, then the body must get something as well. After free time, came the moment of which we had all been so fearful. In uniform, we

had to present ourselves in the meeting room. After a formal welcome, came the exam. Each one of us had to undergo a 15 minute period of oral examination. At 4:00 the doctor joined us for the coffee break, as he so much liked to have coffee with his coffeecake. He spoke of our youth, the people's convictions and the question of the Jews. Then the exam continued. Finally it was my turn. Thank God I knew the answers to the questions asked so I walked out of the room with a weight off my shoulders. I am happy that I passed the written exam with a 1. After dinner we went out with Margret. We walked off joyfully and engaged in hearty banter along the way to Rottach -Egern. This village is situated so beautifully, the streets hugging the shores of the Tegernsee. It is a real mountain village, not as modern as Wiessee, but I think more welcoming. Soon we had to go home again. As Margret told us of her life as an NS [National Socialist] nurse, we found ourselves quickly back home, where the others were still engaged in rehearsal for the farewell evening.

Bad Wiessee, 21 July 1942
The last day in our beautiful "Bavarian Country." All morning we practiced bandaging and carefully checked our first aid kits. After the lunch break we took the second part of the exam, the practical part. Finally it was my turn. First, I had to explain the purpose and application of some medications and instruments. Then we had to bandage each other, serve in the ambulance, resuscitate and a few other things. After completion, after all of our anxieties had quieted down, Dr. Froeden wished us well for our deployments and said farewell. After dinner we all worked feverishly so that at exactly 8:00 the fun could start. We brought in the house parents and the house personnel. After an opening song, the camp's poem—which often brought us to laughter—was presented. The main joke, "The Red Candle" by Weiss Ferdl, came after a series of short charades, poems and songs. That was a real rush. One could

get stomachache from laughter. Then we sat in a circle and played games. It made us so happy that Mr. Duell played like a youngster with us. The medical student, Gundhild Horn, came later as we had a special surprise for her—an earthworm—since she always said, "Then take the poor little worm and go quickly to Uncle Doctor." At 12:30 a.m. when the programmed events came to a close, the ever-caring camp parents provided refreshments. It was a long time before everyone's eyes fell shut and the house became quiet.

Munich, 22 July 1942

Today we were awakened for the last time in the camp. After breakfast we packed our bags and cleaned our rooms. At 9:30 we lowered the flag which was hoisted every morning and which was laid to rest with us every night. Then we had our last meal: potato salad with baked cheese. The house parents had put together a huge sandwich pack for each of us to take with us. To say a proper farewell we went and got Mr. and Mrs. Duell and Anni and Kaethe. We sang for them some fun songs and Margret thanked everyone again for everything. Then we had to leave. A farmer had gotten our things ahead of time. In a specialty rail car, in which were also some mothers of the Berta Schwartz Home, we rode to Gmund. As we sat in the train we all thought, "Too bad that the nice time is over." When I got home, we chatted excitedly, happy to be together again. I was delighted with this deployment where I could show what I have learned.

Munich, 27 July 1942

The important commerce and harbor center Rostov is taken. This morning we were at the large art exhibition in the House of German Art. With catalogue in hand, we perused the large halls in which hang the exhibits of our great artists, a testimony of German creativity during the war. Many of the artists are in the field. Their works are limited to their war experiences. The images they give us of our soldiers in oil paintings, watercolors, busts and statues by the sculptors Thorak and Breker, as well as porcelain and clay works are seen in great variety. The walk through the exhibition hall gives us insight into the artistry of today, which in spite of the war, functions in the same way it did during the years of peace following 1933.

Munich, 30 July 1942
Today it was decided. With three other GD girls from our course, I have been assigned to Dr. Feser. After a long wait it is our turn. Where? That is the big question. The others had quickly gotten their short term camp deployments. But I can make myself available for the next several months to go to a camp in Reichenhall with 161 Rendsburg boys. Kids! Kids! Straight into the youth camp is the right place for us. They often miss their mothers, especially when sick, and that is where we come in as GD girls. "Assistant Mothers of the Homeland" is what they call us.

Bad Reichenhall, 3 August 1942
After a hot train ride, I just arrived in beautiful Bad Reichenhall which will be my new home for three months. For now, I am settled into the camp teacher's quarters, since he is on vacation right now. There are a lot of people here. To direct so many young boys is an art, but it seems to me that here discipline and order reign. We just came from lunch, which was served in a large hall. For me everything is so new. The entire environment is different than in Wiessee, but with time I will get used to it. After I wrote the first few sentences, a young boy came and asked for a nurse. When I went to the doctors room with him, a whole herd came and wanted to be treated. *"Essigsauretonerdeverband"* [acetic acid clay dressing, an old German remedy] came into action. The peeling of potatoes alone claimed three victims and for me, my precious adhesive

bandages. But they are so cute, these ten and eleven year olds, when they come so trustingly to me. I hope that I will fulfill their expectations and serve as a substitute for their mothers on both their sickly and healthy days. This afternoon I went to the hospital with Mr. Henschel to visit a sick boy. One with a throat illness is already lying in the sickbay. The first day in the KLV [*Kinderlandverschickung*] camp is over.

Bad Reichenhall, 4 August 1942

Today the dance started early in the morning. The sick and the pretend-sick showed up. But no one is excited about the oatmeal. Little Herbert has had enough and does not act sick anymore. All of the little requests and grievances are quickly taken care of. After the sports period there was a lot of confusion. A boy who had fallen on his back was brought in. An elastic band soon brought him soothing comfort. Now his case does not seem to be so severe. I will be glad when I have a single sickroom to attend instead of one on every floor. One cannot be more than one place at a time. But slowly everything is all falling into place. Health Service Adviser Dr. Schmitt was here at noon today. He is a real Uncle Doctor with bushy eyebrows, but very kindhearted. We now are supposed to get a NS nurse as a helper. That will be fine with me.

Bad Reichenhall, 5 August 1942

The morning routine keeps everyone on the run. The old patients have to be cared for, and with the new ones we have to think of what to do next. But this job is a lot of fun, especially when I see that the boys get better quickly. It would be too bad if their stay was ruined by an illness. Now it is evening; our patients are all taken care of. In addition to the healthcare, we sometimes have to deal with the homesickness which shows up, especially during an illness. We GD girls are in the right place here. We can comfort and cajole, and this helps the pain go away. I am happy, therefore, to be in the middle of this duty that is so important, yet pleasant.

Bad Reichenhall, 6 August 1942
Today I experienced a great joy. Sophie Schlesinger, a former classmate and GD *Mädel* in Wiessee, visited me. She is in a *Mädel* camp near-by. I am happy that I am with boys and that I fit well in this camp, because Sophie is not enthusiastic about hers.

Bad Reichenhall, 7 August 1942
Yesterday the news hit us hard. The boy who is in the hospital has polio, and so the camp had to be quarantined. That is awful for the boys. If there is not another case then the quarantine will not last long. Until now the camp experience has been joyful and entertaining for the boys. No matter what, my regular duties persist and keep me very busy. The kids are apparently not used to our warmer climate and get illnesses that do not touch our robust southern Germans.

Bad Reichenhall, 8 August 1942
Today the decision came down: for 14 days the camp will be quarantined. The boys may possibly be able to take a few field trips if they can be done without meeting up with outside people. The situation is, Thank God, better than it might have been. The boys and I enjoyed the sun for the first time today. The mountains seemed close and clear, the way I love them. The first week in the camp is almost over. What all have I been able to learn and observe? Much that I find useful. Hopefully the next few weeks will bring me the same joy and fulfillment in my work. Good Luck!

Bad Reichenhall, 9 August 1942
Today *Vati* was supposed to come. That is what was planned, but the quarantine put the kibosh on that. But we both took it with humor and look forward to seeing each other again soon.

I went to Thunsee with Mr. Henschel in the afternoon, after my patients were taken care of. The way getting there was beautiful, especially the views all around. Thunsee, itself, lies there so lovely, like a miniature Koenigsee. The path along the Thunsee goes past the Water Lilly Pond. Soon we began our return, this time on the valley path. This walk made me aware all over again how fond I am of my Bavarian mountains. They attract many tourists with their beauty and charm, my beautiful Land of Bavaria!

Bad Reichenhall, 12 August 1942
Finally my own room! Up until now, I got to sleep on a trial basis in the camp teacher's room. Now I feel even better. *Mutti*'s picture, my hedgehog, some flowers, just as I have it at home; it is now cozier. All day there was absolutely nothing going on, no patients; therefore, it was hurry-scurry when the boys came back from swimming. Sprained foot, sore throat, puss pockets, glass chips in the foot etc. But by being in good spirits and using a bit of humor, I was able to help both myself and the boys.

Bad Reichenhall, 13 August 1942
Today was truly a tragic day. A boy ran away. I would never have thought him capable of doing this; he seemed to be a nice sweet boy. But in a blink of an eye he was gone. Well, he will probably be caught soon. Rosel, my roommate when we were in Wiessee, who is now in Freilassing, gave me a surprise visit, even though she could not stay long. In the afternoon, Nurse Franziska Freund came and introduced herself as a camp nurse. I think I will get along well with her; she gives such a motherly impression. Well, let us hope that all goes well.

Bad Reichenhall, 17 August 1942
Now I am no longer alone. Nurse Franziska has joined us in the camp. Although I am no longer alone, I sure would like to

be. We get along well but I am used to being alone. Yesterday Mr. Burzig, the camp teacher, came back from a vacation. He is just as quiet as Mr. Hentschel, maybe even quieter. That is why I feel so comfortable here in the circle of people who are quiet, yet have good senses of humor. Last Sunday we had beautiful weather. Mr. Hentschel and I first went to the Predigtstuhltalstation and looked with amazement at this technical wonder. This is the most daring cable railway in Germany. Boldly it sways from post to post. Then we marched on to the beautifully located Saalach Lake. It fits so well in this magnificent landscape. The southern sky steel blue, the singular clouds snow white, the mountains clothed in dark green forests; in addition to all of this, the lake—a picture of peace undisturbed by any sound. Along the Saalach shore the path continued on to Berchtesgaden. Mount Reiterberg lay in front of us and Mount Predigtstuhl beneath us, as well as the wildly foaming Saarlach. This picture even grabbed H.H. [*Herr Hentschel*], who ordinarily does not find much pleasure in viewing our landscape. Too bad we had to turn around since it would soon be mealtime at the camp. Deeply satisfied, we returned home from this wonderful hike.

Bad Reichenhall 19 August 1942
An expansive English-American attempt to land near Dieppe was pushed back by the German troops. By 10:00 p.m. there was not one armed enemy left on the land. The *Führer* appointed Dr. Thierack as *Reichsminister* of Justice.

Bad Reichenhall, 20 August 1942
Now I am happy again. All has turned out well. I will stay with my boys; Nurse Franziska goes back to her old camp and only comes when I call her. I would have been very sorry if I would have had to leave my boys. They have become very attached to me and ask me to help them with other than health problems. Sometimes a somewhat worn out pair of pants will

get silently mended and the delighted expression of the pants'
owner is the best thanks I could hope for.

Bad Reichenhall, 26 August 1942

I have not written in a long time, but so many events are
coming at me. Pretty soon I will have to say farewell to my
boys' camp. It is hard to say good-bye even though I was in the
camp only a short time. New obligations call me. I am called as
a *Gesundheitsdienst-Mädel* [Health Service Girl] to pick hops.
Everything will be new, but I will learn a lot. When I am
allowed to organize a camp, all of these experiences will be
very helpful to me. So, keep your head up, Lulu! There was
chaos until everything was sorted out. Yesterday morning I
went to Munich. It was a great surprise for my mother. She
would have never thought that I could come home so
suddenly. I was pretty hurt when I heard Dr. Feser's order.
Away from my boys and into the unknown. But duty is duty.
In the evening I went to Reichenhall in good company. Even
here there are sad and long faces. My suitcase sits there ready
for the trip. A new segment begins.

Fahlenbach, 27 August 1942

Finally I have landed at my deployment place. After a hot train
ride I arrived at the Wolnzach station. Here I found out that I
belonged in Koenigsfeld-Fahlenbach. The train was leaving
very late so, after long consideration, I decided to walk. "The
summer is hot, and the streets are long, but we still march far."
This song went well with my hike. After a one-hour march, I
was in Koenigsfeld and after another half hour I was in
Fahlenbach, where I was to reside in the school house by the
mountainside. The room is bright, cheerful and inviting. It is so
nice and quiet around us, a relief after the hustle and bustle of
the last few days. A train races by only now and again.
Otherwise, peace. Wherever I look hops, hops and more hops.
Everywhere they are plucking diligently and new hordes of

helpers, who are sorely needed, keep coming. Let us hope that my deployment is successful again this time.

Fahlenbach, 30 August 1942

I have already been in the Holledau for four days now; time just flies by. The daily program is so well scheduled and organized that one does not even think of what time or what day it is. On Saturday morning I hiked over to Wolnzach to a health care conference. To my surprise, I saw I was the youngest GD girl of the group. Heidi Hommel, the coordinator for Traunstein, does not mind. Yesterday, Sunday morning, I joined the girls in the hops fields. My hands are witness to the fact that I plucked diligently. After making my early afternoon rounds, I went to Niederlauterbach hoping to visit Ilse, Ingrid and the home keeper. That trip, however, was in vain. So I marched over to the train station, which was a good half hour away from the town. After dinner [presumably at the train station] I went home [back to Fahlenbach] where I had a wonderful chat with the teacher and his family.

Fahlenbach, 31 August 1942

Today I got a great surprise. As I was sitting there having lunch, who should come through the door? Manny! *Mutti* and *Vati* sent him to me. He brought several things that I urgently needed. *Mutti* seems very worried about her daughter. But Manny will tell her everything is all right. Maybe the girls from Koenigsfeld will help so that we can all leave at the same time. Heidi has to leave right now. That is too bad. She was a great comrade. Now I am dead tired. First I held a lecture in the Fahlenbach ward giving the girls advice on how to avoid certain things and how to better perform certain others. Then I quickly went down to Koenigsfeld and made my rounds there. It was a lot more crowded there but we quickly took care of everything to my satisfaction and that of the patients, as well.

Fahlenbach, 1 September 1942

Three years of war! Who would have imagined that when the invasion against Poland started. Three years war! We can be proud of the results. Poland, Norway, Denmark, Belgium, Holland, Occupied France, Greece, Yugoslavia, Crete, Tobruck and, above all, the eastern invasion, are the most important milestones of this Second World War. In all of Europe, only England and Russia are still standing. Almost all of the European states side with us; better yet, they march with us. Let us think of the legions of friendly states in the East, from the Spanish Blue Division to the volunteers of Holland, Belgium etc. Our soldiers have accomplished a lot. Let us remember their hardships and sacrifices of the past winter. One fortress after another was captured and more of them will be. Let us hope that the final victory will soon be won and that the people, in harmony and tranquility, for the well-being of all, maintain the peace.

Wolnzach-Markt, 6 September 1942

Today I am sitting again in yet another place. The work finally done, my entire unit left yesterday morning. The last few days were really hard. In summer heat with no rain to cool the air, the girls still brought in all the hops. Some farmers finished before their deadlines, but those who did not were assisted by these girls who continued to pick. With so much work to be done, no one had time to think of getting sick. I am happy that the girls of Division 2 made it through the harvest without getting sick. On Saturday morning, yesterday, at 11:00 was the GD final conference. It was determined that I will remain in Wolnzach-Markt until the set time for going home. After a heartfelt farewell from the main teacher, the grandfather and Buzzi, who took such good care of me, I moved into new quarters which I joyfully share with Marianne Unger, the GD girl from Ingolstadt. There is no more work here. I hope I can leave soon.

Munich, 8 September 1942
Last night I rode from Wolnzach-Markt to Munich. I am so happy to be home. Yesterday during our farewell, I got a great surprise. I was given the first money I ever earned. Daily earnings in the sum of 6 Mark, with room and breakfast paid. This is quite a lot of money, especially since I did not expect to be paid anything at all. In the afternoon, I visited my *Jungmädel* and then went to the office. Here I met my future boss, an old frontline nurse, and the camp doctor. Then I was directed to Dr. Feser, who ordered that I have two days of rest. On Friday the journey will begin again. This time, unfortunately, I will be in a girls camp; moreover, in Einsiedl on Walchen Lake. Again, I will start life in a new camp with new duties.

Einsiedl am Walchensee, 11 September 1942
After a brief visit at home, the train took me to Kochel. After a lengthy argument, I finally ended up on the bus to Mittenwald. The drive ascending the Kesselberg was absolutely beautiful, as it followed along and rose above deep blue Walchen Lake. The village of Walchensee lay behind us. The bus managed another hill before it went downward toward the new home which lay in front of me, Hotel Einsiedl am Walchensee — a beautiful piece of land, with the house directly on the lake. While we eat, our view goes to the surrounding mountains. Forests, forests, forests wherever I look. An artist would be charmed by the blue of sky and lake, by the forests and mountains. One cannot get enough of it; moreover, there is the wonderful silence. Only some ringing cowbells interrupt the silence. The house itself is ideally situated. Every room has its own balcony. The girls feel comfortable here and already look healthier. I almost did not get to stay in this camp because when I got here, besides the head nurse, there was also a DRK [German Red Cross] helper. The confusion was explained when we found out that Nurse Wally has orders to leave soon for another duty. In the meantime, Head Nurse Wela and

Nurse Wally are very kind and make my life in the camp easier. Especially Head Nurse Wela, who has gone through a lot of hardship lately. I know the camp leader from the BDM. There she led a JM group. The two other teachers are just as nice. I will get along well with the leaders. But, to tell the truth, I would much prefer a boys' camp.

Einsiedl, 13 September 1942
I am sitting on the balcony of my room. Five steps ahead, beyond the street, the forest starts with its dark green glimmer. Only seldom does a car or bicycle drive by. Otherwise the heavenly silence. That which I had feared, happened yesterday: quarantine. Little Anneliese has scarlet fever and so the camp was put on lock down. I always come at the right time! No parents are allowed for ten days. Also, the girls that slept in the same room as Anneliese have to be isolated; a second ward had to be established. This means more work, but we are confident that everything will be all right. The head nurse, the helper and I also have to eat separate from the others. We hope there will be no second case so that the lock down can be lifted soon.

Einsiedl, 14 September 1942
Establishment of the European Youth Organization in Vienna. *Reichsmarschall* Goering orders the weekly meat and bread rations to be increased as of October 19th. Today was again a wonderful fall day. Last night, the three of us took a long walk on the shore of the lake. We have to enjoy the nice days; here it will soon be cool and rainy. I just returned from the lake, an expansive area in which one can really swim. I was in my element again. A sailboat that was anchored in the middle of the lake called to me. What a pleasure this is. As I swam back, a thunder storm began. The last sunrays made the lake appear like liquid gold. A swim such as this refreshes, and renews a joyful attitude toward our work. We were informed that Nurse

Wally will be with us through September 20th and will then have to go to another camp.

Einsiedl, 20 September 1942

One week of work, eagerly performed, lies behind me. Mornings we cleaned the wards, cared for the sick and took walks with the isolates, which brought joy and recovery to us as well as to them. We bathed twenty girls on Wednesday, another twenty on Thursday. That was something. It was clearly something fun. Wash heads, soap up the girls and then rub them dry. No two girls were alike. Each body is designed differently, but all are well built. They are also gaining weight here. During the bathing procedure, one gets to know the girls better and more quickly. I sense that already they are developing trust in me. Nurse Wally had to finally leave today. She was a good friend to me and to the head nurse. We will miss her sorely.

Einsiedl, 21 September 1942

Munich has now had its first big attack. The damage that the English did to our city is severe; heavy are the sacrifices brought upon our civilian population. Impatiently, I waited for a report from my mother. Even though some things in the apartment building were damaged, we did not, at least, have any injured. Manny has been deployed to help with the clean-up. Please God, do not let there be any more damage, and may the English spare our city even though they are dropping papers from their airplanes prophesying that the city will be destroyed.

Einsiedl, 25 September 1942

I have been in this camp for fourteen days already. The time just flies by. I adjusted quickly and already feel very comfortable here. Finally, I have my own space. Flowers on the table and the dresser, pictures of my loved ones, my true friend the hedgehog and the small calendar — that tells me each day how much longer I will be here — make it cozier and more like home. This is what one needs here. After work you need a place of your own, guaranteed to be private so you can really relax. Those who were quarantined are now allowed out. Our old ward is always overcrowded. Truly sick girls are in separate rooms. The day goes by very quickly, which is exactly the way we like it. One task begins where the other left off. Our ward is neither sad nor depressed. Our encouraging words and lighthearted jokes enliven the girls, letting them forget their ailments. I am glad every time a girl leaves the ward healthy.

Einsiedl, 30 September 1942
Wearer of the highest German medal for bravery, never defeated, Captain Marseille, died in a flight accident.

Einsiedl, 1 October 1942
Last night the *Führer* spoke for the opening ceremony of the KWHW [War Winter Relief] 1942-1943. After that, Dr. Goebbels gave his account of the present situation. With biting sarcasm, the *Führer* characterized our enemy. He thanked Front and Homeland for coordinating their efforts. Thunderous applause often interrupted the speech of the *Führer*, who was only in Berlin for a few hours. The days just fly by. Again, we have completed many days full of hard work. We spent all of Tuesday washing and hanging out to dry the clothes of ninety girls and leaders. This was three weeks of laundry and, obviously, was a lot of work. It was a joy to see how quickly they dried in the fall sun and wind. Wednesday we had to finish off the second half of the laundry and, on top of that, bathe the girls. This meant working very fast in order to get everything done. In between, the sick needed medicine, bandaging, heating pads etc. Every evening we take a walk in the surrounding area. A nice ending to the work day. But the

best reward for all our work is the good-night song sung to us by the girls. Throughout, I see that the girls are getting closer to me and that they trust me. Yesterday the message came that the girls will be leaving the camp by October 15th. What will happen with me then, I do not yet know. Maybe I can stay because immediately girls from Hamburg will be coming. Let us see what the future brings.

Einsiedl, 3 October 1942
Today the girls are hiking up the Simmets Mountain. There will at least be quiet in the house so that it can be cleaned. Yesterday I was asked if I would like to continue my GDM service in the HLV [*Heimatland Verschickung*, Homeland Evacuation]. Finally, we GD girls can do work on the Homeland frontier. If there are more air raids we can help the injured and homeless by bringing them to a secure place etc. This provides a wonderful opportunity for us to show our all-around capabilities. With a happy heart I said "Yes."

Einsiedl, 4 October 1942
"In the East the enemy will be defeated and then God have Mercy! Then we will continue our discussion in England. As things stand today the blockade, leading to our starvation, which the enemy hoped to mount, is not possible." [From the Thanksgiving Day speech of the *Reichsmarschall*.] Thanksgiving Day: For this occasion, our girls hiked to the Walchensee and sang there. Brilliantly their echoes sounded as they climbed the road. The good weather is holding on through today. *Mutti* is already with *Vati* in Traunstein. Manny is picking potatoes; seems to be somewhere near Eichstaett. I am curious what all he will have to tell.

Einsiedl, 9 October 1942
Today I took the head nurse to the train station. She had a feeling that she would have to go to Vienna soon. The husband

of her dead friend is there, critically ill, and so she had to leave quickly. Now I manage the ward all alone, which I do not mind. At 5:30 in the morning, in streaming rain, we went to catch the bus in Walchensee. In complete darkness the rain was a bit scary but soon we got there, even if we were shaking from the cold. In Kochel, the head nurse had to wait a long time for her connection to Munich, but then the journey went quickly. It seems that the weather here is turning bad. Leaves are falling from the trees in bundles. It is good that we can keep ourselves busy by crafting. This makes the time fly by. Gerda, the camp leader, went back to Hamburg. The tears fell. Yesterday was her birthday party as well as a farewell party. Our little festivity had as its theme, "How jolly are the people in the Oberland." We had a lively program of yodelers, dances, storytelling and farewell charades. Now Helga will be in charge of the camp until it closes.

Einsiedl, 11 October 1942

Dr. Feser was just here for an inspection. First my heart fell into my pockets because I was so nervous. But soon I pulled myself together. I always have everything in order. The ward was tip top. The medicine and instrument cabinets, which he inspected very carefully, left nothing to desire. The medicine bottles and ointment tubes stood there in a row like soldiers. My patients were happy and satisfied. What else could I want? I can even go home for a few days after the camp closes. Yippee!

Einsiedl, 17 October 1942

I have now been here at the camp for five weeks. Since Monday my ward has been empty. This rare situation made deep cleaning possible. Now everything shines from cleanliness. In the ward, where beds are empty, there is no work to be done. Camp girls still need to be bathed and their rooms cleaned. The crafting that we do causes the days to go by more quickly than we like. I am sitting right now downstairs in the dining room, which gives me the opportunity to get closer to the girls. Each one insists that I promise to sit with her on the train. The camp was nice, but I am already filling with excitement at the thought of getting home.

Munich, 22 October 1942

Now I am back at home in Munich. I think about my time at the camp. It brought happiness and pain, but all of that is as nothing compared to the sense of being "home." The last few days [at the camp] had been spent in preparation for the farewell afternoon, which we spent together in wonderful harmony. Our guests, neighbors from Einsiedl and Obernach, really enjoyed being with us. The highpoint was the camp song, in which everyone was mentioned. The verse about me: "On the second floor is the ward! You will always find Wolfhilde there. Bathing children, combing lice, nothing bothers her. She seemed to be crafting all the time!" After the especially good dinner, came the surprise for the home parents. Color films, taken by Mr. Stoeffelmeier, were shown. This was great, our beautiful Homeland in color photos. After this artistic enjoyment, came something for the stomach. Apple cake with cocoa and pralines, prepared earlier, were now served. It was difficult to settle down the girls for bed but eventually tiredness overwhelmed them. After the girls had been put to bed, we leaders each received a painted tile as a remembrance of our stay in Walchensee. Today we separated ourselves from this beautiful mountainous world which now lay covered in snow. *Mutti* does not want to let me leave again. I hope to get a satisfying job in Munich, where, upon my return home this time, I was greeted with an air raid alarm.

Munich, 4 November 1942

After my "Vacation" I have returned to the working world. I

landed in the health department of the Hochland area. It is interesting to get to know this versatile institution which has so many subdivisions. I now know how much work it is to fulfill the necessities and requirements of each KLV camp. My day was spent writing, organizing, registering etc., as well as taking phone calls from the camps and the health department. This proverb applies here: "Where you stand does not matter; where you stand is crucial."

Munich, 7 November 1942
Just now I took the head nurse to the train station after she had spent yesterday with us. She had been traveling from Vienna back to Kochel until, in the afternoon, she stopped by to see Dr. Feser who transferred her to the expanded Medical Center in Urfeld until her camp girls arrive in Walchensee. Now she is gone after we had a few nice hours together. I have finished training for the variety of duties that I now fulfill. Every day brings something new. One can learn a lot here.

Munich, 8 November 1942
Today I celebrate my 17th birthday. Very early in the morning *Mutti* came with my birthday present table, which was again so nice. The book by Norbert Koch, *The Dykemaster*, and a Hoffmann picture book of the *Führer*'s 50th birthday made me as happy as did the three Gothic, Renaissance and Baroque picture albums, the pictures of the *Eichenlaub* wearers, Petra's wooden plate, handkerchiefs and, last but not least, the sweets. It was such a good day for crafting that I out-did myself. My old Advent candle holder was cleaned up. I started a Christmas pyramid and am already excited in anticipation of how it will turn in the brightness of the lighted candles. Now begins again the time that I so love, with long winter evenings. Soon it will be Advent. The beautiful, mysterious season approaches.

Munich, 9 November 1942

From the *Führer's* speech yesterday in front of the Old Guard: "Think without exception, man and woman, only about this, that in this war, the 'to be or not be' of the Germans will be determined. And when you understand this, then every one of your thoughts and actions will be a prayer for our Germany."

Munich, 10 November 1942

Concert series: Tonight I went to the concert in the Tonhalle. Our area orchestra under Director Trapp performed their first concert. They did it well and our applause at the end of the cheerful themes showed them that we were satisfied with their presentation. The soloist, Luise Lahnstaett, was loudly applauded when her performance reached its highpoint, and she was given a magnificent bouquet of flowers. With doubled enthusiasm, the young musicians will go back to work in order to soon give us additional evidence of their ability.

Munich, 11 November 1942

German troops cross over the demarcation line into Unoccupied France to protect the French territory against the possibility of a British-American landing attempt in south France. Italian troops occupied Corsica. The *Führer's* proclamation to the French people stated that the German Armed Forces do not come as an enemy of the French, nor of their soldiers.

Munich, 14 November 1942

My work in the health department ended yesterday. Tomorrow school will begin again with its offerings of old classics and new-era subjects. Rich are my impressions that I gathered during my work assignment. The farewell from my coworkers, with whom I had shared both pleasure and pain, had been touching. Today I crafted a lot in order to finish all the candleholders, angels etc. so that the soldiers of the Army hospitals will have them to enjoy on the first Sunday of Advent. "To give is better than to receive." The meaning of this sentence I felt many times when I went to the city to buy presents for my loved ones and my friends. I am always happy when I can find something appropriate for them.

Munich, 15 November 1942

Today there was school again, a concept we found hard to grasp. The transition was not so rapid, even though we were all returning happily to our classrooms. Prof. Zweckstaetter spoke in memory of Garri who would still be with us had not destiny so suddenly taken her from us. Manny and I just came from a concert for the Hitler Youth in the Tonhalle performed by the Munich Philharmonic conducted by Oswald Kabasta. This evening was another great experience. The high point was the masterly performed and conducted *Fifth Symphony* of Anton Dvorak. Aroused to a state of jubilation, we rewarded the conductor and his musicians with bountiful applause and many flowers.

Munich, 16 November 1942

German and Italian troops land in Tunisia in accord with an agreement made with them by the French government.

Munich, 22 November 1942

On Remembrance Sunday [*Totensonntag*, Day of the Dead; honoring fallen soldiers], Annemarie Moelders, mother of our unforgettable aviation hero [Werner Moelders], and Ernst Baudin, father of two fallen sons, spoke during the ceremony. Mrs. Moelders spoke in remembrance of her son, who set an example for the entire country and who continues to live on in our hearts. She consoled the mothers who, like herself, had to go through difficult times. Her son Victor is a prisoner of the English; bravely she tries to overcome her grief. In innumerable ways, the love of the entire country supports her.

One example is that Werner's grave in the Invaliden Cemetery [Berlin] is constantly bedecked with red roses, his favorite flower. Ernst Baudin consoled the fathers who mourn their sons' heroic deaths. He is proud of his sons, who died heroically. They will continue to live within us. Through them we must become stronger so that we can be their equals and completely fill their shoes. Now the package lies in front of me, ready to be sent. It contains 100 small messages of joy. A hundred candles will burn; many soldiers will think of their loved ones when the Advent candles shine their bright light. I am happy that I could help a bit toward making this beautiful season more enjoyable for the wounded soldiers.

Munich, 26 November 1942

I just came back from the theater, where *Caesar* by Hans Schwarz was performed. The work, with a wonderful cast, showed us the life and influence of the leader who made Rome great. In spite of historical errors, this work got a lot of applause, often erupting spontaneously, and, at the end, intended to thank the exceptional actors.

Munich, 27 November 1942

German troops took over the up to now unoccupied war harbor of Toulon in order to forestall [effects of] broken promises of the commanders of the French fleet. Contrary to commands of the French government, lower ranking commanders sank parts of their own fleet. The *Führer* orders demobilization of the French military units. In the document "From the writings of the *Führer* to Marshal Petain," we read: "I close this letter with the hope that with this a joint venture can begin, from which we expect from the French nothing but insight into the common fate of Europe—and loyalty." I got news that my Advent package arrived safely and brought a lot of joy to the soldiers. With this, the bearers of joy [the 100 candles] fulfilled their purpose.

Munich, 29 November 1942

Today the theater group presented *The Abduction from the Seraglio* by Mozart. Our white blouses shone festively in contrast to the boys' blue uniforms. This piece received our complete approval because all of the roles were so well cast. Singers were often applauded immediately, even though the opera was still in progress. They gave their best so that we can better understand the immortal work of our great composer. Flowers for the actresses and constant applause thanked all those who presented this wonderful afternoon to us. Dr. Feser had a son and heir, Peter.

Munich, 2 December 1942

In a speech the *Duce* stated: "For the Italian people there is only one duty, namely, Fight. I mean fight shoulder to shoulder with the allies; fight together with Germany."

Munich, 3 December 1942

When I returned from school today, a great surprise awaited me. The autograph of Colonel General Dietl, our mountain commander in the very north, had arrived. In an enclosed letter he thanks me for my best wishes. I am proud and happy that I now own his signature.

Munich, 4 December 1942

Again another part of the Christmas work is done. The head nurse ordered calendar men and children's toys. Now they lay before me, the quaint *Sepperln* [Seppel, hand puppet character in the Kasperle stories, clothed Bavarian style with a green hat] which hold their hearts in their hands; the crudely-fashioned little dog, which will soon be giving great joy to a small child.

Munich, 6 December 1942

After chorus practice we listened to a lecture by two women leaders in the National Labor Service. They told us about the

Labor Service, especially the career path for women leaders. A film highlighted what they had said and also explained the entire operation of the camp, its outdoors layout and uses of free time. We need to be considering all these things since the time for our compulsory Labor Service is drawing near.

Munich, 10 December 1942
House music hour. This year our house music program is based on our old master composer, Johann Sebastian Bach. All facets are being rigorously explored in duets, trios and quartets. Old music, performed by our own classmates, resounds through the halls.

Munich, 12 December 1942
Today the, for us too short, trimester is over. We will not be getting our report cards. Because of this, instruction will be even more intense during the next quarter. As every year, the little ones invited us to attend their Christmas-stories program. It is so cute to see the girls still in their child-like behavior; their performances are so genuine and they are so serious about everything. One could see how much they enjoyed our applause. After the lowering of the flag, we added a farewell to our Happy New Year and Christmas wishes. We, of the old 5-C, waited for Mrs. Kleber. She is going to get married after Christmas and will leave us, which we all regret. We really liked her, but she is going to follow her husband to an unfamiliar city. She will make his children a good mother. We will be with her for the last time on her wedding day.

Munich, 13 December 1942
Today I was occupied with crafting. *Mutti's* present is finally finished. Erna's ordered game is also ready. For Hanna's little doll we made a winter Dirndl [Bavarian peasant dress]. She will probably enjoy it as this is unknown in Berlin.

Munich, 18 December 1942

Christmas comes closer, but it is still not cold. We have the house cleaning behind us. All gifts are ready; the tree, cookies and sweets bought. Our anticipation heightens as Christmas draws nearer. Nowhere else is this festival more celebrated and deeply heartfelt than it is in Germany. Everyone everywhere is working hard in preparation. In the East, West and North, even in the South, they try to magically convert a cypress into a Christmas tree. Whether in an Army hospital, the barracks, in the family or in a community, on Holy Night the people will assemble around the Christmas tree and be filled with joy at its brilliance. Our thoughts go to the Front as the soldier thinks of his loved ones at home. On this evening, every German feels closer to all the others.

Munich, 19 December 1942

The *Führer* welcomed Count Ciano and Marshal Caballero on December 18th and 19th to military and political conferences in his headquarters. On December 19th the *Führer* also received French Prime Minister Pierre Laval together with Count Ciano.

Munich, 21 December 1942

As I was about to start writing in my journal yesterday, the sirens sounded. The only thing to do was to get down into the cellar. Soon occupants of the entire building were there together. Then we heard the sounds of light and heavy flak mixed with the bomb strikes. Factories and the military hospitals at the Rondel were struck heavily. Twenty-four people gave their lives, among them entire families whose fathers are in the East. The Flak shooting lasted over an hour. Ten airplanes were shot down.

Munich, 24 December 1942

Christmas Eve. How slowly does time go by when one is awaiting exciting things. Finally we are ready: the two

Christmas trees spread their sweet aroma; they glitter with their Christmas decorations. Secrecy crackles in all the rooms; no one dare go from one to the other. *Vati* lights the candles; Manny and I stand in front of the door. As we enter, *Mutti* plays [on the piano] the old German song about the Holy Night [Franz Gruber's "Silent Night"]. Then, the passing out of the gifts begins. Manny is happy over his books, a nice tie and cufflinks. His present, a motor, has not yet arrived, but, when it does, it will bring him a lot of joy. Then, my turn. From *Vati*, books: *German Girls in the War Workforce*, and *The Führer Frees the Sudetenland*. Also I bought myself books: *Vom Kaiserhof zur Reichskanzlei*, *Women's Destiny — Women's Accomplishments*, and the novel trilogy, *Paracelsus*. Hilde Wolfe pleased me with the book *The Heredity of Bjoerndal*; Lore Bartel made me a book cover and gave me the master book about Leonardo DaVinci. From the head nurse I received coasters for a liquor set, which was a souvenir from Vienna. A hand carved picture frame with a matching sweets bowl. Manny completed my collection with pictures of *Eichenlaub* wearers. But the present from *Mutti* was not yet uncovered. What could it be? On red silk lay a beautiful necklace of amber, the German gold. My deepest wish was granted. *Vati* was happy with cigarettes, a shirt and neckties. After the uncovering of gifts, I lit the candles on my tree [in my room]. The small figurines peek out from behind the angel hair. My pyramid turns itself in the heat of the candles. Manny gave *Mutti* some lotion, a bath mat and some toiletries. [For Manny] I guessed right with the books about the Navy; he was ecstatic with them. *Vati* approvingly inspected, with the eye of a connoisseur, the tie he had requested. When I took the blanket off the couch, there lay before *Mutti* the two pillows that I had finished for her. Her joy was great, which is the best thanks for a job well done. The lights were turned off; everyone left happily with their treasures. [Later] in the evening we listened to the Christmas broadcast, which had its high point in the speech from Dr. Goebbels. Soldiers from

Stalingrad, Tunis, Narvik and Nizza, from Rschev, from the North Sea or Mediterranean Seacoast, in patrol vessels and from airplanes, spoke with their families at home. The father to his son, the mother to her boy, sisters to brothers. Husbands and wives and children were overjoyed that they could communicate this way by radio. Home and Front were firmly united. Dr. Goebbels greeted them all, especially the Germans in foreign countries and overseas. They stand in constant struggle for their ethnic identity, but in this night they think even more of their Homeland, of Germany. This is how we are all united in our belief, all Germans with the same mind set.

> Christmas lights! In cold dark night, a light is
> brought to us; it gives such radiant shine into our
> world, oh, light in the dark night, open up your
> strength! Fill our time with your glory. Do not let
> us rest sooner, until our being and doing, may
> happen in the light, and we stand before you. Oh,
> light, fill us fully with loving radiance! Cover our
> entire affliction, and be our morning red! Shine
> through our hearts, glorify sorrow and pain: let us
> stand in the light until we go from here.
>
> Christmas 1942
> Hermine Stolz

Munich, 27 December 1942
Yesterday morning Baerbel Luyken stopped by and invited me to her place for the afternoon. This was an invitation I gladly accepted, and we spent several pleasant hours chatting together. We had not seen each other for a year; so many things had happened which were well worth talking about. Soon her father joined us; he was happy to have his daughter home for a few days. On Easter she will finish her teacher-apprenticeship and come to the rural women's school in Strassmoos. From there she will be able to come to Munich

more often. Mrs. Kleber's wedding took place this morning at 10:30. Many friends and acquaintances, many students including us from 6C, gathered. After the pastor's sermon, the confirmation and the following mass, we went to the Sacristy, to give the newlyweds our best wishes. There our teacher stood, next to her stately husband, surrounded by a large crowd of children, her own two and those of her brothers and sisters. She is happy, which helps her to deal with her emotional parting from us.

Munich, 28 December 1942
An evening in the German Theater: The Christmas program offered wonderful acrobatics, comic jokes, parodies, dance, singing and magic. This program was put together very well and earned great applause.

Munich, New Year's Eve 1942
The Old Year nears its end. In my mind, it passes through me in review. Hard fought battles, requiring constant preparedness at the Front and in the Homeland, ended in victory. For the first time, we girls of the 7th upper grade stood in a place where we could do the job of a soldier or woman worker who could then go to the Front. Next year even more will be expected from us, but we will always feel satisfaction knowing that whatever we do is for Germany. For the fourth time the wish matures in us that freedom may come. To make this happen, we have to be untiringly active.

New Year's Wish
With wide open views
With courageous hearts and happy souls
We want to stand in life
Working and partying simultaneously,
As if we stood majestically on a high mountain.

Hermine Stolz

i. Res. Laz. Freudental 1942
im Reservelazarett Freudental 1942

[written while at the Auxiliary
Military Hospital in Freudental 1942]

1943

**The objective of our war is to secure
the freedom of our people,
the boundaries of our realm
and the surety of our future.
In a word,
the objective of our war
is a stable Germany.**

Hermann Goering

Munich, 1 January 1943

The New Year has now begun; what will it bring for us? It will
be hard. Maybe it will bring resolution; maybe it will continue
to demand more sacrifices from us. But Homeland and Front
are united, whatever may come. The *Führer* knows only
fighting, work and anxiety. If we can, we want to lift some of
the burden from him.

Munich, 12 January 1943

School began today. It does not bring much that is new. We
will have to work very hard to reach our goals. But this, too,
we will manage.

Munich, 1 February 1943

I have not put an entry in my diary for a long time. Time
passes by quickly and every day something new is expected
from us. The fight in the East continues with inexorable
harshness. We hear daily of the soldiers' heroic battle in
Stalingrad where they resist a thousand fold superior force,
where they sacrifice themselves to stop the Russian troops. On

other Fronts, also, the fighting continues. Even if we have to give up some strongholds, we will still win, and the final victory will be ours. In order to reach this goal, men and women from 16 to 65 have had to join in the total war effort. Who knows how long we will still be in school. Whatever our new obligations may be, we will take them on gladly because we know how necessary it is. I registered myself today with the Party, to which I will be admitted on April 21. Right now I am working with the *Bann* [Regiment] doing GD Inspection. I have to be Meta Meyer's assistant and help her with the GD duties. I will be helping her tonight.

Munich, 3 February 1943
Stalingrad fell today. Faithful to their country's oath, these men endured until their last breath, held back six Russian armies and killed over 300,000 Russians. The end of the glorious 6th Army was a huge sacrifice but it will not have been in vain. Stalingrad is now a Beacon for Action, spurring on our efforts. The 6th Army is not done for. Divisions of the new Army are being organized: "Long Live the 6th Army!"

Munich, 6 February 1943
Meeting of the *Bann* GD Girls in the Regional Community House. Dr. Gisela Burgdorf, the area doctor, introduced us to Anneliese Suerth who is the new area GD adviser since Margret, "our dear old house," left to be married. After a few opening words about the meaning and the purpose of this conference, we Regiment GD girls were informed about our upcoming duties. Area doctor, Dr. Feser, took the floor to speak in more detail. He told us of many satisfying jobs available right here in Munich. Qualified GD girls are to be allowed to help in the Schwabing Hospital where they will learn a great deal as they are working. Moreover, he wants to establish a GD girl leadership school connected directly to a hospital. We now want to found a GD Association in Munich,

to strengthen our organization even further. Hopefully we will be able to do it.

Munich, 7 February 1943
Today the Girls Conference continued. After a ceremonial morning assembly, we deepened our concerns about various district units by speaking of matters which lay heavy on our hearts. Concluding the Conference, Area Leader Edith Ludwig spoke to us for a short while. This evening we will all go to see *Iphigenia of Delphi* by G. Hauptmann.

Munich, 8 February 1943
Yesterday's theater presentation provided a festive touch to the GD Conference, which has been especially informational and helpful to me. Tonight I helped with check-ups again. Everything went hand in hand so that not a lot of time was lost with every girl. Afterwards I organized my GD apron and hat for my deployment in the theater tomorrow.

Munich, 9 February 1943
Today in school was the "Day of the Working Youth." We gathered in the auditorium for a song to the flag and the school principal's speech about our obligations in school, in our parents' home and to our Fatherland. Group Leader of Ring I, Ursel Weidemann, then spoke about our deployments, our increasing achievements and about discipline. Our nation's anthems closed this special program. In the afternoon I had a meeting with Ursel about a GD course which will be starting at Munich North. A medical student will teach the class to the girls from Ring II. *Iphigenia in Taurus* was performed for us in the theater. The presentation of this immortal work by Goethe maintained its special effect through first-class acting by the cast. Anna Kerstin played Iphigenia and received great applause for her outstanding skill. This performance demonstrates again the German will to keep alive not only

such theater presentations but our entire artistic culture, even in the fourth year of war. And our enemies want to destroy something like that!

Munich, 12 February 1943

Fairy Tale Parent Evening in the Student House. Through invitation of my old group I went with Manny to the Fairy Tale Parent Evening of Ring II. The evening went smoothly, the girls trying really hard to present a well-managed show. Great applause rewarded the young actresses who put on such a lively and unaffected production of fairy tales, charade and circus.

Munich, 14 February 1943

I am just returning home from a session of GD studies-review. Two students spoke on the subjects of nutrition and hygiene. Then came the news that I had already known about since Sunday. We are being allowed to volunteer in the hospital. My colleague and I were the first to sign up. Our eagerness is beyond description. We understand that the work will be hard and that we will have to learn quickly, but the good thing is: "We help."

Munich, 20 February 1943

Theater series: *Don Pasquale.* We truly enjoyed this lively opera by Donizetti. The catchy music, paired with the masterful artistry of the singers, drew forth our full applause. The flowers for Mrs. Anni von Grusevyk expressed our gratitude for this artistic experience.

Munich, 25 February 1943

Last night there were two air raid alarms, but there were no aircraft near us. Nuremberg got hit.

Munich, 26 February 1943

Last night, also, there was an air raid alarm. One could hear flak shooting only far away. It must look like wasteland in Cologne after this latest attack which destroyed at least eight hospitals. Our hospital deployment will begin after Easter.

Munich, 18 March 1943

I have to dig really deep to describe the events of the last week. Overnight from the 9th to the 10th, Munich was horribly damaged by a severe English attack. The sirens went off half an hour before midnight. We had barely gotten to the cellar when the flak shooting started — and continued for the next two hours. The destruction was terrible. I made myself available to our local group, even during the alarm. By the time I got to the Hofkuechengarten, the homeless from Galeriestrasse were already gathered there. On that street the destruction is serious. It is thought that even our work place has been destroyed. The people sat there quietly composed, grateful for any help. The first round of duty was done at 5:30 and I could go home. Many people had become homeless in just a few hours. When I got back to school, I heard of the big losses that hit Stupsi. She lost just about everything but, thank God, she got out alive and well. None of our minds were on the class work. We wanted to help, and it was like redemption to get the command of the school principal, which ordered us to duty with the Regiment. We went home quickly, changed into our work clothes and off we went. Everywhere, the picture of destruction! The Dom [Cathedral, the *Frauenkirche*] stands in imminent danger of collapse. Everywhere are shards of glass and destroyed homes. The Regiment separated our class [for different duties]. I led a group to the Nymphenburg Castle. We were welcomed joyously. Bread had to be cut, dishes had to be washed and food had to be handed out. Soon we were right in the middle of it and were happy that we could help. There was quite a commotion when the food got there: semolina grits with meat. We worked according to plan: one washed dishes, another passed out the bread, the third the tea and the others the food. By 8:00 p.m. everything was done and we went home. The next morning began a new work day. All girls worked very hard, which made me very happy. First off, we moved over to the Prinzenhof and pitched in with mugs and pots, milk and food. After a jolly ride on a pick-up truck we arrived at the Prinzenhof: "Order of 1,800 meals," announced the office leader of the NSV [*National Sozialistische Volkswohlfart*, National Socialist People's Welfare]. "This can become interesting," we all thought. We arranged ourselves quickly and worked without a hitch. With the food came also the first guests. Everything had to move quickly now. After the homeless came the military, then the working men. Dinner disappeared in the blink of an eye. After we finished cleaning everything, we had a short break that we truly deserved. On Friday we had the same hubbub. I had the bread cutting duty. The job went chop-chop and the finger went into the bread-cutting machine. Bleeding stopped quickly, finger bandaged and then I just kept going. Unfortunately, the cut opened up and I had to give up my duty in Nymphenburg. But I am still happy that I could help the people who have lost everything and to assist their transition into a new life. A worthy grave was prepared for the victims of the terror attack. The funeral — total number of dead 205 — was attended by a great many people.

Munich, 23 March 1943
I received sad news today when I got home from school; Head Nurse Ursula Sitzkelitz died. Her death was unexpected and must have happened quite suddenly. I am glad that, for a while, I was able to provide support and cheer for her and that our exchange of letters brought her joy. Our brief friendship was built on reciprocated love.

Munich, 25 March 1943
Theater series: *Emilia Galotti* at the Schauspielhaus. The splendidly produced and excellently presented performance sparked our applause, which continually increased up to the very end. An extraordinary evening.

Munich, 27 March 1943
Eighty girls awaited their graduation. Parents and students came for the farewell festivities. Two Bach choirs initiated the special program. After a piano solo, a graduating student expressed thanks from the class to the teachers and parents. My class members and I all thought the same: Next year one of us will stand at the podium. Next year....

Munich, 4 April 1943
Big Rally at Circus Krone in recognition of Munich's *Gesundheitsdienst Mädel* [Health Service Girls, part of the BDM, *Bund deutscher Mädel*, League of German Girls, itself part of the Hitler Youth]. We GD girls [*Gesundheitsdienst Mädel*] went on duty in the Circus Krone building and really had plenty to do. At first the girls had to overcome their shyness but then they swung into action. We were called from one direction or another to bring the sick to the hospital tent. It filled us with pride that we were able to handle this deployment through our own strength. Regional Leader Giesler and County Leader Lederer requested that we assist the mothers who have many children with their routine housekeeping chores in order to relieve them of their concerns about their youngsters [apparently evacuees temporarily housed at Circus Krone]. Ever since this Sunday, the whole population of Munich knows that here we have German girls with German hearts who want to help wherever in Munich we are needed. After the Proclamation, an enormous demonstration in which 8,100 girls took part, we marched through the city to the heroes' statue in front of the Army Museum. Laying of the wreaths in

remembrance of our fallen closed the fulfilling afternoon.

Munich, 10 April 1943
Theater visit: *Peer Gynt* by Ibsen in the free translation by Dietrich Eckhart.

Munich, 12 April 1943
First GD duty in the northern sector of the city. Even though not many girls were there, those that came were very useful and take seriously their work in public health. Let us hope that we will be able to fulfill our duty in this new assignment.

Munich, 13 April 1943
Concert in the Tonhalle with Oswald Kabasta. He conducted Wagner's *Overture to Tannhaeuser*, *Till Eulenspiegel* by Richard Strauss and Beethoven's *Third Symphony*, *The Eroica*. Our excitement was evident in the drawn out applause at the end. A Hitler Youth handed the Maestro a beautiful bouquet of flowers. A wonderful evening!

Munich, 15 April 1943
When we got back from a theater afternoon in school yesterday, we found that a letter had arrived in which Theo announced he would visit. We were so happy! In the evening, we went to the train station. But it seemed that no Theo had arrived. *Vati* and I got home to realize that, when neither one of us had spotted him at the station, Theo had gone on ahead of us and was already home. Time flew by as we shared stories. Midnight had long passed when, there! the howl of sirens. Down into the cellar. But it seems that nothing serious happened. Too bad that Theo had to return to Berlin early in the morning. We hope he will return again very soon.

Munich, 18 April 1943
As of today I am a Party member. We young Party-initiates were taken into the Party in a ceremony in front of the

Feldherrnhalle during County Munich's celebration of the *Führer*'s birthday. County Leader Lederer, after a speech in which he brought to mind revered tenets, pledged us into the Party by leading us in recitation of this oath: "We commit ourselves to fulfilling the demands of the *Führer* and promise to do so faithfully and responsibly as long as we shall live. We will prove worthy of the trust the *Führer* places in us." After everyone had taken the oath, the Local Group Leader welcomed each of us into the Party with a hand shake and by distributing Party insignia.

Munich, 22 April 1943

The school doors will be closed for a short time. In all-out war the rule is "Your school is now wherever you can best work for victory." After this vacation, an achievement contest will begin. The aim for each of us will be to improve our scholarship. The contest will reach its climax when the student judged to be the highest achiever is awarded the victory medal. Last night, for the first time in a long while, I had the post of school security night-watch. We settled ourselves in comfortably. One can sleep well even on hard straw.

Munich, 2 May 1943

County Council in Fuerstenfeldbruck. With Anneliese Suerth I went to the meeting in Fuerstenfeldbruck. This was the first time the GD girls worked there, and they were so happy to be in their apron-and-hat uniforms. Too bad for them that there was not a lot of work to do. The regiment leader was proud of her *Jungmädel* and of the older girls who sang to the regional leader and received 10 accordions in return. I could speak with Anneliese about anything that had to do with us GD girls. Looking back, this County Council was very useful for me.

Munich, 3 May 1943

School starts again tomorrow, which means a lot of hard work.

But this will not be so hard for me since I have set the goal of becoming a physician and will work very hard towards that achievement. GD school in Berchtesgaden opened.

Munich, 29 May 1943

I have just come from the theater: Goethe's *Faust I*. For quite some time now, a symbolic act precedes each performance. All stand up and salute the middle section where the injured soldiers have taken their seats: a greeting to the honored citizens of the nation. After that the performance begins. Great applause rewards the actors who through their outstanding performance drew us deeply into Goethe's tragedy.

Munich, 7 June 1943

Local group meeting. Since I am now a Party member of our local group, I received an invitation to this year's Party Conference. After a welcome from the local group leader, Regional Speaker Party Member Meister spoke about the duties of National Socialists during times of war. Our jobs will be easier if we continually keep in mind the early struggles of the National Socialist Party.

Munich, 8 June 1943

Theater series: *Robinson Shall Not Die*. This play by Friedrich Forster takes us into the poverty stricken life of Daniel Defoe, author of the timeless *Robinson Crusoe*. In flowing fashion, the last years of his life are played out. A wayward son leaves his father behind in poverty, stealing his last treasure—the handwritten Robinson manuscript—and selling it. After a series of imaginative adventures involving children, the manuscript is returned to the original owner. The children declare, "Robinson shall not die." We thanked the actors from the bottom of our hearts for this seemingly effortless performance, especially Gustaf Waldau, Inge Schmitt and the children.

Munich, 22 June 1943

Second year at war with the Soviet Union. Two long years have passed since that day when the *Führer* held back the Soviets and saved Germany and Europe from the danger of the East. Two long years of privation for our fighters at the East Front who made it through hard winters and endured muddy seasons in scalding heat. They fight for our peace and protect us from the horrors of Bolshevism.

Munich, 3 July 1943

County Munich Roll Call: loyalty promises to the *Führer*. We regiment GD advisors provided health care security for the incoming leaders; unfortunately nothing happened. After welcoming words from the county leader, Regional Leader Giesler spoke encouraging words about the youth and their care, the youth who have grown so close to his heart. Our spirited applause thanked him for his words. His speech was an accounting report: much has been done already, but much more still has to be accomplished. After such a rousing speech, one feels renewed strength for the struggle which each day brings.

Munich, 4 July 1943

Big rally in front of the Feldherrnhalle with Paul Giesler and Dr. [Robert] Ley. A radiant sunny summer day, the sun was shining down hot on the big plaza; the southern blue sky showed no sign of clouds. In spite of the intense heat, we *Mädels* did not show many signs of nausea. In agreement with the DRK [*Deutsches Rotes Kreuz*, German Red Cross], we brought afflicted people to the DRK meeting place where they would get further treatment. Dr. Ley highlighted for us the struggles which the populations who live in the bomb-targeted areas have to live with daily. Hate towards the English, those murderers and fire bombers, increases steadily. How can we remain peaceful when these murderers and fire bombers destroy our Cathedral in Cologne; aim senselessly at our hospitals, children's homes and churches; at residential areas and suburban communities; daily claiming so many lives. We will freely breathe a sigh of relief when revenge is extracted for all these criminal deeds. After the speech by the Reich Organization Leader, applauded with great approval, came the parade in review before the Region Leader and his guest, followed by the closing concert in the courtyard. County Munich Roll Call is an acknowledgement of Homeland loyalty to the Front, an acknowledgement of our loyalty to the *Führer*. Munich stands before Greater Germany, even before the entire world, showing how our city and its people have been sullied with shameful rumors. We stand together: the Capital of the National Socialist Movement.

Munich, 10 July 1943
Area sport games 1943. Today Petrus [mythological weather deity] is definitely not on our side. Our sport games are rained out. Today, Saturday, were the regiment and area final competitions. Aside from treating small wounds and scrapes, there was nothing much for our GD girls to do.

Munich, 11 July 1943
Still today it rains without interruption. In the stadium there was uncertainty as to whether to call it off or keep it going. But in the end the presentations and the games were stopped. Thank God, matters with the Berchtesgaden GD School are now cleared up. We are being allowed to visit the school and to study and work in the Dietrich Eckart Hospital. I am already so excited about this.

Munich, 12 July 1943
Anneliese Suerth wanted to come to my GD job tonight but, after some back and forth, we decided to go to the concert of Spielschar [amateur performers] Hochland in the courtyard of

the Ministry of Culture. The landscaping there was beautiful. The boys and girls of the Spielschar were positioned beyond the green lawn and the fountain while their comrades in the area orchestra played half-hidden by hedges. Great applause rewarded the young musicians and singers whose madrigals and folk songs rang out into the tepid summer night. With this, the program celebrating the 15th anniversary of the Hochland Area ended.

Munich, 14 July 1943
The 1942-1943 school year has now ended. For us, it was only a very short one since the first trimester was almost completely cancelled. When classes resumed at Easter, Area Leader Emil challenged the Munich high schools to an achievement competition under the motto "Book and Sword." All students of the school now met in the assembly hall for the victory celebration during which the *Siegernadel* [Victor's Needle, oval shaped] award would be given. After the "Parisian Entrance March" and the song "Oh Germany High in Honors," our headmaster spoke about the purpose and goal of the achievement competition. Our class ranks third out of the 25 classes. For the seventh grade this is surely a great achievement. With pride, Hilde picked up the document. Then each of the three best students in each class received the *Siegernadel*. These are the best students of the entire school. Once we returned to our classrooms, Professor Zweckstaetter handed out the additional *Nadel* medals: I ranked 14th so I am in the upper half. Loaded with our report cards, we separated with best wishes for our recuperation until we come together again [as seniors] for the last stretch.

Munich, 15 July 1943
Today the decision was made that we are not being allowed to go to Berchtesgaden but will stay in our school at the Hochland camp. Hopefully, there will be something to do in

the hospital ward. We are mad at Feser in the depths of our souls. Vengeance would be sweet.

Munich, 3 August 1943

Tomorrow we will have been on vacation for three weeks. At the last minute I was not allowed to go to the Hochland camp. So I pass my time reading, writing and doing Christmas needlework, because during school I have little time for all that while juggling my job and school work. Anyway, the air raid protection measures have to be continually strengthened. Take away sand, fill up buckets of water etc., preventive measures that are necessary due to the ever increasing number of air attacks. Hamburg was the hardest hit of the all the western Reich cities which are being bombed. People from the bombed out areas come to us for help, bringing with them what little they still have. They go on to live in the mountain villages, hoping to recover at least their health. These are wounds brought on by this war. We must, however, remain strong and carry in our hearts hatred for our enemies who do not want a united Reich. Even as I write these sentences, the sirens are howling "Air Raid!"

Munich, 15 August 1943

It is quiet here now since Manny left. He became an Air Force assistant with the Flak [anti-aircraft spotting]. At the same time he gets 18 hours of classroom instruction. Soon his education will be completed and he will be assigned directly to the Flak. For *Mutti* it is very hard as Manny is just 16½ years old. This sacrifice is demanded of us and we will have to bear it.

Munich, 18 August 1943

Munich looks like a bee swarm. Since the awful attacks on Hamburg, everything has gone crazy. Furniture, clothing, etc. are being sent to the countryside. Authorities and offices move to the country. Mothers with children up to the age of two are required to leave; those with children up to 10 years may leave if they wish. Entire schools go into the KLV. I wonder what they are going to do with my school. Last Monday was the deployment debriefing of the Hops Council. I will not join the hops harvest now but will accompany a KLV transport. Another new assignment, which will surely bring me joy — especially since my colleague will be going with me. We have prepared well in case of catastrophe. Suitable GD girls are being pulled in for catastrophe duty. They support the DRK [*Deutsches Rotes Kreuz*, German Red Cross] and all other emergency personnel.

Munich, 19 August 1943
Little has changed at school. Everyone except Hanni and Irmi Giesen returned. I don't think things are going all that badly. It is only the agitators and the rumor mongers who cause such disruption. In the West and North of the Reich, the people stand tall and courageous in spite of all their losses. We must also be and stay that way. Then everything will come to a good end.

Munich, 20 August 1943
For us GD girls, the long awaited deployment has come: hops and KLV transport. Today I am extremely tired, yet I still want to tell about my eventful day. In the morning we packed bags with medicine, bandages, etc. at the Virchow Pharmacy. After a long back and forth during baggage check, it finally came down to our just making it onto the train at the very last minute. After a hot train ride, we arrived at the familiar Wolnzach train station which, for me, held so many memories. After lunch, *Frau* Dr. Willms and the medical students arrived and the handing out of the medicine could begin. The GD girls journey on to their deployment by bicycle, car or train. Soon they will have settled into their work, which will bring them as much joy as it did me last year. When I am finished with my

transports, I will follow and take over the Health Department headquarters as a "nurse." My colleague and I went on to Wolnzach-Markt, emptied our suitcases etc. The "Congo Express" brought us to W.B. After another hot trip, we were back in Munich. Tomorrow our real duties begin.

Bad Wiessee, 21 August 1943

We managed our first transport. At 10:30 a.m., as we arrived at the Holzkirchner train station, children and mothers were assembling for passage. Anxieties calmed as the children found their places. Soon we heard the announcement, "GD girls come here." Amidst all this confusion, it was natural that a child with severe heart problems had gotten overly excited and nausea was the result. If only the train had left on time. But it did not leave until 12:30. After the grief of her first farewell was overcome, my little patient got better. Happily she looked at the world that flew by us outside. In Gmund we had to transfer and after a two hour delay, we boarded the bus. One of the teachers was the sister of Zwerk. We both had to collect ourselves not to start laughing. In the Hotel Albrecht a good meal waited for us; then we went to our quarters. Haus Schrader lies directly on the lake shore and is attractively furnished. The girls are certain to like it here. After dinner, the two of us strolled around this old village, so familiar to us from last year. Later we met Mr. Hoster with his wife and son — a cute boy, the little Werner. At the Restaurant Post, we passed a few happy hours in the company of the teachers. On the way home the cloudless, clear starry sky arched over us. Our first transport is over.

Munich, 22 August 1943

I am just getting home. The nest is empty. So I made myself comfortable. This morning at 7:00 [still in Bad Wiessee] we slipped out of the house to the pier in our bathing suits. Swimming was wonderful, the sun was shining, the sky was clear and bright, and all around there was not a person in sight. Refreshed, we came back on shore, got dressed and went with the others to breakfast. Afterwards we said good bye to the teachers, and my colleague went swimming again. Later we were brought to the ferry heading for Tegernsee. The two of us were very tired and had to fight to keep awake during the hot train ride. Now I sit on the cool balcony and write. Tomorrow will again bring something new.

Munich, 23 August 1943

After initial misunderstandings about the transport etc., we found the right train, this time occupied by boys. We were sure there would be no difficulties, and there weren't. Too bad that it rained. From Bruckmuehl we rode back to Munich in a special train going by way of Rosenheim. Tomorrow is a day of rest. Then we will be off again.

Berchtesgaden, 25 August 1943

Transport to Berchtesgaden. In the morning at 9:30 we started a trip to Berchtesgaden. Good that we were able to get through this time, otherwise we would not have been able to take care of small maladies that pop up here and there. After a comfortable train ride we arrived in Berchtesgaden. Petrus seemed to have been a good friend, even though the mountains lay in a haze. In high spirits, we rode the train heading for KVL Camp Hochwald, in company with those going to the KLV Camp in Schoenau. The girls have it really nice here. The house has a practical arrangement and is furnished attractively. In addition, there is plenty of open space for outdoor activities and the vistas are gorgeous. Here they can recover in safety. This is a beautiful bit of land, our Berchtesgaden, with its mountains and lakes and meadows and forests, all encompassed in heavenly peace. I truly treasure this jewel of our Homeland. But now Petrus is very mad; it is raining down naughty boys. The mountains cannot be seen.

Too bad; it could have been so nice. Let's hope for better tomorrow.

Munich, 26 August 1943
Yesterday we did manage to get back to Munich. The weather grew steadily worse; the prospects of getting some food grew slimmer. After a long ride we finally arrived in Munich. After a short intermission I lay in my featherbed and slept the sleep of the righteous. This morning we recorded our trip expenses. We both plan on going to harvest hops. We really want to work since we are not in school.

Wolnzach-Markt, 29 August 1943
We have safely landed in the Holledau. The weather is rainy and muggy but just perfect for picking. I have already comfortably adjusted to being in the Health Center. There is usually hops work only in the mornings; afternoons and evenings we have appointment hours. But then it is really intense and that puts me in my element. This is how it should be all day; then it would be right for me. One helps the doctor — who is a really great guy — handle prescriptions, bandages and massages. It is a shame that, from all that, one does not actually learn very much. I secretly hope for deployment to a hospital. Now the morning cleaning of the infirmary is over, the patients have been taken care of and the dull period sets in. But I must comfort myself with the maxim: "It does not matter where you are deployed; what matters is how you accept it."

Wolnzach-Markt, 31 August 1943
Life here goes on in its own way without worrying about the outside world. The only thing of importance here is the hops and that they must be harvested at any cost. It is good though that I can listen to the radio at night, to know what is happening in the world. Here in the Health Center work also

continues apace. After morning appointments, cleaning of the infirmary, instrument sterilization, lunch, more appointments and dinner, we still have evening appointment hours and treatment of the bedridden. Our ward is currently over-occupied. But this entire work assignment brings me happiness and joy. It is rewarding to see the healing process in action, especially on days when a patient can be discharged as healthy. We are not too impressed when a patient lacks the restraint to keep from crying out during a check-up. Our Health Center functions with quiet perseverance.

Wolnzach-Markt, 2 September 1943
Today I am still very tired. Last night I was on duty in the Health Center until 1 a.m. Also the night before that, when usually it is only until 11:00 p.m. At least there was a bed of straw to lay on in the sick-bay. So it is still nice. Last night a nurse and I took a boy with a fractured upper arm to the hospital in Pfaffenhofen. I felt sorry for the boy because of all the bouncing around, but he bravely suppressed and denied every pain. Then we picked up an injured boy in Koenigsfeld and brought him to the Health Center. I overcame my tiredness after napping from 6 to 9:30 a.m. The infirmary shines from cleanliness and everyone is in a good mood. The reporters were just here. A big crowd of them followed Heinz Mueller here and enthusiastically they wrote down what *Frau* Dr. Willms told them about the health care of these deployed boys and girls. We awaited the Region Leader who did not, after all, come to our Health Center. Instead, there was a big rally at the market place where Paul Giesler spoke to the youth about the importance of their deployments.

> Precisely in such hard times as these we have
> to double our sense of unity, and we will do it.
> We are mortal, but Germany must live.
>
>   Adolf Hitler

Munich, 4 September 1943

My hometown Munich has me again. I did not plan to come home until tomorrow night, but unfortunately, I was obligated to take my colleague to the Schwabing Hospital. The poor girl fractured her fibula for the second time, again in the left leg. So I packed my things and rode to Munich in an ambulance with my patient, along with three more girls who joined us. In the Schwabing Hospital Hilda was attended very quickly. The other three were taken to the auxiliary hospital on Maria Ward St. Then the more difficult task stood before me: informing Hilde's parents. But this was soon taken care of. It was a big surprise for *Mutti* to see me so soon again. The deployment time, which I enjoyed so much, is now over. Again, I was able to learn much and see many new things during these deployments, and to become familiar with new types of treatment. Moreover, I was able to assist in doing important work.

Munich, 6 September 1943

I am not happy about going to school, even though I do not need to review much. It is just hard to get used to again. The circle of comrades, who work towards the same goal during the next half-year before we go out into the world, has grown smaller.

Munich, 7 September 1943

Terror raid on Munich. Just after 12:00 the sirens went off. Not long after that, the first bombs fell and the flak fire started up. A sudden strong spurt of air pressure led us to think that a high-explosive bomb had fallen close by. When the air was somewhat clear, the security control determined that the only damage was broken windows, but a lot of them. It must be very bad in the southern part of the city. Phosphorous, incendiary and percussion bombs all came down in great numbers. Property damage is extensive. Fifty-three airplanes were shot down during the bombing run, one of which is credited to Manny's battery. *Mutti* is now in the Region's kitchen cooking for the homeless. In an exemplary manner, the needs of the homeless are being met. The bearing, courage and determination of the people are outstanding. The people of Munich like to whine but, when required, know how to stand strong.

Munich, 10 September 1943

Just now the national anthems are being played. The *Führer* speaks from his headquarters to the German people to tell about the collapse of Italy. Since Mussolini's capture on July 25th, a new kind of treason has been played out by the Italian King and Marshal Badoglio. Italy concluded a cease fire with the Allies, leaving its own former partners in a bind. The *Führer* immediately took counter measures. German troops took Rome and put down the Resistance everywhere. "Our" Rommel is now in Italy with his division to re-establish order and peace. With this, on top of all the bombing terror, we in the Homeland have to bond ourselves even closer together. All Germans have the same will: "*Führer* dictates; we obey."

Munich, 11 September 1943

We had to say farewell again to our teacher, who was once more drafted. It was hard for him and for us. We will have to finish the last five months without him, under the guidance of a new teacher whom we do not know. As a farewell gift, we gave him a "goodie basket" for which we had all chipped in. Who would not enjoy a present like that? The last two hours we spent just talking and talking. Any harsh feeling there may ever have been between him and his class is forgotten. Only the pleasant hours stay alive in our memories. We parted from each other with both sides expressing their best wishes.

Munich, 12 September 1943
Now I am the homemaker, already for the fifth day, because *Mutti* is still occupied in the NSV [*National Sozialistische Volkswohlfahrt*, National Socialist Welfare] kitchen. With faultless organization, they cook for ten thousand. They prepare a simple but nourishing casserole which is distributed from there to the many homeless shelters. In this, the NSV really performs something great. Here, the free provisions; there, the renewed dispatch of women and children to the country side. The Party fulfills the *Führer's* demands; it sets the example.

Munich, 14 September 1943
The world is still overjoyed at the news of the *Duce's* rescue by the *Waffen* SS and the paratroopers. With a bold surprise attack, *Obersturmführer* Skorzeny and his 12 men got an unwounded Mussolini into our hands and then on to safety. Even the enemies have to admit that the Germans reward loyalty with loyalty. They returned to the Italians their *Führer* in order to make the situation once again what it was before. The nation of Italy again fights beside its allies.

Munich, 18 September 1943
Main rehearsal for the Day of Military Training 1943, which was supposed to coincide with the beginning day of the work week in the Hochland area. At first the weather was nice. Then came such a sudden rain storm that we had to seek shelter in the waiting room of the Flak soldiers, which they kindly allowed us to use. In return we had to sing Upper Bavarian songs to them, which they, as northern Germans, really enjoyed. Our joint practice with the assistant medical officers [*Feldscher*] did not take place. The best we can do is hope that there will be good weather tomorrow.

Munich, 19 September 1943

Even today it appeared that Petrus would balk, until he thought better of it. The presentations started at 9:30 after the Region Leader arrived with his guests. Today the infantry's drill field presented a different spectacle than the usual. The boys in all their various formations showed what they could do, showed the spirit which lies within them, their joy at participating in all technical and military things. Presented were: model airplanes and gliders, gymnastics exhibits, field and bivouac skills, obstacle relay race, driving prowess of the Motor-Hitler Youth, operation of a Flak-helpers battery which is under attack, laying of cable by the Communication-Hitler Youth, not to mention our *Feldscher*-GD *Mädel* units which alternated with one another in demonstrations that gave insight into the work of the Hitler Youth under war conditions. After these presentations, a parade of all the Hitler Youth group formations, enlivening the entire field, marched in review in front of Region Leader von Epp and other dignitaries. Manny was marching with his battery.

Munich, 4 October 1943

Again, there was a heavy terror attack on Munich. This time we had unbelievable luck. Explosive benzene and phosphorous bombs fell just 200 meters from us. After the attack, I went to the office of my area group to find out what my deployment orders would be. The office had been completely destroyed. The watchword was "Do what you can on your own." We walked out after the all-clear to see the desolation of our apartment. We could not clean up anything because the light did not work so we went downstairs to help there with the bucket brigade. After two hours of effort we realized that there was nothing that could be done. Then we took to watching that fire did not jump to the next house with the next strong wind; again we built a bucket brigade and continued. When the danger was under control there, we went upstairs and lay down for two hours. First we had to move mortar pieces off our beds. One dare not even think about what was destroyed by this attack: the Opera House, part of the [Royal] Residence, whole blocks of homes, hospitals and schools. Senseless destruction wherever one looks. In the apartment we are mostly done with the clean-up. We carried mortar down by the bucketful. The ceilings fell down in all the rooms; doors and windows were blown out; all the window glass was broken. But we live and still have a roof over our head—something which many others no longer have.

Munich, 15 October 1943
Life goes on. Everyone tries to set up their home in the best way possible. We have "moved out" of the large living room and picked my room to live in. This way it is warmer as we still have no windows. Only in my room were the windows replaced right away. Work goes on. Only the ruins remind us of what has happened.

Garmisch-Partenkirchen, 17 October 1943
Regiment GD Leader Conference 1943 in Garmisch. We soon felt at home in the beautifully furnished Pension. I was already acquainted with a few of the people, but most of them were new to me. Our heads were really spinning with all the new things: a reference file and a disaster response plan patterned after the North German model. From such a conference, one finds the strength to keep on working. One feels that what we accomplish daily through the GD is not for naught; rather, we feel that we must daily work even harder to achieve the standard taken for granted in other regions. We just got back from an informal hike to Partnach Gorge, which provided an opportunity for chatting. You get so much closer when you can talk about your sorrows, share advice. This togetherness gave us all courage. At 7:00 p.m. we boarded the train back to Munich.

Munich, 28 October 1943

Duties at school, home and work continue, with expectations increasing daily. School is nearing its end. In eight months we will be through. But until then, we still have to work hard. When we finally graduate, the first goal in life will have been accomplished as we go into our chosen careers. I have done my train station duties two times already. The hours at work just fly by. Where there is a mother bringing her young children to the train, milk has to be warmed up. A young girl traveling by herself may need some advice and returning soldiers have to be directed to the Red Cross. Even though I get home extremely tired at night, I know with certainty that I was of help to other German people. I was an example to them of how the youth want to help them and that we do so with happy hearts. I could see how a cheerful word from one of us brought a smile to brighten a mother's tired face, how delighted she was that we took her children from her, giving her some time to relax and get her chores done without worrying about the children. My GD girls are happy to provide this service. My "big girls" have just been replaced by younger ones, signaling that the long awaited hospital deployment is about to begin. Let us hope this is true. If not, we will be doing a nursing course instead, taught at the main campus on Hildegard St. This will give us theoretic knowledge along with the practical.

Munich, 8 November 1943

For the 5th time we are celebrating my birthday during wartime. Let us hope that the next one will fall within the longed-for era of peace. On my birthday table I found the candle wreath: 18 candles radiating their glowing light. Excited, I saw my books: *Men against Death and Devil* by Rudolf Thiel; the *Behring-Memorial Book* by Philips University, Marburg-on-the-Lahn; *History of the Berlin Opera* and *Life of Prince Eugene*. Inge delighted me with a beautiful handkerchief, Manny with the *Eichenlaubtraegern* [photos of heroes to whom the Oak Leaves medal had been awarded], Evi with a gorgeous bouquet of roses.

Munich, 9 November 1943

Today is the 20th anniversary of the March to the Feldherrnhalle [*Putsch*] of 1923. Yesterday, to everyone's joy, the *Führer* addressed his Old Guard in the Loewenbraeukeller. In a rousing speech the *Führer* explained our situation and the policy determined by it into the foreseeable future: "Onward to victory; we do not capitulate." I have just turned 18. For me a new year of life is beginning. What will it bring? Graduation, RAD [*Reicharbeitsdienst*, Reich Labor Service], KHD [*Kriegshilfedienst*, War Auxiliary Service]? Bertel wrote in her book, "Try to live, dare to be happy." Goethe.

Munich, 26 November 1943

Actually I am extremely tired, but still I will write down today's experiences. The *Führer* called the working youth to the KBWK [*Kriegsberufswettkampf*, War Career Competition]. Reich Youth Leader Arthur Axmann was to speak to us on this occasion. The Hitler Youth of Munich met in the large assembly hall of the Freimann national railway repair station at 5:00. The colleague and I who were there on GD duty maneuvered a great spot for ourselves and stood in the first row of the parade line up. After words of greeting from a Hitler Youth, the Reich Youth Leader requested of all working youth that we take part in the KBWK. He spoke about the conduct of the country's youth during the terror attacks, while on war deployment and in their professions. The singing by the youth of their song "Forward, forward" sounded like an answer to Axmann's speech. I had barely gotten home after a long wet and cold walk, when the alarm sounded. No choice but to go down into the cellar. The terror attacks are on the increase. The Reich's capital, especially, has endured terrible terror attacks lately. The morale of its population is peerless [an example for all].

Munich, 28 November 1943

Today we celebrate the first Sunday in Advent of this year. My work program was very full today but I was able to finish it all well. The stuffed elephant for little Helga is finished; the pyramid, *Mutti*'s toy, was put up again; the package for the soldiers at the Front made ready to send. I did some embroidery and completed my school work. This is the kind of Sunday that I like, when one can happily putter. Before we went to bed, the candles were lit and their heat slowly turned the Christmas pyramid. First Advent.

Munich, 5 December 1943

Second Advent Sunday. Today we finally received the long awaited news from *Vati*, who was called back into the military November 24th [11 days ago]. Right now he is still in Belgium. Who knows where he will go from there. For now, he is doing well; he is healthy. We are slowly getting used to being alone. Along with *Vati*'s letter, there was also mail from DRK Head Nurse Hermine Stolz. She asked me to send her theatrical pieces which she can have performed for Christmas. She has, in the meantime, taken over the management of a military hospital in the French Vosges and is happy with her job. I hope I can fulfill her wish.

Munich, 15 December 1943

The classroom in the Main Campus School was decorated festively with pine greens and small stars today. We had a short break after the first class, which was about medicines and the filling of prescriptions. The girls were sent out so we could finish the last decorating and arranging. A pine wreath was put in the middle of a table on a white tablecloth with small angels and dwarfs and candlesticks of pine greens all around. We lit the candles, opened the doors wide and the girls came in with radiant expressions on their faces. Christmas songs rang out; poems and Christmas stories were shared. Miss

Obermeier, our gracious teacher, was surprised by the small package which she found at her place. At the end of our simple pre-Christmas party, Miss Obermeier said, "Even during these hard times when terror attacks threaten the German people hourly, we must keep in our hearts the German ways and celebrate our most beautiful holiday, Christmas, in meaningful simplicity."

Munich, 18 December 1943

The Christmas trimester is over. Our last days of vacation have begun. We intend to savor them. In the evening we celebrated our Nikolaus Day. Weeks before, we had already made plans, crafted and written little rhymes to make our party as nice as possible. Mrs. Neigele, the Region Children Group Leader, lent us the lighted arch with the Germanic symbols. We made candlesticks of pine cones and greens. Name place-cards made the tables look festive. The best thank you for our efforts and work was that all were so very happy and in great spirits. Dr. Feser came, with Hilde Moser and Evi, to thank us. He was also very happy about our simple but effective party, enabled through modest means. The highlight of the evening was when the "stern" Nikolaus arrived. There were reprimands for everyone's smallest of sins, so many things to laugh about, since even the most insignificant of incidents were brought up. Then we went into the "Sack," that is to say the *Krabbelsack* [grab bag of presents]. After Nikolaus departed the unofficial part of the festivity started; snacking on cookies, apples and nuts which had been donated by Dr. Feser. Manny, who had played Nikolaus so very well, was invited for this. To relax, we played some parlor games in which Dr. Feser took part. Sometimes it was so funny that our midriffs hurt from laughing. Too bad Dr. Feser and his companions had to leave. In his short speech he said that there is increasing need for us girls to replace the boys, who are having to leave earlier than planned. Having become hungry through all the game playing, we ate the rest of the cookies. A volunteer work colleague took over the cleaning and put everything back in order. With happy, open hearts we went back home. "Be joyful, the Christ child is coming soon."

Munich, 19 December 1943

Fourth Sunday in Advent, only five more days until Christmas. *Vati* has been ordered to Sylt, where he has long hoped to be assigned. There he will get to know the ocean, the "wild North Sea." He is also doing well otherwise. This will be the first Christmas without him, but thousands of others share the same destiny.

Munich, 24 December 1943

Christmas 1943; 5th War Christmas. Manny put up the Christmas tree. I decorated it the way *Vati* had always done it. Although we are already half grown up little people, we got caught up in the joy and excitement of the gift sharing. Finally we got to that point. Manny hummed some verses of the Christmas songs on and off. Even though it was the 5th war Christmas, there were plenty of items on the Christmas present table. On Manny's space, he found a beautifully handcrafted money bag, an electric shaver, books and his sweets. *Mutti* gave me a brooch, re-worked from what used to be earrings, and some stationery with my name printed on it. My poor thoughtless mother really made a big mistake here. She had it printed Thierschstrasse 33 instead of 34, but this did not cause me to enjoy it any less. *Vati* also granted me a long held wish: bookshelves made of Italian marble, also books. Manny's traditional present: the *Eichenlaubtraeger*. My colleague gave me a beautifully carved wooden box in which, resting on cotton, was a ring identical to the one she wears. After graduation we will have the date engraved. Inge gave me a beautifully hand crafted book cover, perfect for my being a bookworm. Evi delighted me with a comb and mirror set for my purse, Petra with a napkin holder, Lore with a poetry book by Gerhard Schumann, Fanni with a leather tissue holder. Not to be forgotten is Aunt Ida's present: a book all about classic authors. *Mutti* was thrilled with Manny's bookmark, which he gave her along with a writing pad. To *Mutti* I gave a coffee warmer and a small blanket which I worked in Bruegger crochet. While listening to the Christmas broadcast, which united Homeland and Front, we thought of our distant *Vati* and how he might be spending the holiday. We hoped that he received at least one of our letters. Since he was deployed he has not received a single sign of life from us. Surely he is thinking of us as we think of him. At 9:00 p.m. Dr. Goebbels delivered his traditional Christmas speech in which he emphasized the solidarity of all Germans. On this night, Front and Homeland stand in even closer union. "High night of clear stars, which stand like wide bridges, today the world must renew itself like a newborn child." [Opening lines of the National Socialist Christmas song "Hohe Nacht der klaren Sterne" which first appeared in a 1936 Hans Baumann song collection.] Fifth Christmas at war.

Munich, 29 December 1943
The old year is nearing its end. It is not at all wintry today. First it rains and then it is cold again, but no snow covers the roofs all around. I pass the vacation time by reading, writing and crafting. Visitors come, visits are made, and so the time passes. Soon I will have to start with the studying. It is my ambition to graduate near the top of my class.

Munich, 31 December 1943
Overnight it has become winter. Outside it is storming and snowing. *Frau Holle* [deity from an earlier culture; now folkloric] is working very hard. I could watch this awesome snowstorm for hours. The snow lays down a white blanket over everything. It completely covers the ruins, covers them

with the blanket of snow. Now winter is really here. Yesterday afternoon my colleague was here and we passed some happy hours together. Another letter came from *Vati*; the communication system now works. He tells of the Christmas festivities which he celebrated with his comrades. He will soon be going to a Maritime College, and then he hopes to be deployed back to Munich. Perhaps it will come to pass.

New Year's Eve Summary of 1943

I look back over the year which brought us many bad times and very few that were good. One thing it did for sure was to bring the entire German population together in a united effort for all-out war. Women and old men had to go to work either in the factories or to replace soldiers in offices and command posts. We now stand at that point in time where we must make it through, no matter how hard the going. The terror keeps getting worse. Even in southern Germany, our beautiful Innsbruck is heavily bombarded. The Reich's capital suffered heavy damages. Still, in all of these cities life goes on with the people going about their work ever tougher and more determined. We know we have to stand firm. Even as one stronghold after the other is lost, the people in 1943 do not have to starve; after each bombing, they are taken care of and the children are kept safe. The best proof of our affirmation of life is the increase in number of births. Our people want to live. In order to be able to live in peace, we have to fight this battle until the final victory is won. I am adding a year-end report:

1/1/43

From the *Führer*'s proclamation for the New Year: "There is no doubt that at the end of this war the National Socialist State will exist as an imperturbable and indestructible block in Europe."

1/9/43

Announcement of the Japanese imperial government: "The National government of the Republic of China today declared war on the British Empire and the USA."

1/20/43

Agreement between Germany and Japan on economic collaboration.

1/30/43

Tenth year anniversary of the seizure of power [by the National Socialists]. At a Rally in the Sportpalast, *Reichsminister* Dr. Goebbels reads a proclamation from the *Führer*.

2/3/43

"The battle of Stalingrad is over. Faithful to their oath until the last breath, the 6th Army under the exemplary leadership of *Generalfeldmarschall* Paulus succumbed to the superiority of the enemy and disfavor of the circumstances. The sacrifice of the Army was not for naught. They died so Germany may live."

2/5/43

Conference of the national and regional leaders to confirm the unity of all the powers of the nation for total warfare. On February 7th the *Führer* spoke to an assembly of Party leaders.

2/18/43

Total mobilization of the Homeland. At a huge Sportpalast Rally, Dr. Goebbels set forth the measures for making full use of all our strengths for the all-out war: freeing of soldiers for the Front, freeing of workers for the armament industry, introduction of far reaching work duties for women. In his speech, Dr. Goebbels exhorted, "I give voice to my conviction that Germany, through the tragic blow of fate at Stalingrad, has been vindicated to its very core. Therefore, the watchword becomes: Now! People, rise up! Storm, break loose!"

2/20/43

From the *Führer*'s proclamation on the 23rd anniversary of the founding of the Party: "Gigantic masses of the German people unconditionally agree with the New Reich's ideas and the National Socialistic conception. The Party became the immutable embodiment of this power and today it is the guarantor not only of victory but also for the preservation of our nation's future."

3/21/43

In his speech for Veterans Day in the Berlin *Zeughaus* [Armory], the *Führer* announces the World War II casualties to date: Each of 542,000 German men died a hero's death.

3/25/43

Reichsführer von Tschammer und Osten [von Tschammer und Osten is all one surname] died after a long illness.

4/13/43

The world is informed about the Bolshevistic crimes committed at Katyn. Corpses of about 12,000 Polish officers, shot by the Bolshevists, were found in mass graves in the forest of Katyn near Smolensk.

5/2/43

SA Chief of Staff Viktor Luetzenberg died due to injuries in a motor vehicle accident.

5/13/43

The African campaign is over. The OKW [*Oberkommando der Wehrmacht*, Supreme Command of the Armed Forces] announces: "The heroic battle of the German and Italian fighters in Africa came to an honorable end today. The last of the opposition groups in the area around Tunis had to quit, after going for days without water or provisions and after they used up all their ammunition. Surrender was due to the lack of necessities, not to assaults by the enemy which had encountered again and again the superiority of our arms. In spite of all their difficulties, the German and Italian fighters in Africa completed their objectives. Because of the opposition by our troops, the enemy had to engage in bitter months-long struggles for every foot of soil and had to keep its strongest forces engaged in North Africa where it incurred severe human and material losses. Thus occupied, the enemy could not fight as strong at other fronts and that became a great advantage for our united forces. The *Führer* sent a radio message to our troops."

6/5/43
At a large Rally in the Berlin Sportpalast, nine working men were awarded the *Ritterkreuz zum Kriegsverdienstkreuz*. *Reichsminister* Speer gave a speech about the accomplishments of the munitions industry while *Reichsminister* Dr. Goebbels outlined the political military situation.

6/12/43
The German garrison on the Mediterranean island of Pantelleria surrendered. The following day, Lampedusa also surrendered.

6/26/43
Reichsminister Dr. Goebbels opens the 7th great art exhibition in the House of German Art in Munich.

7/7/43
The OKW reports: "The battle in the region of Belgorod and Orel has taken on gigantic form. For some time now there have been descriptions of unheard of numbers of Bolshevist tanks lost; on some days they lost 300, 400, even 500 or more tanks."

7/8/43
The Indian Independence League of India in East Asia has

formed an Army under the name Indian National Army. Subhas Chandra Bose is their commander.

7/10/43
During the night of 7/10, the enemy began an assault on Sicily with strong naval and air forces.

7/14/43
During their series of air raids, the British destroyed historic monuments of Aachen.

7/17/43
The number of foreign workmen in the German war industry is said to be 12.1 million. At the beginning of the war, the number was only 500,000.

7/20/43
Large mass graves near Vinnytsia [in the Ukraine] were researched by an international commission of well-known forensic medicine experts. Their conclusion was that most of the victims had received shots in the back of their necks and had been buried over five years ago in these 110 mass graves.

7/22/43
In the military news, mention is made of the entire Front from the Sea of Azov to the Orel battlefield.

7/23/43
The enemy broadens its great attacks along the East Front. Simultaneously, attacks began at the Kuban Bridgehead and south of Lake Ladoga.

7/25/43
During the night there was a British terror attack against Hamburg. It caused heavy human losses and severe damage to residential areas, cultural and public buildings.

7/26/43

The Italian government's official press representative, Agency Stefani, announces: "The King and Kaiser of Italy has accepted from Benito Mussolini an offer of resignation as the Chancellor and President. The King named the Marshal of Italy, Badoglio, as his successor." In truth, Mussolini was removed, arrested and abducted against his will through cowardly betrayal. The betrayer lied in his first public speech by saying, "The war continues." His first internal Italian measure was to declare a brutal state of emergency.

7/28/43

Enemy bomb squads continued their heavy raids against the city of Hamburg.

7/31/43

Fighting becomes heavier on the main battlefields along the East Front.

8/2/43

One hundred twenty five American aircraft tried to attack the Rumanian oil reservoir. "Over half of the aircraft did not return."

8/17/43

The OKW announces that a planned withdrawal from Sicily has been in progress over the last fourteen days.

8/18/43

The *Führer* designated SA *Obergruppenführer* Wilhelm Schepmann, who had been the leader of the SA Group Sachsen, to manage SA affairs as Chief of Staff.

8/23/43

Charkov, which has been occupied and reoccupied several times throughout the eastward drive and is now only a field of ruins, was cleared again according to plan.

8/24/43
Once again, during the night, mighty British bomber squadrons carried out a heavy strike against the Reich's capital.

8/25/43
The *Führer* appointed *Reichsminister* of the Interior Dr. Frick as Reich Protector of Bohemia and Moravia. To the position vacated by Dr. Frick, he appointed Reich SS Leader Himmler. He appointed current Secretary of State and Reich Protector of Bohemia and Moravia, Karl Hermann Frank, to simultaneously hold the positions of Minister of State and Reich Minister for Bohemia and Moravia.

8/28/43
The King of Bulgaria, Tsar Boris III, the unifier of his people, died after a short grave illness. The seven year old successor to the throne, Prince Simeon, ascends to the throne as Simeon III. A regency is set up.

8/30/43
In harsh battles, fought without cessation in the East since July 5th , it has still been impossible for the Soviet Union, even with all their investments of lost lives and sacrifice of material items, to penetrate the German Front. Wherever German retreats have been made, they have proceeded in disciplined fashion, after the destruction of all objects which could be of use to the enemy.

9/1/43
Strong British air force attack on Berlin.

9/3/43
English troops land at the SW point of Calabria.

9/4/43
Renewal of terror attacks on Berlin.

9/8/43
The ignominious treason of the Badoglio government against its German brother in arms is made known. Back on September 3rd this coward sneakily made a peace treaty with Eisenhower. The OKW announces: "In south France, Italy and in the Balkans, where German and Italian troops were fighting together, the Badoglio government put in place directives which it felt necessary.

9/10/43
The OKW announces: "The Italian armed forces no longer exist." The *Führer* spoke on the radio to the German people about the Italian events.

9/12/43
A special message announced: The *Duce* has been liberated. The agreed extradition to the Americans is hereby prevented. Benito Mussolini again has taken over the highest leadership of Fascism.

9/19/43
After complete destruction of all important military plants, the troops were drawn back from Calabria and Capulia to be united with divisions in the region of Salerno. Immediately after he was freed, the *Duce* visited the *Führer* for several days.

9/22/43
General Commissioner of White Ruthenium, Region Leader Wilhelm Kube, was the victim of a Bolshevistic murderous attack in Minsk.

10/2/43
After extensive destruction of all significant war facilities,

Naples was left for the enemy.

10/5/43

Sardinia and Corsica are evacuated as ordered. The island of Kos was occupied in a two day battle.

10/8/43

At a conference of national and regional leaders, the *Führer* said, "Our whole population knows that we are in a period of 'to be or not to be'."

10/9/43

During the retreat of the Front in the East, Kuban Bridgehead was abandoned.

10/22/43

It was announced that the *Führer* welcomed members of the Bulgarian governmental council, Prince Cyril [Simeon II's uncle] and Bogdan Philov [a statesman].

10/31/43

At the *Reichsberufswettkampf* [National Vocational Competition], the *Führer* made a proclamation: "For the war effort, one needs commitment in the job. Your achievements in the National Vocational Competition are proof of your unshakable belief in victory."

11/3/43

As a remembrance of the heroic battles on the Kuban Bridge Head, the *Führer* established a Kuban Medal.

11/8/43

On the evening before the anniversary of the March to the Feldherrnhalle [the *Putsch*], the *Führer* spoke in Munich. In conclusion he said, "That which we now lose in blood will later be returned to our people. It is in new homes that a million people can be given back their existence."

11/13/43
The OKW announces the successful landing of German troops on the island of Kos. In addition, we are making great counterattack advancements in the area of Zhitomir.

11/23/43
Zhitomir taken. Island of Samos occupied. Bomber squadrons mounted a heavy terror attack on the Reich's capital. Through the dropping of many explosive and incendiary bombs, several areas of the city were devastated. Irreplaceable art galleries were destroyed.

11/28/43
During a speech at the opening of the new youth film series, *Reichsminister* Dr. Goebbels said, "There are no more stirring demands in Germany than to retaliate against the criminals from the Thames, with interest and compounding interest, for what they do to us. The German people can rest assured that we work day and night with feverish energy preparing this retaliation."

11/29/43
The *Führer* spoke to 20,000 young officers about their duties in the Army, Navy and Air Force.

12/4/43
During a new terror attack on Berlin, 53 enemy airplanes were shot down. A workshop was held for journalists.

12/9/43
In a speech before the German railway men, Dr. Goebbels said, "None of us even think of succumbing to the enemy's terror."

12/11/43
The art treasures of the cloister Montemassino were handed over to the Pope's administration. Sixty million was the result of the December 5th door to door collection for the KWHW. This was the answer of the German people to the terror attacks, the highest sum yet ever to have been collected.

12/19/43
Tenth year anniversary of the *Kraft durch Freude Werkes* [Strength through Joy organization].

12/24/43
On Christmas Eve, Dr. Goebbels addresses a radio speech to the German people. The *Führer* gives *Reichsminister* Speer the post-war task of rebuilding the cities damaged through bomb attacks. Planning and preparation shall start immediately. Through expansion of their attacks to further areas, the Russians began their winter offensive.

12/26/43
While engaging in an attack on a convoy destined for the Soviet Union, the battleship *Scharnhorst* was sunk in the North Sea, with the brave crew firing until their last shell was gone.

12/27/43
The *Führer* awarded the Grenadier-Regiment 199 "List" [named for Julius List, WWI commander of a unit in which Hitler served] a shoulder stripe with the inscription "Infantry Regiment 'List'" as a high honor for its heroic fight. The next to last Commander, *Eichenlaubtraeger* Josef Heindl, who fell on October 10th, was a workmate of *Vati*'s.

12/29/43
The destruction of communist gangs from the Balkans went according to plan with great losses for the bandits.

12/31/43

Reichsminister Dr. Goebbels gave a New Year's speech to the German people: "Gathered around the *Führer*, we German people stand at the end of this hard year of war ready to take a bold step into the unknown future. We know it will be **our** future. Fate does not **give** it to us; we have to fight for it ourselves."

1944

**Our single prayer to our God
should not be that he gives us
victory, but that he would rather
justly assess our courage, our
bravery, our hard work and our
sacrifices.**

Adolf Hitler

Munich, 1 January 1944
Now we write the year 1944. After the *Führer*'s words, we can
look confidently into the future that will surely still bring us
hard times but, in the end, victory.

Munich, 10 January 1944
Today was the last vacation day. Tomorrow the "serious side
of life" begins again. I just returned home from a GD
deployment. The Reich Chamber of Pharmacists requested GD
girls to help with the sudden pile-up of work. So at 2:00, six of
us GD girls found ourselves in the Seidl Street office. They
were expecting us there and quickly put us to work. Stamp,
sort and stamp again. Little by little almost all the workers
dropped by to observe this new arrangement. They were all
very kind to us, most of all, the Chamber's manager. When the
job was done, we were "paid." Helper's salary 0.50 per hour.
In this way, our work was given a bit of recognition. With our
help it will be possible, in the shortest amount of time, to send
out to pharmacies throughout Germany the materials which
are warehoused in Munich. This way, these valuable goods are

spread throughout several areas and are less vulnerable to being destroyed by bombs.

Munich, 12 January 1944

The school opened its gates again. For us, it is the last time. The rush to the finish has begun and hopefully will result in graduation for all of us. Service in the RAD [*Reichs Arbeit Dienst*, National Labor Service] continues. We gladly do our duties. What we do is not much and is not grand, yet we know we are doing work that has to be done. Now I sit here in the comfortable classroom of the *Mutterschule* [Main Campus School] and wait for my girls. It won't be long before we have finished the course.

Munich, 16 January 1944

Finally it was clarified with the RAD. I was picked for the student *Ausgleichdienst* [service alternative to being in the military]. At least now I know where I stand. On Monday I will go before the Student Council. Hopefully my dream will come true and I will go to an auxiliary KLV hospital, preferably to the auxiliary hospital Berta in Reichenhall. I know I could learn a lot working with *Frau* Dr. Willms. Events quickly stumbled over one another; the Student Council did not allow me to go to the KLV. Alternative service is allowed only in the NSV [*Nationalsozialistische Volkswohlfahrt*, National Socialist People's Welfare]. The final exams started today after they had been postponed for an entire month. Our graduation is supposed to take place already on February 15th. The Latin test is behind us; hopefully we passed. Tomorrow the remaining foreign languages will be tested. The momentum we have achieved carries us forward into the unavoidable.

Munich, 31 January 1944

Yesterday was January 30th, the 11th anniversary of the seizure of power. The *Führer* spoke from his headquarters to his people. He spoke confidently of the coming days and months which, while still bringing us some suffering, will also bring victory. We passed our examinations. All of the fuss is over. Now we have twelve days of vacation, which we have truly earned. In eleven days our years of school will come to an end. We are all very comfortable now, enjoying our last days of togetherness.

Munich, 5 February 1944
The days move on and daily bring something new. All the testing fear is over and soon we have to say farewell to those who have been our companions for eight or more years. The Latin exam had to be taken again because a small cheating incident was discovered. But now it is over. Next week we still have a choir practice, but then it is off into life; for me, hopefully to Reichenhall. Outside it is wintry again. The snow falls densely and the wind blows cold. A real winter, just as it should be. *Vati* is in Wilhelmshaven right now at the Administrative School of the War Navy [*Kriegsmarine*, the KM]. Due to the terror attacks on the city, mail is delayed. We worry and hope that nothing bad happens to *Vati*. Not every shot hits its mark.

Munich, 12 February 1944
The finish line has been reached. An eight year long segment of life is over and a new life begins. At 11:00 a.m. teachers and parents gathered in the festively decorated hall. After the performance of a choral piece by Beethoven, Traudel Koesel thanked the parents and teachers on behalf of all the graduates. She spoke a remembrance of our Garri who could not celebrate this day with us. In humorous terms, she described our class's development through the years. After the hymn by Gluck, our principal spoke serious words in keeping with the wartime situation. Seamlessly, without a period of transition, we will step into our next lives, whatever for each that may be. Abrupt

though that may seem, we will do it with happy hearts. My graduating report card had some pleasant surprises for me. I can be proud of my grades. The first step towards my university education is accomplished. Performance of a spring choral number and a song of praise followed the distribution of the report cards. Singing of the national anthems closed the short, serious celebration. Conference for the Regiment (*Bann*) GD leaders. After everyone had arrived, Dr. Hoenig talked about First Aid procedures, illustrated by accounts from his country practice. Florian Seidl recited from his poems, ballads and novels. His exciting way of presenting them brought the stories to life.

Munich, 13 February 1944

My colleague and I picked up Area Girls Leader [*Gebietsmädelführerin*] Inge Piebats at the agreed upon place. It was very exciting to talk with her. The morning meeting was all about preparation for the struggles which lay ahead of us. We girls have to stay strong and brave "come what may." *Frau* Dr. Vogel spoke about "foot problems and incorrect posture," subjects that are good to know about under any circumstances. Dr. Feser updated us about on-going work, covering all important issues and answering questions. A community meal followed. In the evening we all went to hear Horst Taubermann in a song recital.

Berchtesgaden, 15 February 1944

Now I am traveling into real winter. The Berchtesgaden area is already bedecked in its most beautiful snow adornments—and still it snows. After an arduous climb, I arrived at Castle Fuerstenstein, but in vain. Nobody there. At the Four Seasons, nurse Matilda was ready to show me my new home. I was assigned to the Stiftskeller and will also be watching over another camp. This way I will really get to know Berchtesgaden. There is work already: a girl with 40.5 degree-centigrade fever lies in the ward. I expect the doctor any moment. Surely the little one will have to go to the hospital. Now I sit in my room, which I am sharing with another leader, wear my new house slippers and try to get myself settled in. Soon, fulfilling work will make me happy.

Berchtesgaden, 20 February 1944
I have only been here for six days, yet it feels like eternity. I had gotten so comfortable working in the Stiftskeller and now have to move over to the Park Hotel. I am already well acquainted with Berchtesgaden. The daily walk up to the Schoensicht never fails to thrill me. It is so quiet all around, only sleigh bells are heard here and there. The sun shines and immerses the mountains in its mild light. I could gaze forever upon this wintry splendor. My room here is bright and large, has a balcony in front and is on the south side with a view to the Watzmann Mountain. Here there is nothing to remind one of the war and the bombing terror. Peaceful is this picture of nature. I don't have all that much work to do. Tomorrow I will make my first visit to the other camps.

Berchtesgaden, 21 February 1944
I enjoyed a nice afternoon with Bertl yesterday at Lake Koenig [the *Königsee*]. The paths around the lake are very dangerous but we were able to get through as far as the *Malerwinkel* [Painters' Angle, a scenic overlook]. It is surely the most beautiful lake in Germany. Unfathomably dark, it lies there embedded in mountains that are reflected in it. The mood constantly changes, sometimes opaque, other times clear and transparent. The afternoon was a great joy for me. Now I have five camps to visit: Stiftskeller, Schoensicht, Haus Koerber, Bavaria and Park Hotel. Right now accidents are on the increase, as are illnesses brought on by the cold. In between visiting the patients come the hygiene inspections, with much walking involved in both. This is how the days pass quickly, yet seem like an eternity. No matter. Daily I get closer to my

goal.

Berchtesgaden, 26 February 1944
The last few days brought with them plenty of work. Little Berta broke her lower leg. We had quite a ride on the sleigh up to the hospital. And all that for naught. Yesterday we drove up with the car and took her on to Hospital Katrin in Bischofswiesen. Today I took over little Marai and another patient. Now I sit on my balcony enjoying the sight of the beautiful landscape drenched in sunlight. This afternoon I went to the Dietrich-Eckart-Hospital with Brigitte. Thirty-four days until .... The walk to the Dietrich-Eckart-Hospital made me very happy. It, my future workplace, is simply fabulous. Too bad everything is camouflaged, but the entire house seems to be made of glass. The landscape penetrates the rooms. Construction is plain and simple in Upper Bavarian style. It goes well with the surrounding houses and fits into the landscape. It should be a joy to work there.

Berchtesgaden, 28 February 1944
I have been in this new assignment for eight days now and have become quite comfortable with it. My working arrangements totally and completely fulfill me, the staff is cordial and the wintry landscape is beautiful. What more could I want. Last night I got to bed late. Little Amalia got an infected appendix and had to be brought to the hospital. The little one was a real trooper, bumping by car over the hard road to the hospital down below. So every day of accomplishments also brings worries which have to be overcome.

Berchtesgaden, 3 March 1944
Today brings departure. Saying farewell to the girls was very hard for me but was made easier by the joy of knowing what comes next. Oswald was here yesterday afternoon. Just as he

started to leave, Dr. Willms called and said that I have been assigned to her and will be going to Haus Berta in Reichenhall. Oh, I am already so excited. This fulfills my innermost wish. I look forward to working and living in Reichenhall.

Reichenhall, 4 March 1944

Now the mood of the hops harvest is with us again. This locale brings up memories of the close friendships we had back then and provides enough gossip to last for hours. It was a beautiful camaraderie that we formed back then. I did not actually get to the camp. Rather, I learned that my job will be to look after 17 KLV camps. I will really have to hustle in order to do this because seven of the camps are in the Bavarian-Gmein. Where there is a will there is a way. That is what I am here for: to work and to work harder. Anyway, we are compensated by getting to have informal chats with *Frau* Dr. Willms, who took me away from Dr. Feser and welcomed me here so warmly. Today I am very tired from having made my first visits to all the camps. Now I know what my work is to be and am happy that I can really get started on Monday.

Reichenhall, 8 March 1944

Time just flies by. One often does not know how it passes. When I march through the area all alone, tromping through the high snow, I get this happy feeling that I am helping here. I help the children who are away from home by at least being at their side when they are ill. Anyway, at night when I am dead tired, I know my day was not for nothing because the sick children needed me. This knowledge gives me both a sense of elation and of fulfillment. The winter means us well; it snows and snows and simply does not want to stop. I really like the mad rushes I make through the countryside and often return from my rounds looking like a snowman.

Reichenhall, 12 March 1944

Veterans Day. I think of the loved ones far away, of relatives and friends that fell for the *Führer* and for the people. There have been so many who sacrificed their lives. I think of the dead in our Homeland who lost their lives in the daily attacks. I think of all of them today. Their sacrifices should not be for nothing. I already have been in Reichenhall for over eight days. Each day I rejoice that I can work here. I can do the work easily: mornings in Reichenhall, or mornings in Bavarian-Gmain with afternoons in Reichenhall. Soon I will be working closely with Nurse Bertl, from whom I expect to learn a lot. Most evenings we either go out or spend pleasant hours just chatting. "Those who want to work must do so joyfully." This sentence gives direction for our life here. Yesterday came the order for my deployment to Berchtesgaden in the GD school. How happy I am—and to have 20 more days of eager anticipation, all that while still in the company of Dr. Willms.

Reichenhall, 15 March 1944

Actually, I am very saddened but, as long as one can still hope, I suppose it will be all right. The Region Student Leadership [*Gaustudentenführung*] struck a line through my plans: Vacation time not granted. This puts my visit to the GD school in question. Hopefully Anneliese will at least still take me for 13 days during the ward changeover. This would still give me some idea of how things are done there. Maybe it will work. Otherwise life goes on here as usual. Mornings I visit the camps and help with the appointments. Afternoons we do our shopping or, like today, help with the check-ups etc. Tonight in Villa Berta there will be a Variety Show so that our patients will have other things to think about. They practice eagerly and so are diverted from the feelings of homesickness that keep sneaking in despite all our efforts.

Reichenhall, 16 March 1944

Today is Manny's birthday. He is only seventeen years old but already a soldier for the Homeland Flak. He passed his War-Navy [*Kriegsmarine*] exam in Stralsund and will be enlisted in October. His wish is granted. May the new year of life bring him health, happiness and the ability to reach his goal! Last night's Variety Show demonstrated to us the high morale of our patients in House Berta. They really worked very hard to bring us something nice, and accomplish it they did. Often we laughed so hard that we were in tears. Dance recitals, songs, speeches and small theatrical pieces alternated with each other in lively progression. The children will not soon forget this evening. Happy and contented, they allowed us to put them to bed.

Reichenhall, 20 March 1944

The days just fly by, filled with work but also with a sense of peace. I just took over Nurse Gretl's work area, in addition to my own, and now work during the appointment hours. This is teaching me a great deal. Every day brings something new. Dr. Willms is such a good teacher that it makes us want to learn. Munich had another daytime attack, again causing a lot of damage and taking a few human lives as well. There is still no news from *Mutti*, though I am hoping for the best. I just made it through my last ward. This is the fourth time I have been placed in a new setting and this time is the nicest. My comfortable room is next door to that of *Frau* Dr. Willms. Nurse Gretl came back from her vacation and took over for me at the Reichenhall camp so I can completely dedicate myself to appointments and to the Bavarian-Gmein camps. Until April 1st when there will be changes again.

Reichenhall, 23 March 1944

Every day here passes so quickly. Mornings after breakfast: make visits, keep appointments or march to Bavarian-Gmein.

After coffee: check-ups, weighing and measurements. In between, there is emergency care, as today when two patients with broken arms had to immediately be taken to the hospital. There is always something to do: a urinalysis, supervise a blood test, refill bandaging rolls and make the instruments shine from cleanliness. Often, at night, I am very tired. Until I go to bed I sit comfortably with Dr. Willms having deep conversations about the past and about what the future may bring. In another nine days I must again say farewell to lovely people and move on to get acquainted in a new workplace. The last attack on Munich was very hard on our neighborhood; another bomb fell close by. Thank God nothing happened to *Mutti*. I understand that the city looks terrible. *Vati* went back to Sylt, where he likes it very much. Hopefully Manny will be released from the military hospital soon.

Reichenhall, 25 March 1944

Vati is celebrating his 50th birthday today. My thoughts wander over to him in Sylt. From the bottom of my heart I wish that the next years bring him peace and quiet, and that he stays healthy. In House Berta we also have a birthday child. In order to prepare everything, we got up a quarter hour earlier today. *Frau* Dr. Willms got him some postage stamps and a picture of the *Führer*, while we gave him a book. Pine branches and a burning candle were neatly arranged in front of his place at the table. We sang a cheerful song to awaken our birthday child. Dear little Reinholt was overwhelmed with joy.

Reichenhall, 27 March 1944

I have begun my last week in Reichenhall. Outside it is unfriendly, cold and wet. Rain is cleaning the snow away. Here in the house everything goes on the same. Mornings, appointments and ward rounds; afternoons, physical examinations, etc. Everyone pitches in to help because the hospital beds are all full and the two nurses are alone. With everyone's help, the work gets done. Oswald had to enlist, so our small hops group gets smaller and smaller. Another six days — then I, too, will be in a new workplace in new surroundings.

Berchtesgaden, 3 April 1944
I have to reach back in my thoughts in order to record events of the last few days. Those last few days in Reichenhall, filled with work and happiness, went by far too quickly. We, who had become friends so quickly, were united for the last time at a small farewell party. We chatted, did handcrafts and drank tea. On April 1st, for the last time, I worked through the scheduled appointments and made the round of ward visits. In the afternoon I ambled on over to B'gaden with Claire Boehm. Anneliese and Lieselotte Stolz welcomed us warmly and told me that I was to substitute for the school leader. On top of that, on that very first day, Dr. Feser came to visit. It went better than I thought it would. After lunch, the weather being beautiful, we went to Lake Koenig. It was blissful. After this long walk we were all very tired. In the evening, I passed out aprons and caps to enthusiastic recipients. This morning we were awakened early for flag-raising and breakfast, then off to the hospital. There, the head nurse welcomed us and assigned us to the different wards. I go to women's surgery. Nurse Rosemarie showed us our jobs: Pass out the coffee, dust, and then the real nursing duties of bandaging, organizing bandaging carts, cleaning and sterilizing instruments. Then it was time to pass out the midday meal. At 12:30 the job was over. Rich in new impressions, we left the house in which we will be working and learning daily. This afternoon, class instruction will be held at Anneliese's.

Berchtesgaden, 7 April 1944
The days are just rushing by. Mornings in the hospital from 7:00 to 1:00 there is always work to do: fill orders, re-bandage,

move patients to the radiation area or to the operating rooms. In between, serve breakfast, second breakfast and lunch. It seems routine but there is always something new to see if one only opens one's eyes. This morning I was, for the first time, able to watch as a cast was being put on. All hands moved around each other like clockwork until it was all finished. These opportunities to learn through observation are marvelous. These days we are learning a lot about misery and bravery. Soldiers with amputated limbs are thankful for every small assist. Many new ones arrive in our ward with the hardships of their long journeys and the sufferings they bear still written on their faces. Often they can express appreciation with only a hint of a smile, so weak are they. I am happy to be in this job which allows me to help a little.

Berchtesgaden, 10 April 1944
Easter 1944. This year I will not be at home but will celebrate Easter in the company of the GD girls and the wounded soldiers. Saturday we went into the forest and got moss, pine greens and flowers—the first messengers of spring. We arranged all these things decoratively on little plates. In the ward we decorated vases and got everything ready. Yesterday, on Easter Sunday, together with the nurses, we sang songs with morning and spring themes. Along with this joyous Easter salute, we brought the soldiers their Easter plates and put flowers in the vases. The holiday mood lasted all day and was evident even as we worked. After lunch we went up to the Platterhof Mountain. Our greater wish, to see the *Führer*, was not granted. But still, it was a beautiful walk in our world of mountains. In the evening we had free time and soon we went to bed. Today Petrus was mad at us. We wanted to go to Salzburg but had to change our plans because of the weather. There is always so much to write about and so many things to put in order, that we can still make for ourselves a rewarding day. Tomorrow we will go to our jobs with renewed vigor.

Berchtesgaden, 18 April 1944
I have not written for a long time. Instead of taking care of the soldiers, I am lying in bed allowing others to take care of me. I seem to have a terrible cold. I am already doing much better. If I could only return to the girls!

Munich, 26 April 1944
I have to think hard to describe all the events of the last few days. On the 22nd of April I was finally released from the KLV auxiliary hospital after the suspicion of typhoid fever turned out to be nothing, Thank God! The laboratory results were negative. Light of heart, I returned to the Schoenfeldspitze where I was welcomed with cheers. The girls were no longer there, but the *Bann* GD Advisors were holding a conference. Among them was a guest from the Duesseldorf area, *Bann* GD Advisor Hilde Wrossen, who gave us factual information about assignments carried out by GD girls during night bomb attacks. She quickly became a good comrade. It was not easy to get her to tell us how she earned the *Kriegsverdiesnstkreuz* [War Merit Cross]. She always just spoke about her girls. She led the work team— "Immediate Deployment, Transfer, Completion"—to which Claire and I belonged. Many a day and night we spent talking together, but it was so nice just to listen to her. Sunday was a bright beautiful day, so we went to Lake Koenig, making a round trip tour to the Alps by way of St. Bartholomeo. So much beauty abides in our Homeland: a bright blue sky, the mountains that surround the lake and the lake, itself, the deep green Lake Koenig. In the afternoon there were classes. Petrus was also good to us on Monday. Finally, I got to go again to Salzburg, the Mozart city. Immersed in new impressions, I was captured by the charm of this beautiful city: a sea of flowers, happy people everywhere. One cannot help but be happy here where every house is almost a memory of an Age Gone By. In the evening we went to the Landestheater to see *The Golden Dagger*, a Japanese play. The walk home was

beautiful, even though we were so tired and it was so late. A clear night, the sky dotted with stars. We were enjoying ourselves, but for the people in Munich it was a disastrous night. As soon as we got to the Schoenfeldspitze we heard the alert. Munich has suffered a severe attack. I got into the city last night only with great difficulty. Everywhere buildings were burning. I only had one thought: "How will I find my way home?" I went by Hilde's house. Completely destroyed. So it went on. How I heaved a huge sigh of relief when I did not see any fire from the bridge. Even so, we did have some damage. It was burning in the bed room. Fortunately Manny was there. He managed to dampen the fire and put it out, so that the damage is not all that bad. Now my hometown Munich has me back. Where will I be deployed next?

Munich, 28 April 1944
Time hurries by with every day, something new. Even with all the destruction in Munich, life goes on. At the market, fish is sold in the open air. Everywhere people are busy with clean-up work. Business places are repaired only to the extent necessary. Life goes on, and I have gotten used to how things are—except that I miss the mountains. Those were such beautiful times, so rich in new impressions, so full of adventure and practical experience. I hold dear the memories of those times of study and observation, of work and of joyful camaraderie. Whatever my next deployment may be, it will find me ever ready to help and to work.

Munich, 7 May 1944
Today is a really rainy Sunday. I feel so happy within my four walls that the weather cannot ruin my mood. Since Thursday I am an auxiliary worker in the *Beratungsdienst* [Advisory Service] of the *Studentenwerke* [Student Section]. I am so happy that I am together with Hannchen. I am in a writers' pool, and the work is interesting. The soldiers ask about graduation and

study courses. They ask for advice and are happy when we answer them. We build a bridge between the Front and the Homeland. Far away and despite their struggles, the soldiers think about their futures. Even there, in the monotony of the camps, they want to improve themselves. In many camps, schools have been formed. The German cannot be without work. He always has to keep busy. We on the Home Front can help him by providing information. Other times, we write out the lists of our captured soldiers.

Munich, 15 May 1944

By now I am used to my new work environment. In the morning at 8:00 our work begins. Letters are written, brochures are mailed, documents are organized, dictations are given, mail finished, calls answered. In no time noon is here and we are happy to have put a dent in our work. At 2:00 p.m. appointments begin. People looking for counsel have to fill out an application, then they are counseled. We must be versatile because our tasks are different with everyone's case. Through this work we are introduced to the academic life and come in touch with all careers. Every day after closing time, we cross off the day on our calendars, satisfied to have completed another good day. Saturday was payday. For the first time, a real salary: 80 RM per month. This much we never expected. We looked at our pay envelopes with pride. And to think that just three months ago I was still in school.

Munich, 20 May 1944

Yesterday, after a long time, I had GD duties. We GD girls organized our catastrophe plan after the example of our comrades in Duesseldorf. The Northeast group meets in the Circus Krone, the Southeast group at Max-Weber-Platz. Every girl has her bandaging equipment. Next on our agenda is to run the girls through a thorough review. To be thoroughly prepared is of the utmost importance. When duty calls us, we will be just as brave as the thousands of other girls who are helping people injured during the bombing attacks. Performing this first duty brought us yet another joy. We learned that on June 1st our hospital deployment will begin. Every other Sunday, we GD girls will work at the Schwabing Hospital. In three weeks it will be my turn.

Munich, 21 May 1944
Mothers Day. Day to honor the mothers. On this day, the *Mutterehrenrkreuz* [Mother Cross of Honor] is awarded throughout the entire Reich. Proudly we watch the mothers who, even in war and the terrors brought by it, are always in good humor and find the strength to birth children. We think of the mothers who sacrifice their sons for the *Führer* and their Homeland, the mothers in the armament factories, the farm women and the mothers with many children. To them belongs our love, our idolization. A mother is the soul of the family. *„Wenn eine Mutter ihr Kindlein tut wiegen, schaut der Mond in ihre Kammer herein."* ["When a mother rocks her baby, the moon looks into her room." Traditional German song.] *„Mütter, euch sind alle Feuer, Alle Sterne aufgestellt; Mütter, tief in euren Herzen Schlägt das Herz der weiten Welt!"* ["Mothers, you are all fire; you set all the stars in the sky; Mothers, deep in your hearts beats the heart of the whole world!" Third verse of song *Hohe Nacht der klaren Sterne* by Hans Baumann.]

Koenigsdorf, 27 May 1944
Hochland camp, who does not know this camp in the Hochland area? Thousands have had a camping experience there. Now, for three days, all the boy and girl leaders of the Hochland area come together here for a leadership meeting. Claire and I arrived late. Happily making our way, walking through this beautiful spring landscape had been such a pleasure. We had not been in the camp very long when the call came for us to assemble at Adolf Hitler Square to welcome

Gauleiter [Region Leader] Giesler as he arrives. To the accompaniment of trumpet fanfares played by the marching band, he paraded in front of us. Then we moved on to Thing Square where the *Gauleiter*, in his robust manner, spoke to us in words that hit their mark. His speech, which was much after our own hearts, was often interrupted with cheers. In the afternoon, *Oberbannführer* Hiller spoke about "Sports and Games harden your body." Body training has top priority in our education. Party Member Hogwind covered the subject of folkloric song and dance. Giving practical examples, he showed us the difference between German dance and foreign dance. All of us leaders then danced a Polonaise under his direction. We are to learn the German dances again. After dinner, we gathered again for a festive evening at Thing Square where *Hauptmann der Gebirgsjäger* [Captain of the Mountain Fighters] Simmett, who used to be *Bannführer* [Regiment Leader] of Garmisch, spoke to us, his young comrades. After him Emil Klein spoke. For both, the main subject of their speeches was the German understandings of loyalty, honor and bravery. At 8:00 p.m., Retreat was sounded.

Koenigsdorf, 28 May 1944
I survived my first overnight in a tent. At 8:30 a.m. we presented ourselves for the morning program. "Of German Ways" was the subject. The high point was the lecture given by Herbert Boehmer. A performance by the Hochland amateur players rounded out the program. Then we gathered for folkloric dance. Hogwind was a patient master here. In joyous dance the many couples swirled. For an Upper Bavarian girl or boy, folk dance seems to be just the right thing. After lunch SS *Hauptsturmführer* Weinhuber spoke. He gave the camp a political overview of our current situation. Then, in closing, the boys engaged in scouting games and the girls practiced basic gymnastics. After dinner, the Hochland Amateur Players presented a fine Upper Bavarian Evening. Upper Bavarian songs and dances, the *Schuhplattler* danced by 10 year old

Berchtesgaden boys, a beautifully performed charade and a puppet show followed one after the other. Happiness reigned among the boys and girls. Everything fit together: the beautiful landscape, the wonderful weather and the camaraderie of the camp participants. In a relaxed mood, the leaders retired to their camps. We who were from Munich ambled back to the camp that had so quickly become home for us. At dusk we sang songs together until we parted company. The moon shone and there was peace everywhere. A most unusual experience for a big city person!

Koenigsdorf, 29 May 1944
Those lovely days of camaraderie are over. This morning two programs were scheduled. Inge Wuensche spoke on the subject of "Maturing and remaining pure are the highest and hardest arts of life." With carefully chosen but accurate words, she touched on this sensitive subject. Afterwards, there was an exhibition. With this, Inge wanted to interest me again in BDM studies. However, I do not believe that is the path I should follow. I want to continue working in the BDM but stay independent. At 11:00 a.m. we had a final roll call and lowering of the flag at Adolf Hitler Square. The camp flag was lowered to trumpet fanfare. With the flag in our midst we marched past the *Gebietsführer* [Area Leader] and Inge. With that, the camp meeting was over. The days of camaraderie established a new circle of friends. We went back to our homes richer for the experience.

Munich, 3 June 1944
After 6 months of being away *Vati* returned for a vacation. To me, it is as if he had never been gone. Now we will enjoy the few hours we have together.

Munich, 11 June 1944
Today I have returned home rich with impressions. The first

hospital deployment, for which I waited so long, is behind me. The hours were yesterday from 2 p.m. to 7 p.m. and today from 7 a.m. to 2 p.m. I was so happy to be doing this job working with sick people. I listened intently to the orders of the nurse and helped her in every way I could. Make the beds, pass out bed pans, take temperatures and check pulses, pass out the food. Here comfort; there help, feed and encourage. Pass out medicine, prepare syringes; all these things fill up the hours. On top of that we attended to special needs of the patients: incandescent lights, inhalers, rheumatism bandages. I learn about these things in the women's ward which is led by Dr. Feser. I find it rewarding and fulfilling to aid and encourage the sick, helpless people who are bound to their beds. Every second week I will work with the GD girls helping the nurses in the ward. I am already looking forward to the next time. The war situation has changed a lot since I made my last entry. The long talked about invasion of the northern French coast has begun. The Americans already realize that they are attacking our Atlantic Wall in vain. They are having a hard time getting to the coast. They establish bridgeheads in the areas of Cherbourg and Dunkirk but are constantly pushed back by us. The outcome will be known soon.

Munich, 15 June 1944
Within five days Munich had two terror attacks. Both started at 7:30 a.m. Thank God that most of the planes did not come into the City Center but dropped most of their bombs on surrounding areas. Yet the destruction is high and the deaths are many. And it continues without pause. My workplace in the Student House is heavily damaged. After the main clean-up is done, our work continues. The homeless are given all possible assistance and they are well cared for because we are people who live by the motto "All for one, one for all."

Munich, 16 June 1944

Retaliation against England has begun. Without pause, our heaviest explosive charges are fired against London and South England. The V-I rocket—this newly developed, destructive secret weapon, which is just the initial step in Germany's broadened retaliation—surprised our enemies and the entire world. "The unpiloted airplanes" are an enigma to the English. For us they are retaliation for the terror they rained down on our women and children.

Munich, 23 June 1944

Vati's vacation is over. How quickly time has gone by. He left with a heavy heart. But we Germans band together through necessity. All have to help in the victory and for that we all have to make personal sacrifices. We all hope for a quick end to the war and then we will all be together again.

Munich, 1 July 1944

Deep sorrow fills the entire German population. *Generaloberst* Dietl, the hero of Narvik, died in an airplane crash. The most popular General of all, whom the mountain fighters revered like a god, has gone into the big Army beyond. He can no longer fulfill the task given him by the *Führer*, of helping Finland in its battle. The *Führer* himself honored the great soldier, to whom he posthumously awarded the *Schwerter zum Eichenlaub* [Knight's Cross of the Iron Cross with Oak Leaves and Swords], by his presence and oration at the State Funeral. I am proud and happy that I own his signature and a short greeting from him. In regard to Dietl's faith in the *Führer*, his motto was "The harder the battle, the more I trust in him."

Munich, 9 July 1944

How quickly the time does pass. Fourteen days went by so quickly and my deployment is on again for Saturday and Sunday. We are greeted warmly by the nurses and the job begins. Each of us is proud that we can substitute for a nurse who, through our presence, gets to have a rest. For our part, we get to learn how to care for the sick in all kinds of situations where nothing is spared us. We take on all kinds of work and are proud when we are allowed to do something by ourselves, like taking the temperatures and pulses of the entire ward. I still have not dared to give a shot, but I will, for sure, the next time I'm given the chance. On Sunday morning we made sick rounds with Dr. Feser. He was very pleased with how we conducted ourselves and with the beautiful roses given him by one of our colleagues. Once again, a nice deployment.

Munich, 10 July 1944
Now *Mutti* and I are all alone. Manny, who has been in the LWH [*Luftwaffenhelfer*, Air Force Helper] for a year now, went to the RAD [*Reichs Arbeit Dienst*, National Labor Service] in the Protectorate [Czechoslovakia]. He has reached a new point in his life and enters it whole-heartedly. He has always had before his eyes the goal of being an officer in the Navy. *Mutti* had a hard time with the good-bye but she will have to get used to it.

Munich, 12 July 1944
Munich has two terrible terror attacks behind it. Both yesterday and today at midday enemy fighters attacked the city. The north and the west were especially afflicted; partially, also, the south and east. In today's attack, the Student House was set on fire. Try as I might, I couldn't get through to it because of the sea of flames. The number of homeless will be high again but everyone will be taken care of as the whole community pulls together.

Munich, 13 July 1944
For the third time within 48 hours Munich was under the heaviest of attacks. All the impact of the falling bombs was in

our neighborhood, on Thierschstrasse [the von Koenig family lived in one of the two top 5th-floor apartments at #34]. Wave after wave the bombers flew over us. When it finally quieted down a bit, the first surveillance showed that an explosive bomb had hit the building at #38 and a fire bomb had struck the back side of #36. Everyone was running around outside putting out fires and removing what they could from #36. The endangered apartments were emptied quickly. Then #36 just kind of burned down and only very little was salvageable. Everywhere else in the city looked as bad as our street, if not worse. Wherever one looks there are fires, debris and ruins. The number of dead, injured and homeless is bound to be huge. And yet the people bear it bravely. All the people say, "The important thing is that we are still alive." Life, itself, is the most valuable of all mankind's assets. Munich is without power, without water and without gas. Candles, field kitchens and containers of drinking water help to alleviate our desperate needs. And so it goes. In the stores, as long as they can still function, items are sold. Bread is brought in from Wuerzburg and Nuremberg, etc. Special trains leave Munich with mothers, children and the unemployed. Minor damages are repaired by neighbors pooling resources and talents. So we people in Munich, as in other air-raided areas, get on with our lives. If tomorrow, the *Regensburger Domspatzen* [Boys Choir of the Cathedral in Regensburg] were to sing for us, they would have our rapt attention. Even in the midst of ruins, the German people maintain a deep connection with art and are thankful that they have the ability to find consolation in it.

Munich, 16 July 1944

Another heavy terror attack targeted Munich. For the fourth time within a few days, the North Americans dropped incendiary and explosive bombs. And again they landed in our neighborhood. Both Adelgunden and Mannhard streets were badly damaged. But as soon as we heard the all clear, the clean

-up began. Everyone tries to keep their home livable—until the next time. The many people left homeless are thankful for the help that is given to them by the government. Relief Trains, named "Hermann Goering" and "Dr. Goebbels," are now stationed in Munich. They distribute food, hot wine or tea with rum, clothing for entire families, etc. Quick aid was necessary and quick aid came. Even this fourth attack did not take away our lust for life; we go on working.

> Besonders in Mün-
> chen, gegen das der Feind innerhalb von fünf.
> Tagen bei für die eigene Abwehr ungünstiger Wet-
> terlage vier Großangriffe führte, entstan-
> den zum Teil empfindliche Schäden und Verluste.
> Die Haltung der Bevölkerung war
> vorbildlich.

[Translation: "Especially in Munich—considering that the enemy, over a period of five days, launched four heavy bombardments and that the people of Munich carried out their own defense under unfavorable conditions of weather and amidst damages and losses already sustained—the forbearance of the people was exemplary."]

Munich, 18 July 1944

We have just come up again from the basement. In the Tyrol, enemy troops have been turned back. I spent the entire morning putting my books in boxes and sewing coverings around the mattresses and pillows. We brought down to the ground floor as much as we possibly could. Everyone tries to save what they can. By doing these things we are able to do, we lighten responsibilities of the government which has more than enough relief work to do. Undisturbed by the destruction round about, Nature continues to thrive. On my window sill the cactus is in beautiful snow white bloom, with its many

budding sprouts pushing against the hedgehog cactus next to
it. Ah, Nature!

Munich, 19 July 1944
Again, sirens howled over the city. Quite some time later, the
enemy attack began. Thank God it was out at the city limits.
Three hours later the all-clear sounded. What times *Vati* and
Manny must be experiencing! We hope they will soon receive
the letters we have sent. Manny is deployed in Prague, where
he likes it very much. It is going better for him now because he
has become used to military routine.

Munich, 20 July 1944
Assassination attempt on the *Führer's* life. He was not injured.
Providence was on his side. His companions all received
wounds of varying severity. I am so happy that the *Führer* is
alive. What would we do without him? We need him to be
with us yet for a long time to come. The *Führer* lives; may God
be praised. Alarms sounded from 10:30 p.m. to 12:30 a.m., but
without any bombs being dropped on the city.

Munich, 21 July 1944
Munich has made it through the sixth terror attack in 10 days.
Again, bombs of all kinds—explosive, incendiary and
phosphorous—were dropped, destroying everything they
touched. People had to lose their lives. Unfortunately, we GD
girls were not able to help in either the rescue stations or the
homeless shelters. These ongoing attacks are supposed to
weaken us; the plots against the *Führer* are to break our spirit.
Providence determines otherwise. The gratitude and love for
the *Führer* becomes ever stronger. We stand with him,
believing in eventual victory.

Munich, 26 July 1944
Munich has a few days of quiet, except for some alarms that
did not even get us out of bed at night. These days are being

used to rebuild stores and workplaces. Our office has to be completely reassembled. Yesterday we picked out items of office furniture, cleaned them up, transported them to the office and set them up. Soldiers are working everywhere cleaning streets and salvaging furniture. The trains are running again. Water has been restored in several city areas and the lights are burning again. Busy doing all this work, we forget the wreckage around us, the ruins which have transformed our city. Yesterday I saw a movie, the first in a long time. It was good to experience the beauty of the cultural film, be updated by the weekly report documenting current events and view the movie, *I Need You*. It allowed us to forget our surroundings, at least for two hours.

Munich, 27 July 1944
The *Führer* named Dr. Goebbels as *Generalbevollmächtigten* [Plenipotentiary, with full powers] to conduct the total war. Dr. Goebbels just spoke over the German radio. He gave a report of the events of July 20th and their consequences. Total, all-out war effort is now demanded of us. New weapons are to be used as all Fronts make ready for the last strike. "People, to Arms!"

Munich, 29 July 1944
I just read in the newspaper that our Gretl Brugger died during an air raid. Gretl was a steadfast and true comrade who, even with all her other work, continued to serve with the GD girls, who were so close to her heart. With us remain the memories of many happy hours together, which she enriched with her humor and songs. She sacrificed her life for the *Führer* and for the German people whom she so deeply loved. She will continue to live among us.

[Translation: "During the air raid on July 11, 1944, we lost our beloved daughter: Party Comrade Gretl Brugger, Dressmaker. February 7, 1925 – July 18, 1944. Munich. Josef and Anny Brugger and Family."]

Munich, 31 July 1944

Again, Munich was the target for the enemy airplanes. This afternoon at 12:30 came an air raid alarm. Thank God they did not make it into the city but had to drop their bombs in the surrounding suburbs; nonetheless, they again succeeded in desecrating the historic monuments, hospitals and residential areas. I hope the number of dead is not so high this time. We have already sustained huge war losses. As expected, the retirement age for working women was raised to 50 years. All "under the table" work is to cease. In the very short time we may have, every effort must go toward "Weapons and Soldiers."

Munich, 6 August 1944

Today was the funeral service for Gretl Brugger. Hitler Youth House Moelders was decorated festively, with flags of the *Pimpfe* [Wolf Cubs, boys 6-10] giving the room a sense of holiness. Comrades, GD girls and invited guests took their places. Following the introductory music were brief memorial speeches which focused on sacrifice as a test of life. „*Heilig*

Vaterland, in Gefahren" ["Holy Fatherland in Danger," first line of a song by that name written by Rudolf Alexander Schroeder, 1914]. A speaker from the Party eulogized our Gretl, who fell believing in the *Führer* to whom she was devoted. We National Socialists see death not as a punishment but as fulfillment of life. Gretl's mother, Mrs. Brugger, known as "Brugger Mommy" because she rushed to assist whenever there was an emergency, is consoled by knowing that Gretl did not die in vain; she had become a soldier. Tomorrow, so soon, Mrs. Brugger plans to return to her work with the NSV [*National Sozialistische Volkswohlfahrt*, National Socialist People's Welfare], doing so henceforth in honor of her daughter. A brave German mother. After the song by Gretl's close comrades, the service concluded with the national anthems. I am glad that I was able, with my presence, to give the suffering mother a bit of joy. Mrs. Brugger still did not know that, in the meantime, her own mother had passed away.

Berchtesgaden, 12 August 1944

After a long train ride we arrived in our beautiful Berchtesgaden. For three days not to have heard or seen anything from the city, that is wonderful. Still, my thoughts constantly wander back home. Do they have electricity or not? The weather here is beautiful, except that it is very warm. But, from that, there is occasional relief. The girls have gone up to the Platterhof to sing. The two of us, Claire and I, are being truly lazy, lying in the shade and writing letters.

Berchtesgaden, 13 August 1944

Last night brought me another period of contemplation. I went for a walk with one of my little ones. She carries some kind of sorrow, but she is withdrawn. It takes a lot of effort to get closer to her but, in spite of that, I will still try to help her. Instead of saying good night, we set up a play scene. We played doctor's visit, with Erri and Fraenzi as doctors and the rest of us as nurses. We died laughing. Today has been a beautiful day full of sunshine and happiness. In a morning ritual with the flag, we began a day which started out so clear and bright. We were really lazy again: reading, sun-tanning and doing crazy things with the children from the houses around us. At 11a.m. Dr. Feser and *Frau* Dr. Schuetz came to visit the girls in the hospital. Lunch brought them all together in the festively decorated dining room. Dr. Feser spoke about GD duties. Following the afternoon coffee hour, we went to the Aschauer Pond for swimming. It had gotten oppressively humid, so the swim felt great. After dinner, we shared an evening of togetherness focused on "Girls, preserve your honor." Assorted performance-art numbers were followed by the reading of a letter written by a soldier, expressing his thoughts about love and marriage. The candor of his observations stimulated quite a discussion. While, outside, a thunderstorm broke loose, bringing the longed-for cool air, we girls engaged in animated debate as to the pros and cons. The song *„In den Krieg will ich reiten"* ["Into war I want to ride" by Hans Baumann; the full first line reads "Into the war I want to ride before I pluck roses for a bride."] concluded the session. After lowering the flag, we all went quietly to bed. The experiences of this day enriched us.

Berchtesgaden, 14 August 1944
We had to say farewell to the people we met here and to the mountains we loved so much. This morning we went to Reichenhall. Claire packed Margit's things. I visited House Berta, *Frau* Dr. Willms, Gustl, Albina and Nurse Josephine. The hours just rushed past. We arrived in B'gaden where I contacted Hanne's brother and arranged to pick him up at the military hospital at 12:00 and accompany him to B., where Hanne's mother and Irmi awaited us. We enjoyed a jolly hour together. After lunch I visited *Frau* Dr. Wilms in Bischofswiesen. There are so many interests we have in

common that the long way that we traveled back together passed quickly. Dr. Willms spoke about complications which first occurred during treatment of the most common illnesses among the hops workers, and of their cures. Just as I was leaving that train, the one for Munich was called. Now I am on my way back to Munich, to return to my work with renewed strength.

Munich, 16 August 1944

We just came back up from the cellar after an air raid alarm. Thank God it was nothing. I got an infection in the left small toe which, due to the long marches through Berchtesgaden, has not gotten better. Now I am curing it with wraps. Before I go to the hops harvest it has to be well.

Wolnzach-Markt, 25 August 1944

Vacation: what a word. I would never have thought that I would so treasure the meaning of a vacation. Vacation: these are ten days when I can get out of the city, do something other than type. My vacation takes me to the Holledau, as it did last year. This deployment is a time of most rewarding work. Three days are already gone by. Time flies. The GD girls have gone back to their home regions. *Frau* Dr. Willms arrived. After we spent a night sleeping on straw and talking with others in the same situation, we found better lodging. Gretl and I are now moved into our little room.

Wolnzach-Markt, 27 August 1944

Sunday morning. We sit in a guest room of the Hotel Post and write. Right now our view is of the market place and the church, which contrast beautifully against the blue sky. In the foreground are a willow tree and the War Monument. There are hops wagons driving through the market place, church-goers leaving church, men finding their way to the restaurants for small talk. Life in the country goes its way. Yesterday was our big clean-up day. The entire Medical Center shines with as much cleanliness as we found possible to give it. Now we wait for the hospital equipment and the beds.

Wolnzach-Markt, 1 September 1944
First of September—and five years of war. What a five years these have been: filled with victories and setbacks, being bombed, retaliating. At the beginning of the war, there were three war powers; now almost the entire civilized world is involved. At the beginning of this sixth year at war, Germany, though surrounded by danger, is safe and secure, with both Homeland and Front waging all-out war. The outcome will soon be known: victory or downfall. The course of the war affects our family in that *Vati* was drafted again; Manny is away serving with the KHD [*Kriegshilfdienst*, Auxiliary War Service], Felix in France. Our apartment is damaged by the aerial attacks. Many war deployments are behind me. I am overjoyed that I was allowed to prove what I am capable of and that I could help in areas such as the KLV, train station and hospital jobs. Here in Wolnzach one does not notice the war too much. If we did not listen to the Armed Forces Report in the evening, we would not know anything about what is happening in the world. Mornings we have appointments with 60 to 70 patients each day, then station duty. I have the girls' ward until nap time, which includes cooking, cleaning and serving lunch. Or I work the evening shift where we have appointments with 150 to 200 boys and, in between, care for those who are hospitalized. Boys and girls come the entire day with their small complaints. There are many that fake their pain, but those who are really sick are commendably brave. Our ward is mostly full, more boys than girls. The days just fly by, filled with work but also with happiness. During these times there is a wonderful camaraderie. Nurse Tilde is a first-rate person and comrade, as well as being our boss. Bertl and Inge and I are therefore…[next two lines of the *Kriegestagebuch/* Diary are not readable].

Munich, 8 September 1944
My vacation, during which I experienced such pleasant hours of companionship, is over. The farewell lunch that we cooked together tasted twice as good as any we could have had in a restaurant. The homemade cake on the last Sunday was simply wonderful. We spared no effort; we baked and cooked as well as doing our jobs. On Wednesday we all went together to pick hops. *Frau* Dr. Willms and I plucked two containers full. Those were seven gay hours in the hops fields. Yesterday I drove with *Frau* Dr. Willms and Director Keitl zigzagging throughout the hops producing area, known as the Holledau. We went from Pfaffenhofen to Freising and back to Wolnzach. It was very hard for me to leave these good people with whom I shared such a friendly and open relationship. Now I am back in Munich. In the office, the 60 hour work week has been introduced.

Munich, 14 September 1944
The days were once again blessed with both genuine alarms and cuckoo calls. Thank God nothing serious happened. Still, we had to carry the machines up and down, and we did so in good humor. During all these alarms I thought of Hilde who, at this time, lives and works only in air raid situations. She is experiencing so much now, whether it is at a hospital bedside or in the operating room. She enjoys the work because of the opportunity to learn. Whenever we hear about air raids over Bohemia or Moravia I think of our Manny, who will be returning soon. Only 11 more days. I think that, among us, *Vati* still experiences the fewest alarms. His deployment has him sitting on an island, soon to be ravished by storms. *Mutti* took over the management of a soldiers' sewing room and is doing important war work.

Munich, 17 September 1944
After a long time, I am on hospital duty again, finding deep

fulfillment. Work at the hospital ward is strenuous, since some patients in our care are kept permanently in the basement shelter. The new nurses are very nice and our working hours together are very pleasant. I get along especially well with the NS [*National Sozialistische*, National Socialist] nurse. This job continuously brings me new joy. I am happy about all I have learned here that will stand me in good stead in the future. If everything goes well, I will be able to continue working here on a regular basis.

Munich, 22 September 1944

Today, again, was another black day in the history of Munich. The dance started during the noon hour. The train area was hit especially hard. Some of the bunkers received full hits and many people died. Thank God nothing happened to us. I am always so relieved when, at the Monument [the *Max II Denkmal*], I look around the corner [west, down Thierschstrasse, in the first block, on the south side of the street] and see that our home-castle [fifth-floor apartment at #34] is still standing. Life goes on.

Munich, 26 September 1944

We are in great fear for Manny. Since September 8th we have not heard anything from him. He is supposed to come home this week. We hope for the best. Thank God, the awesome Hannchen has come back. Everything is so much more fun when we are together. Our work goes on. Academic consultations are now limited to the permanent war invalids and to the temporarily disabled soldiers, since only they are allowed to study. I do not know if we will have to move to Erlangen, since the University is to be relocated there. I also wait for news of my colleague from whom I have not heard for some time. She lives in danger under constant alarm, but there is also the possibility that the mail got lost. I hope nothing has happened to her.

Munich, 27 September 1944

Once again we mourn the loss of a dear comrade. Hilde was freed from her severe ailments. During my last deployment I had visited her. Again, her hopes were high, since her condition had not changed for either better or worse. She never would have made a full recovery and her infirmity would have hindered her career. Her parents are in great pain. She was their only daughter; moreover, a sweet and brave one, always happy and ready to help, really a good comrade. In the GD she found peace and happiness. She had been at all of the camps, took part in all of the service evenings and was always in good spirits. She will always be in our memories. I expressed my condolences to her parents in a letter since it is very important to me that I take part in the funeral of one who was so dear to me, even if I cannot be there in person. I think of her with deep sorrow.

Gott, der Lenker aller Geschicke, hat unsere edle, einzige Tochter und Schwester

Hildegard Hilsendegen

Absolventin der Städt. Oberschule
am St.-Anna-Platz

im Blütenalter von 19 Jahren nach schwerem, geduldig ertragenem Leiden in die ewige Heimat geholt.
München (Welfenstr. 1/I), 27. 9. 1944.
In unsagbarem Weh: Die trostlosen Eltern Otto u. Franziska Hilsendegen; Stiefbruder Alfred Hamann u. Verw.
Beerdigung: 29. 9. 44, 15 Uhr, Ostfriedhof. Der Gottesdienst wird am Grabe bekanntgegeben.

[Translation: "God, the Ruler of all history, took to the everlasting home our noble and only daughter and sister, Hildegard Hilsendegen, at the young age of only 19, after she had patiently endured much suffering. She was a graduate of the City High School at St. Anna Square. With unbearable pain: the inconsolable parents Otto and Franziska Hilsendegen, step-brother Albert Hamsun and family. Munich (Welfenstr. 1/I). 27 September 1944. Funeral September 29th at 3:00 p.m. in the East Cemetery. The religious service will be held at the gravesite."]

Munich, 29 September 1944
Today brings with it a farewell. Irmi Helmbrechts has to go to Salzburg, the Mozart City, with Dr. Schuh. After the office closed, we set a nice coffee table and passed a few hours chatting happily. It is a strange thing to say good-bye. One can never find quite the right words to say. Irmi is not going far away but, still, a nice person is gone from our work circle. We wish her a lot of luck in her new job.

Munich, 1 October 1944
Twelve hours of hospital duty lies behind me. Yesterday I gave my first injection but it was not too bad once I overcame my fear. Today I helped Dr. Feser as he checked someone's glucose level in the laboratory. He explained a lot to me and afterward I helped him with a blood test. Then he made an intravenous injection. Work was pretty easy this time because we only had a few patients. It was really pleasant again. It is Thanksgiving Day. The people thank the farmers who, even with all their difficulties and hard work, make sure that everyone has everything they need.

Munich, 2 October 1944
Wedding Anniversary for *Mutti* and *Vati*. Twenty-two years ago they took the marriage vows which produced Manny and me. Two more siblings would have complemented our family, but such was not to be our destiny. Twenty-two long years filled with sorrows and worries, yet also with happiness and hopes. In the last years we would have been better off financially, but then the war came. *Vati* was drafted, was allowed to come back and, since 24 November 1943, is in the

service again. We hope from our hearts that we will be able to spend their next anniversary day together.

Munich, 4 October 1944

Scarcely 12 days passed before this new attack on Munich. In the office, the usual scene: broken windows, dirt and cold. Thank God nothing happened at home. But many other city areas were hit hard. Nymphenburg with its castle, the train station and the Pasing area show signs of terrible damage. The gas is off again; we have not had it since the July attacks, another problem to overcome. The entire Homeland suffers from these attacks, now more than ever, since the enemy surrounds all the borders of the Reich. Since they cannot defeat us with weapons, they are trying psychological attacks. The people of Munich, usually a quiet folk, are gradually working up a rage against these air gangsters. I find this a joy to behold.

Munich, 6 October 1944

To our surprise Manny came home. Last night he came from Bruenn. Now his time in the KHD [*Kriegshilfdienst*, Auxiliary War Service] is over. Work there demanded many hard hours from him but also gave him the joy of seeing other places and making friends with both boy and girl comrades. Now he has a new goal in sight, which will come really soon. The nice thing about this is that he will be going to Flensburg-Moravia, one hour away from *Vati*, so the two of them will be able to meet more often. In the North, two; in the South, the other two. We will be taking good advantage of the short time Manny is here.

Munich, 12 October 1944

Today Manny left again. So short was the time of togetherness. He is already so excited about school, about new comrades, all of whom have the same goal, and the new duties and jobs that the Navy will require of him. When the war began, Manny was a small 12 year old child, and now he is drafted. By January he will be on a ship facing battle at the Front. The soldier's luck shall accompany him. This is my innermost wish for him as he leaves.

Gmund am Tegernsee, 14 October 1944

I sit on the balcony of the Villa Mark. In front of me lies the Tegernsee in bright blue sunshine. The surrounding mountains wear colorful fall dress in striking contrast to the pine forests. Everything is dunked in the mild light of the sun which reflects off the towers of the Tegernsee Monastery on the other side of the lake. All around it is wonderfully still, which feels really good after the noise of the big city and the train ride, which required patience. Everything here is so peaceful and lovely; nothing disturbs the joy of nature. Next to the house a creek murmurs, cow bells ring, otherwise silence. Our Alpine foothills, mountains and lakes, forests and meadows, this is how it is in our beloved Bavaria. Here in the school everything seems disorganized. I am the first and only one here. No one knows anything about a conference. This could be interesting. I wonder what comes next.

Munich, 15 October 1944

I had to go back home again. After a long adventurous ride, I arrived home at midnight unexpected by *Mutti*, who did not hear my knocking. I did not gain entry until 6:30 a.m. To bed, as fast as I could get there, after first stuffing myself. At noon I got up, well rested. Now I am writing letters and working on my memory book, which contains pictures of our GD girls and of my deployments. It is really fun to gather the pictures together, a task that brings me joy. The news just stated that Field Marshal Erwin Rommel died from his injuries. That the life of a great soldier should find its end in that way! A National Socialist, a true commander, he led his armies to a string of victories in Africa until the Italians put an end to his advance. Recovered from his illnesses, he became Inspector of

Military Facilities. In France he received a severe head injury during an air raid. I am proud to own his autograph.

Munich, 18 October 1944
On this day 131 years ago, the "Battle of the Nations" [1813, Napoleon, *Völkerschlacht*] found its victorious end. Victory came as a result of the *Volkssturm* [People's Army]. Following that model, the *Führer* announced today that a *Volkssturm* has been organized which includes all men between the ages of 16 and 60 who are fit for military service. They will stay in their present jobs, training in their spare time, being drafted as needed. The enemy is at Germany's borders. Germany gathers all its human power to ward off the attack and, when the time is right, to turn the tide back in our favor. "People, to Arms!"

Munich, 20 October 1944
Once again the sirens sounded over the city. On Monday the lovely Mozart city on the Salzach was attacked. The Mozart House, the Cathedral and Mozarteum were destroyed. Which city was hit today? After two hours the alarm was over. Surely it had been Regensburg's turn.

Munich, 22 October 1944
Today was a really good Sunday to stay at home, at least for me. I have almost finished Manny's Christmas present, a small mascot. A seaman has to have his talisman. Hopefully he will enjoy the Dirndl from Bavaria. In the afternoon a family from Kuestrin, who could not find a place to stay in Munich, came to us and warmed up. They slept downstairs with the Kainz family. I felt sorry for the small child. At least they are warm now. Tomorrow mother and child will be evacuated. The father is going back to the Stalin Front knowing that his wife and child are safe.

Munich, 23 October 1944
Alarm. It seems that Regensburg and Augsburg have been hit again. On all Fronts we are holding back the enemy which is using every possible means to force our surrender. That is why the bombing attacks have become heavier. We will resist, because we have to.

Munich, 27 October 1944
Manny wrote an enthusiastic letter about his life now, which is hard and strict but allows him the daily satisfaction of being in the career of his choice. He will reach his goal, as he has put his body and soul into this.

Munich, 28 October 1944
Hospital duty in Schwabing. Unfortunately not much was happening there. There was little to do because the entire building is cold since the boiler room was hit on October 4th. Head Nurse Ingeria sent us home. Next time there will be work again and I am already looking forward to it. Alarm. Several fighter planes over the city. Heavy flak fire but it seems that no bombs fell.

Munich, 29 October 1944
Terror attack over Munich. Full Alarm. At 11:30 p.m. the first bombs fell. In our neighborhood nothing was damaged. Also last night bombs were dropped.

Munich, 31 October 1944
My colleague is back again. Excitedly she told of her work in Bad Duerkheim. The farewell was hard for her. Hopefully she will find satisfaction in her new job which brings her into the *Ausgleichsdienst* [Alternative Service; compulsory service required of those not in the military]. Now she is here again and the long separation is over. Hilde is trying to courageously endure the pain over the loss which affects her entire family.

Her uncle, aunt and their children were killed in Sunday's attack on Schellingstrasse. An entire family was lost. Yet life must go on and we who survive must cling ever more closely to each other.

Munich, 3 November 1944
Air raid. The sirens had barely begun to howl when the concert started. Through it all, Hanna and I both ran breathlessly to our homes. Hospitals, and other targets, were under attack. An hour later came another alarm. This is the way it is all of the time now. Single rogue planes swoop over the city and drop bombs in such a whirlwind that we do not even have time to get to the basement. Yesterday our Air Defense racked up a great victory. Out of the total 132 planes that flew over Germany, 128 four-engine planes were shot down. Hopefully we can now stand up against these air raids. I only work in the office two or three times a week now; the rest of the time I work at the Schwabing Hospital. I am tremendously excited. Because I learn a so much more there in just one morning and, besides, I am kept very busy.

Munich, 4 November 1944
Terror attack on Munich. During lunchtime combined enemy forces attacked Munich, indiscriminately dropping explosive and incendiary bombs. There was vast destruction, especially in the southern and western parts of the city, and loss of human life. So it was stated in the news. How much misery and pain was inflicted, not to mention the vast amount of destruction! Yet it has to go on. The trains will be quickly repaired, doors and windows boarded up. The most important things will be taken care of.

Munich, 8 November 1944
Nineteenth birthday. For the sixth time I am celebrating my birthday during war. The book by August Heisler, *Still a*

Country Doctor, a biography of Hoelderlin, a money gift from *Vati*, *Ritterkreuzträger* from Manny, a Bavarian art print, a beautiful doily and some sweets completed the birthday table. The last year was rich in experiences: In February, graduation; the KLV time in Berchtesgaden and Reichenhall, then the visit to the physician assistant leadership school. I got to see Salzburg and Lake Koenig and get to know them. My alternate non-military service began and took me into counseling. Bombs destroyed our city. We moved with our jobs two times. After three short vacation days in Berchtesgaden, I went to the hops fields. The year that lies behind me is a year full of work, but also of rewarding experiences and fond memories. What will the new one bring? I move forward unperturbed, to continue doing my duties for the *Führer* and for our people.

Munich, 9 November 1944

November 9th, 1944. We remember those who died on November 9th, 1923. The writing on the Memorial means the same now as it did then: "And still, you won." As it was then, with victory accomplished at the end of the long battle, so will it be at the end of this war.

Munich, 12 November 1944

Today I came home from work very tired but still it was a really nice day. I like it very much in our ward. There is always a bit-of-this or a bit-of-that to do. Yesterday two new patients were admitted, one right after the other. One patient soon died. It is a strange feeling to watch someone die and not be able to help. That she was freed from her agony is consolation for the son who accompanied her. Today I experienced my first air raid alarm at the hospital. The patients that could walk were hastily dressed, the others quickly brought to the elevators. In tandem, the most important instruments were put on a cart and also taken to the basement. Thank God that no bombs fell. Due to the alarm, all work was delayed yet we still managed to complete our scheduled work on time. I am glad that I can now come here to help every day of the week. Today we commemorate the anniversary of those who died November 9th, 1933. We remember also the many soldiers who died during the World War and the war now, and those who were sacrificed during the air raids. The *Volkssturmmänner* [men of the Peoples' Army] were sworn in. Throughout the entire Reich the battalions marched: old men and Hitler Youth, men of all professions and of all ages. In Munich, *Gauleiter* [Region Leader] Giesler laid wreaths from the *Führer* at the Monument and at the 16 coffins in the Temple of Honor. The rally took place at 2:00 p.m. in the old conference room of the Circus Krone. *Gauleiter* Giesler addressed the men. Afterwards, *Reichsminister* H. Himmler read the proclamation of the *Führer*. Swearing in of the *Volkssturmmänner* ended the ceremony. "Battle Cry" by Dietrich Eckart [written 1919/23]captured the spirit of the *Volkssturm*:

> Storm, storm, storm.
> Ring out the bells from tower to tower!
> Ring out so that sparks begin to spray.
> Judas appears, planning to take over the kingdom.
> Ring out, that the bloody ropes redden with blood.
> All around is nothing but fire and torture and death.
> Ring out, Storm, that the earth rears up
> Under the thunder of liberating revenge.
> Woe to the people who still daydream!
> Germany, awake!

Munich, 14 November 1944

Again, the days have been filled with alarms. Today there was a horrendous attack on our city. It is always frightening until we get to Hanna's, but it is worth the effort because of the security we have in this basement. Bombs came down very close by. Once again, we had really good luck. Thank God nothing happened at home. The Prinzregenten Theater was hit.

In Schwabing and in the Westend it must also be very bad. Now that it is becoming so cold, we already suffer enough when windows are broken and roofs are blown off.

Munich, 19 November 1944

It is a beautiful bright November day outside, yet there is no peace or joy. We live in fear of the fighter pilots, with good cause. We already have three hours of precautionary alarms behind us, plus one short full alarm. Perhaps the rest of the day will be quiet. I have not let things bother me and continued to do crafts: a stationery folder and a small photo album for Manny, two more photo albums, all from my supply box. It gives me great joy when something nice comes from my crafting and I can make someone close to me happy. In the evening I started a small doily for the head nurse in the ward. While I work on them, my thoughts go out to the people for whom I am making these small surprises; I am connected with them in thought. Especially during these hard times, Christmas should be celebrated as a German time of reflection. This celebration will give us strength. Among the ruins and destruction, we will come to a true sense of who we are. We are Germans.

Munich, 22 November 1944

Terror attack. Today Munich was once again the target of an enemy bomb attack. The Cathedral, the old, dear landmark of our Homeland, and the St. Michaels church, one of the most beautiful Renaissance churches in the world, are the sacrifices. Nothing pains the *Münchners* more than to see how their Cathedral with the world famous double steeples, which welcome us from afar as we approach Munich again upon our return, become a sacrifice to the terrifying bombs. Hospitals, schools, public buildings, etc. were destroyed as well. Human losses were also heavy. One piece after another of our beautiful Munich disappears. It fills one with furious, frenzied rage and intensifies the hatred against the murderers who destroy these marvels of western culture. Out of this springs enhanced strength to fight against our enemies to the very last.

Munich, 25 November 1944
Hospital duty. These 14 days were long, because I had always counted on being able to work during the week. Now it was time again. Admitting and discharging patients kept us very busy. I was allowed to watch a pleurisy puncture. Dr. Feser explained x-rays to me. Then there were many other different things to get done. We went home at night feeling satisfied.

Munich, 26 November 1944
GD Roll Call at the German Museum. This morning the GD girls from Munich gathered at the German Museum. Dr. Feser spoke to us about the rights and obligations of the GD girls, and about the varied challenges that this war poses for us. He thanked us for the work we have done so far and spurred us towards new activities. Songs and a speech about "The Brave Heart" completed this special meeting. The GD girls were then allowed to go off with Anneliese. I am happy that I am involved in the GD [*Gesundheits Dienst*, Health Service], doing a job that I enjoy and into which I can completely submerge myself.

Munich, 27 November 1944
Today I am really tired. Again Munich was the target for enemy terror attacks during the morning hours. This time they even hit our area. The NSV regional office, the St. Anna Primary School and the Lyceum, the bordering homes opposite Steindorfstrasse, everywhere, there were explosive bomb craters and huge fires. Today I would have been working at the Schwabing Hospital but, now, helping in the Homeless Shelter became much more important. We handed out food all day. Sandwiches were made and coffee poured. It just went on

and on. All these people had to be quickly and appropriately helped. Some are thankful, the others are dissatisfied. One gets to know human nature.

Munich, 28 November 1944

A day goes by so quickly when one continuously works at helping others: answering innumerable questions, passing out food, fruit and cigarettes. One gets to know one's "clientele," rejoices with them when they have finally found shelter, comforts them as sorrow overtakes them when they become aware of having lost loved ones. To have given this warmth and comfort to so many people makes me happy and glad. Even though I am dead tired at night, I am happy.

Munich, 3 December 1944

First Sunday in Advent. For the sixth time in this war comes the silent, secretive pre-Christmas season. This time, even if the people have great worries and have suffered through the many air raids, we think back on Christmases we enjoyed in better times. I sewed two lace doilies on a piece of gold cardboard and made a new photo album. Then I worked on a *Rauschgoldengel* [angel made of gold pleated paper], after that, made small pictures that can be embroidered with yarn by children's hands. This is how my day went by so fast. Soon it will be time to light the candles of the pyramid, which then turns itself in the heat. *„Für uns ist eine Zeit angekommen, die bringt uns grosse Freud"*["For us a time has come that brings us great joy" — 1939 Christmas song by Paul Hermann].

Munich, 9 December 1944

Another week full of work and alarms has gone by. But everything went well, and after the alarms we went back to the office. Today I worked in Schwabing again. Traudl, who had always worked with me in the ward, now lies in room number 46. It is ironic. Thank God she is doing better. The job at the hospital bedsides continues to bring me joy. I am especially happy when I can follow through on something all by myself and bring relief to the patients without having to ask long questions of the nurses. The work-loads of the nurses have doubled. Ten patients are lying in the basement, and there is constant back and forth between the ward and the basement.

Munich, 10 December 1944

Second Sunday in Advent. There were all kinds of different jobs that had to be done in the ward, and the alarms made us late with our schedules. When we finally finished passing out the soup, the all-clear sounded and we were able to migrate up from the basement. Petra, whom I had not seen since our farewell, was here this afternoon. She works in a pharmacy as an apprentice. Time passed very quickly as we talked about our old school times and our friends, now scattered to the winds. Liese, formerly a maid here, also visited me. She is now with the Flak. She expects to be transferred; to the West or the East? It is always nice to get together and talk with people you haven't seen for a long time. Especially in these times, one seeks to draw the bond of friendship tighter.

Munich, 15 December 1944

Time passes so quickly; days just fly by when they are so full. When I get home from the office at night, then we eat and afterwards the sweetest hours of the day begin. I listen to the radio and write Christmas letters that will go to all my loved ones with whom I still have a connection. Today on my "household" day, I will get out my photos and send them to *Vati* and Manny. Then I will purchase a train ticket to Berchtesgaden. I am so looking forward to two days in the mountains. Hopefully Tommy will not ruin my plans.

Munich, 16 December 1944

Now I cannot go to B'gaden anyway. The road was completely

destroyed yesterday. So I will stay here and continue to work on my small Christmas surprises, so that they will finally get finished.

Munich, 17 December 1944
Today I am really in the Christmas spirit. I have written my Christmas letters to all my friends throughout the country. I crafted a small Christmas/engagement present for Hanna and put together my packages.

Munich, 18 December 1944
I am dead tired, but I still want to recount the events of last night and today. Last night at 10 p.m., the sirens jolted us out of our wonderful Christmas spirit and sent us down to the basement for the third time today. We had barely gotten down below when it started. Without a break the bombs fell. It was really awful; it had never been this bad before. A mine must have come down close by. Finally this hell stopped and we could go outside to check on the conditions. How did it look there!! The buildings at Steinsdorfstrasse numbers five, six and seven had simply disappeared. The corner house, number eight, was completely engulfed in flames. Our apartment was in total chaos; no doors or windows anymore, walls crumbled, ceilings fallen down. It was a sad picture of destruction. There wasn't much we could do. We took out the age-old winter windows so that at least one side would hold off the winter cold. In the morning we went to the Homeless Shelter to help pass out food and other necessities. Our lives play out now between the Homeless Shelter and our apartment.

Munich, 22 December 1944
In two days it will be Christmas. Only a few people give any thought to it, yet the holiday still lies within them like a spell. We will celebrate it together with the homeless who have lost everything. We nailed shut all doors in the apartment as best

we could and put new blackout covering on the windows. So we go on living and working, trying to get back on track.

Munich, 24 December 1944

Christmas Eve. What a magical phrase in every sense. In the morning *Mutti* and I decorated our small tree. I neatly tidied up the room. The big Christmas tree at the Homeless Shelter we already decorated yesterday. The dinner was a cold meal and everyone was surprised at the large portions. We all really liked it. Also, the tables were very nicely decorated. Apples, pine branches and candles on white paper gave a very festive impression. When the children came, the candles on the tree were lit. Everyone was enchanted by the sight of the lighted tree, which for us Germans is a symbol and sign of reappearing light. After we cleaned up everything, we went home. The six candles on our tree shone for us for Christmas. We thought of *Vati* who has to be away in his comrade circle for the second time. We thought especially of Manny who may, at this very hour, be going to sea. We have not heard from him for weeks. The book by Margarete Rohrer, *In War against Wounds and Illness*; *Shining Country* by Louis Trenker; Holbeins Works; a photo album; two ceramic vases and cookies made me happy. *Mutti* got stationery and a food stamp case. Though the gift table was very simple this year, we both still had a lot of joy. We only have one wish: that we may continue to live and work. What happens next is up to all of us. Sixth German Christmas at war.

Munich, 31 December 1944

New Year's Eve, end of the old year. Snow lies everywhere outside; quietly the snowflakes fall, blanketing the rubble and the ruins. Christmas week was spent working and helping out where I could. Letters from friends and relatives came, telling how they spent their Christmas and sending best wishes for the New Year. The old year brought sorrow to so much of mankind, to the individual, to the entire population. After the first shock, we got back up on our feet and bravely continued lives ruled by the laws of war. This year, for the most part, *Mutti* and I spent all alone. *Vati* is in Sylt. Manny—first with the RAD, then in Flensburg—now cruises on the high sea. This was his wish, so he is happy with what he is doing and we have to accept it. Sometimes mail does not come for weeks. May fate be kind to him! He is very happy to have the small talisman I sent him and he may need it. The old year nears its end. For everyone, it was full of hard work and much worry. For me it was rich in new experiences. What the New Year 1945 will bring, we do not know. We trust in the future and will continue to work within our belief that Germany will be victorious. I quote from a poem [1938] by Agnes Miegel:

>*„Laß in deine Hand,*
>*Führer, uns vor aller Welt bekennen;*
>*Du und wir,*
>*nie mehr zu trennen*
>*stehen ein für unser deutsches Land."*

["Let us in your hand, *Führer*, acknowledge before the world; you and we never to part, we will be there for our German Country."] With these words let us enter into the New Year, into the year of strong hearts.

1945

**With a broad unfettered view,
with courageous hearts and happy souls
we want to take our stands in life
working and playing alike
as if we were raised up on a high mountain.**

Hermine Stolz

Munich, 3 January 1945

The New Year has begun and with it "The Seriousness of Life." At the office we have to start all over again. A table, a few chairs, that is all we have. We take dictation at the office but have to do the typing at home on a portable typewriter. This is how it will have to be for a while. Just 12 weeks to go in the counseling office to complete my compulsory non-military service. Then I will be turned over to the employment office. Hopefully they will find for me employment that is better suited to my interests, where I can learn more and work more meaningfully than I am doing now in the office. Before that time comes, Hanna will marry. The preparations keep us all in suspense. What I am doing for her right now is knitting the front parts of the jackets. After that, I have to craft a small wedding present for her. The time until the 27th will go by in no time at all.

Munich, 6 January 1945

The first hospital duty in the New Year. All the rooms are still festively decorated. Nativity scenes and Christmas trees bring the Christmas magic into the hospital rooms. There was plenty of work today. There are 20 female patients in the basement and just as many upstairs. This means we have to work fast if we want to give each one a fair amount of care. One always learns something in new situations and becomes more self-reliant in the process. When there is so much work to be done, one is required to make more independent decisions. Traudl is still lying in #46. Thank God she is getting better.

Munich, 7 January 1945
Today I am really tired. Once again, work in Schwabing was very strenuous. In addition to the work, I had to walk back and forth since there was no bus available today. Still, I think of those hours with inner satisfaction and I am looking forward to the next time.

Munich, 8 January 1945
Terror attacks on Munich. The sirens sounded last night at 8 p.m. We had just barely made it into the basement with our air raid backpacks when the concert began. One strike after another for a solid 45 minutes shook the basement walls; then silence set in. Above ground, everything was lit up like daylight from the many fires. Our home had been spared. Then came new waves of attack; everyone back to the basements. For the second time the sirens resounded. People had to leave their burning homes behind and seek basement cover. On went the awful concert of whistling and wheezing bombs which now fell continuously. These two attacks lasted for three hours. What have they made of Munich? A heap of rubble. Our quarter was not hit so hard this time. We are caring for 300-400 homeless. City Center, Schwabing, wherever one looks, heaps of rubble and raging fires. It is a sad picture of destruction. Hanna's neighborhood was hit very hard. Our workplace was once again totally destroyed. At the moment everything seems hopeless. There is no bread and no food. There is no newspaper, no means of transportation. Salvaged

furniture lies in the snow-covered streets. Ambulances of the NSV make their way through the rubble. The firemen worked feverishly but the water often froze and they could not extinguish the fires. Munich has finally become a Frontline city.

Munich, 14 January 1945

Life in the city is gradually returning to some kind of order. Winter with its cruel, bitter cold doubles our misfortune. People pull their last possessions behind them on sleds looking for some shelter. Great is the misery throughout the city. Earth moving equipment is used to recover bodies of the dead. Soldiers and prisoners clean out homes, clear the streets. Here and there, newspaper saleswomen have set up improvised stands, often just a chair, with the newspapers on top. In no time at all they are all sold. We turn our attention to the West, where our soldiers are once again advancing; to the East, where they are engaged in hard-fought defense. Looking at the larger view, one can, for a few moments, forget the heavy burdens of the last days. Provisions in the shelters are exhausted. There is a lot of work to be done and we still do it with joy, to help these poor people as best we can.

Munich, 15 January 1945

Finally I am doing a hospital shift on a week day. Our ward is overly full, 70 female patients, of whom 20 are in the basement. This means we must be clear headed and fast on our feet. We begin by changing bandages, facilitating radiation and giving injections that were ordered on the day before. Then there are appointments and new orders to fill. Somewhere in there, second breakfast is served; at 11:00, lunch. One has to pass meals out quickly so that the patients in the basement also receive warm food. One has to be careful that everyone receives the right thing. Those with diabetes get a fruit juice; those with a fever are brought something light to eat, etc. That which helps the one may harm the other. As soon as all the food was distributed, we took care of the health insurance. Then the total migration to the basement begins. Patients that are unable to walk are placed on cots, stretchers and lawn chairs and are brought to the elevator until everyone is finally downstairs. A cart with such necessary instruments as a microscope and Polari meter, along with all the patients' health histories, is prepared. There is a bandage cart and other carts for injections, infusions, blood work etc. so all the treatments can be continued downstairs. My work day was over around 2:00 p.m. Working directly with sick people [which I like to do], not with disgusting world data files.

Munich, 18 January 1945

Again I was allowed to work at the hospital. In the office there is nothing to do. One just sits around in the cold with no work being done anyway. This morning was, once again, jam packed with work. It went by quickly because so many were pitching in to help. When one can come more often, one gets to know the patients better and then knows exactly who needs this and who needs that. One does not have to ask for help so often and is able to accomplish much independently.

Munich, 20 January 1945

Today I had hospital duty the entire day. To get there, I waited at 6:30 a.m. for the *Fliegender Gauleiter* [Flying Region Leader; probably a play on *Fliegender Holländer/ The Flying Dutschman*, an opera by Wagner] which is what the people of Munich call the temporary train from the Odeonsplatz to Hohehnzollernstrasse. Jesting aside, we are very glad to have this train! Female patients were brought to the bathing room and to radiology. Beds were stripped. In between these routine assignments, new orders were filled. After lunch we had to secure the hospital. We brought the sick downstairs and re-made the beds upstairs. I helped the head nurse in jotting down the curves. At 3:00 p.m. we got the all clear. Since there was not a whole lot left to do, we did a deep clean of the station's closet area. Our ward has been assigned two nurses from the Alsace area. They lived in Kolmar and had to return to the Reich. I like them very much. They are perfect models of the NS nurse; moreover, one can tell at a glance that they have been well schooled. They miss Alsace, the embodiment of the Reich. We work well together with them.

Munich, 28 January 1945

The week has once again passed by quickly. *Mutti* had an attack of sciatica on Monday morning and couldn't move so I stayed home and did the grocery shopping for our small household. Thank God her condition improved enough so that she could get up again. Hanna's birthday present is going to be finished soon. I am constantly with her in my thoughts. She has become a woman now. I wish her all the best from the bottom of my heart on her life's path next to her husband. "Holy is the hour, as holy as a prayer, as one from our circle goes off to new alliances, quietly and hopefully." G. Schumann wrote this song for marriage. Hanna herself entered into marriage with this Germanic saying: *"Mit Wille dein Eigen"* [with your own will].

Munich, 30 January 1945

Once again it came to pass. Hospital duty on a work day during the morning hours. Now we are many student nurses, and the time at work passes quickly. Since I have not felt well for some time now, I had Hilde take a blood sample from me. Dr. Feser gave me a thorough physical, prepared a transfusion !!! and checked a urine sample. We will get the final results on Thursday and will probably have to take x-rays. It is not going to be so bad, *Unkraut verdirbt nicht* [Weeds do not wither: German proverb].

Munich, 1 February 1945
Hospital duty. Today I had to walk a lot. We could tell that
Traudel was gone again because, otherwise, we said,
"Trautchen will do it." Now it is left up to the student nurses
and me. The blood test was completely normal so that no x-
rays have to be taken. It seems to be a kidney infection so I just
have to keep myself warm and watch for it not to get worse.
Dr. Feser wrote me a prescription for Albuzid.

Munich, 3 February 1945
Days that are not completely filled with work seem to drag on
so much longer. Today was not like that; it went by as quickly
as a breeze. While every morning is more or less the same,
there is also constantly variety. This kind of work will never
bore me. The walks I make to the pharmacy, to the library, to
the administration offices etc. grant me insight into the
operation of this big hospital. Traudl did not return, although
all of us had hoped she would. The wedding announcement of
Irma Wayer lies in front of me. Finally her wish has come true;
her fiancée returned. At the same time as Jenna, she, too,
became a woman. My best wishes accompany her on her life's
journey with her husband, a doctor.

Munich, 8 February 1945
Finally we received news from Baerbel again. She is working
as an apprentice on an estate up in the Northeast. They
experience hourly alarms, yet keep on with their work day
after day. Over Christmas she got engaged to a certified farmer
who studies in Goettingen. She will build her happiness after
the war and most likely retain her ties to her country and her
people, whom she so loves. She goes her way firmly and
confidently. It is a true joy to read her letters. One should show
them to the people of Munich who waver and are now
becoming scared. The danger from the East is great but we
have to stick together in order to secure the very existence of

our people. It may be that we stand alone but we will do it, cost what it may.

Munich, 10 February 1945
One year ago today the gates of the school closed behind us and we entered life with eager anticipation. All of the graduates will be thinking about that today. My thoughts hover over the rows of seats, stopping at each to consider what its then-occupant is doing and accomplishing now: Our Wayerlein just got married. She is giving up her studies. Right now she is working at Rodenstock in the science department. Dieps is in the KLV in Bad Toelz. I do not envy her in this position. Ursel was in the Sudetengau with the RAD and has now gone into the Air Force, stationed in the West with a searchlight battery. Lorle is in the health department of the Student Services but is looking for another job which will satisfy her more. Erna Hort and Gretlies Dosch are in the Sudetengau with the RAD, working in a munitions factory as KHD girls. Inge is in Oberammergau and works there in a factory as part of her student war deployment. After her time in the RAD, Liese went into the Air Force and had had frequent reassignments. She is still her old sweet self. Irmgard is in Oberhofen, interning in a pharmacy. Mopsels, once a medical student, moved up to being a state-credentialed telegrapher who meets the demands of her job with her own great humor. Lilli is busy in the household of her aunt. Nobody has heard from Erna Buss, although we believe she is in Vienna. Remtschperl is with Siemens, working in cable. Her training as an actress has to take a place in the background for now. Hilde, my former colleague, now works at the Schwabing Hospital as head of the office for *Ausgleichsdienst* [compulsory non-military service]. Stupsi is in the protectorate serving in the RAD. Times are really rough there and she is hoping for her early release. Jenna, my faithful companion in the counseling service, got married and will probably not study very much anymore. She will be looking for a way to busy

herself in Berchtesgaden. Karin became a DRK helper. She is doing an apprenticeship in Reichenhall at this time. Frenchi was in the Sudetengau as a KHD worker and is now in Illertissen at the camp leadership school. Anneliese Kraus also went into the Air Force after her RAD time and pushes bravely through all the miseries. Ljuka, since she cannot continue her studies, will probably just lie around on her lazy bum. Marion is working half-days at the Schongau airport; the rest of the time she helps her father in his medical practice. Ruth is in Weilheim at the NSV County Office, Gabi works in a NSV kindergarten and Lotte is employed in a pharmacy. Those would be all of my fellow travelers over those eight long years. Every one of us is trying to fulfill the expectations placed on us. We enjoyed a somewhat regulated education and can now fully demonstrate our abilities. Wherever we all are now, that grounding in old camaraderie unites us. They all write to me. We had a golden school time. My studies, when I get to them, will be even nicer.

Munich, 24 February 1945

Twenty-five years ago the [Nazi] Party was founded at the Hofbraeuhaus in Munich. For 25 years the Party has worked, fought and won. Now it is going through its hardest test, with some Party members becoming inconsistent because luck is not on our side right now. Because of this the Party members who are steadfast must, now more than ever, hold together and drag the rest of the people along with them. The general membership meeting of our local group works under this dictate. The *Führer* will be in Munich today to speak to his old comrades, the Old Guard. I am anxious to hear his words, which will revitalize us all to keep the oath we pledged. Yesterday's Accountability Report, given by the Local Group Leader, stated that out of the 420 buildings in this jurisdiction [*Ortsgruppe*], 180 are still standing, and the population went from 20,000 down to 2,500. Our *Ortsgruppe* [locale] has certainly suffered but continues to fulfill its pledged obligations. We have always mastered any situation.

Munich, 25 February 1945

Terror attack on Munich.   For the second time this year, Munich was the target of a severe bombing raid. Once again the concert was on.   There—rumble, rumble—two attacks right close by. Then we heard another and wondered where it could have been, Adelgunden or Thierschstrasse? *Mutti* went up when it was quite dark. Thierschstrasse numbers 39, 41 and 43 had been hit; Adelgunden Street number 1 totally demolished. Two bombs went into the Isar [River] and one exploded at the turnabout. Above ground power wires were down. Duds fell on number 43, as well as on Hildegard Street 38. So, our local area had again been hit. Two hundred homeless are being cared for at the Neptune Café.

Munich, 28 February 1945

More and more fugitives from the eastern and western parts of the Reich are reporting to the provision shelters. These people have wandered for many days, able to bring with them only a few things. They have suffered great deprivation and are very needy, but are happy that, within the Reich, they were able to save themselves from the Bolshevists and the Americans. It is against these poor homeless that the terror attacks mainly take place, especially in Dresden and Berlin.

Munich, 1 March 1945

We have finally received another letter from Manny. His letter, dated February 10th, demonstrates his bright enthusiasm. "Dear *Mutti*! You must have been shocked when you first heard on the radio, 'the heavy battleship *Lützow*!' No sooner on board and already sent out on a mission. Now I am back in port but hoping the command 'Seaworthy; clear the decks for battle!' will soon be given again. It really shook when our 28 centimeter turrets fired. My station is next to the right turret. It is like a bomb shelter, but it is wonderful. The provisions are great. The cook is good enough to compete with you. For breakfast, 40 grams of butter and 40 grams of pork fat; for lunch 100 grams of canned meat, potato salad and sauce; for dinner, meatballs, 100 grams of spinach, potatoes and gravy. Impeccably prepared. Forty grams of butter! Like God in France. We eat well because the work, especially while out at sea, is hard. But the time will come when we are all at home together again eating Russian eggs with mayonnaise. So, stick it out for now and everything will fall into place. The terror is just beginning: the great offensives from the East and West. But we will hold out. You have had several alarms in last days. They were supposed to leave you alone. We wait for them and will show them our sharp teeth. Ships with fugitives come into our harbor daily and we are ordered to help them. We witness scenes which escalate our immeasurable rage, but not a syllable of complaint crosses the lips of our brave comrades from East Prussia. We all have our hopes up for victory. I will close now, warmly greeting you and Lulu with thousands of kisses from your sailor Manny who, in his spirit, imagines our being together again. Anticipation is the best kind of joy! Stay courageous!"

Munich, 8 March 1945
After a few soft breezy days seemed to announce spring, it has become winter again outside. The snow falls in thick flakes. *Frau Holle* is efficiently shaking out her feather beds. Tree and branch wear their white load. The ruins and wreckage have been covered over. All around us there is a thick pelt of snow as the flakes keep on falling; some in wonderful swirls, others, still and even. "It snows."

Munich, 9 March 1945
Finally, today, Lore Bartel came for a visit. The last time we

saw each other was at our graduation. Since then she has been in Geisenhausen-by-Landshut in the RAD; moving then into the KHD to work as a streetcar conductor. She wore the same trim uniform as the Munich conductors and it looks very good on her. The hours flew by as we enjoyed lively chats about the past which had held us together for eight years and of old comrades who are spread out all over the world. Lore is the same as she used to be. She, like me, has had many solitary hours because she is not like the other girls in her camp who have only men and dance melodies in their heads and do not think any deeper, the type we reject. At Easter, her KHD service will be over. It was, for us both, a nice get-together.

Munich, 10 March 1945
After 5 weeks, my first day to work at the hospital again. I re-connected with several old acquaintances, by that I mean several old patients who had wondered about my long absence. Twelve hour work day. That is a long time but it still went by very quickly. We have a few terrible cases of pneumonia which required our extra attention. Some patients, hard hit by rheumatism, could hardly move and had to be fed. Being bathed and using a bedpan are torments to them. They are so thankful when we treated them carefully and show some concern. I think they like me very much; so, for me, the 12 hours caring for the sick were not in vain. I may be dead tired but I am satisfied.

Munich, 11 March 1945
Heldengedanktag [Veterans Memorial Day]. On this day we think of those who lost their lives for Germany. Every family thinks of their own dead and, beyond that, we all think of the men of the nation who lost their lives. This year Dietl and Rommel fell and are mourned by the entire population. At this time we also think of the many who died from the air raid attacks. Gerhart Schumann wrote the "Song of the Dead:" "The

army of the dead is forever marching towards you. But always we are near. Forever, there stands the tower of admonition. You are spared from death, because we died for you. When you do your duty righteously, you raise us up into the light."

Munich, 17 March 1945
The days are just flying past and before I can turn around, Saturday is here again. Again, work at the Schwabing Hospital brought me much joy. I was allowed to do all the injections that came up throughout the day. I have completely overcome my inhibitions and can do them very well now. In other ways, also, I am able to work much more independently. This, more than anything, is a source of constant joy. Traudl came. She looks fresh and healthy once again. She passed her pharmaceutical exam and is hoping to get a position in Schwabing. Hilde is sick. Her stomach is out of order. But still, she got up once again and went to work. An incorrigible rascal.

Munich, 19 March 1945
Today I received news that the DRK head nurse, Hermine Stolz , lost her life during a terror attack on Heilbronn. I am so saddened by it. We saw each other and spoke to one another for only one good hour in 1942 on our way from Munich to Rosenheim. Out of this encounter, we developed an exchange of letters, which we both enjoyed. For Christmas in 1942, I hand crafted Christmas ornaments for her military hospital in Freudental. In 1943 I got her textbooks which she used with a theater group during Christmas time. In 1944 she could no longer take a part in this because, earlier in December, she gave her life for her country which she so loved. I will carry with me the memories of a woman who was a true mother to the injured and, to those who worked for her, a role model of professionalism.

Munich, 24 March 1945
We had daily alarms throughout this entire week, each one

often lasting four to five hours. During these warm spring days, it was a true blessing when one could spend some time in the sun. There was an air raid alarm today while I was working at the hospital. Fortunately all the patients were down in the basement when this familiar concert began. Nothing happened at the hospital itself; we got off with just the scare. Thank God nothing happened at home either. The airport in Vienna was hit.

Munich, 25 March 1945
Today is *Vati*'s birthday. My thoughts wander towards him in Sylt. May he live his next year in leisurely good health. May his wish of seeing Germany victorious come true. The way it is right now, it does not seem possible. It takes a lot of will power to still believe we can win. The enemy to the west is at Darmstadt; everywhere, the Rhine has been overtaken. There is a break in the battles to the east, the quiet before the storm. One does not know what to think. The rations have had to be shortened drastically. The terrible bombings continue. I still try to believe in our victory because if we lose we give up the meaning of our lives.

Munich, 30 March 1945
Today is Good Friday. Easter, the festivity for spring, is at our front door. In spite of the six years of war, I made a few preparations. I blew out five eggs, boiled the eggshells in onion peel water so that they turned a glowing yellow and then I painted them. They all turned out different. Then I pulled a thread through them and hung the Easter eggs on a forsythia branch. The Easter greeting is finished. With modest means, I still achieved a beautiful effect.

Munich, 31 March 1945
Hospital duty. There were blossoming branches in all the rooms. Easter nests with brightly colored eggs. Along with the

usual nurses' ward duties, we organized everything so that there was peace and quiet for Easter. Right in the middle of the day came the usual alarm, which does not even upset us anymore. Linz got bombarded. Dr. Feser had to perform a pleurisy puncture which we were allowed to watch. Two patients had to be brought to the operations bunker to be bandaged up. Another was taken to the ear, nose and throat doctor. So, the day flew by. After exchanging the best of Easter wishes, we all went home.

Munich, 1 April 1945
Easter. The festival of joy and of spring. Festival for the children. Memories of childhood awaken: Easter egg hunts in the Museum gardens, our own little Easter bunny. Our Easter greetings decorate the room. In the afternoon we went to a concert in the Prinzregententheater. Finally, to be able to listen to some music again and to be among festively dressed people. It was an uplifting experience. Today is also April 1st. Yet no one is in the mood for pranks. The Russians have penetrated the Viennese Neustadt. One sees no holding of the line and turning of the tide. But the heart tells us, "Stick it out." It is hard to control the defeatists among us who spread rumors and cause unrest. After such news, the carefree hours spent at the concert worked like a dream. I put my faith in the *Führer*. He will continue to guide us; he knows what he is doing.

Munich, 7 April 1945
Twelve hours of hospital duty are behind me once again; four of them, of course, under alarm and in the basement. But who does this bother anymore. My indecisiveness is because my work situation has not been resolved. I do not know what I should do. Should I still register for special assignments, for which I qualify, or should I go into the DRK, or should I work half days in the hospital, half days in the office. Or, should I wait to see how the situation develops. But this "wait and see"

wears one down. Much better would be a job that would not allow me time to think. With time, will come the solution.

Munich, 9 April 1945
Terror attack over Munich. Yesterday evening, the nuisance, single plane raiders dropped bombs. This afternoon Munich experienced a heavy terror attack which destroyed many suburbs. For the first time, a new alarm signal, "acute air raid," was given. We are going to have to get used to the many small and full alarms because the Fronts are closing in on us.

Munich, 11 April 1945
A new attack tried to completely destroy the city. Bombs were dropped without rhyme or reason, and now even on areas further away from Munich. Low flyers attack the trains, and the farmers in the fields are being shot at. Due to this it is hard to get field hands. A simple trip becomes a dangerous venture. The Fronts are closing deeper into Germany, with the Russians in Vienna and the English in the West; nonetheless, the enemy is everywhere faced with the resistant will of people who will not allow themselves to be defeated. The soul of our struggle for freedom lies within the *Werwolf* [special forces trained to operate secretly behind enemy lines], the Hitler Youth and the *Volkssturm* [Peoples' Army]. Their goal is to bomb the enemy's supplies behind their Frontline and to overwhelm them with losses.

Munich, 13 April 1945
I received good news, even though today is the thirteenth, which makes me exuberant. I am to do an internship. Surgeon Dr. Kittel, region leader of our students, is looking for someone to write down data while also being able to do nursing duty. This puts me in line, right where I wanted to be. I feel like I have been freed of all the dark thoughts I've recently had. One only needs to have a goal to steer towards with will and love.

The American President Roosevelt died of a brain hemorrhage. What other surprises will the turns in this war bring?

Munich, 14 April 1945
One should not get too excited too soon. Things often turn out differently than one has supposed they would. Now *Frau* Dr. Mueggenburg is not letting me go. But I do hope that I can still make it happen. What would she have done if I had been approved to study or if I had gone to the KLV? The decision will be made on Monday. There was not much going on in the hospital today. I could only come in the afternoon. Our older mothers from the refugee train are so frugal and accommodating; they do not make everything such a big deal, as other old women do.

Munich, 20 April 1945
Today is the *Führer's* 56th birthday. Today, in this tensest of times, we all think of him. It is he who has led us imperturbably and steadfastly, faithful and true, through these hard war years and who will continue to lead us forward. May he keep his strength and good health and be able to ward off any challenges. Dr. Goebbels touchingly recalled the many speeches of the *Führer*. I agree with all my heart to what he then said, "May he always be what he is to us now and always has been: Our Hitler!"

Munich, 21 April 1945
Today is *Mutti's* birthday. I wish her the best, especially health, from the bottom of my heart. May this next year grant her innermost wish of victory and, with that, Manny's return; she misses him very much. This was another eventful day. There was not much to do in the ward because a transport was sent to Reichenhall yesterday. All the work got done quickly and everything was good. Then, at 11:00, the air raid alarm sounded. We had barely gotten the sick to the basement when

it all began. We had to carry the gurneys down because the elevator had already shut down. With one delivered, we hurried back up; even more quickly, back down. The building shook; even in the basement we could feel the shaking. The building at Maennerbau 3 was destroyed when it was hit. There was a time-bomb just outside our office. When the alarm was over, Dr. Feser processed the patients who were being released. We had to work really hard to take in all the injured from Maennerbau 7. Again, a heavy terror attack sweeping over our city.

Munich, 22 April 1945
Liese was just here to ask for my advice. She was put on leave by the Flak and does not know where to go from here. I gave her a Latin book and a Biology book to take with her. She has to continue learning and working for herself. In a year she has forgotten all she had learned. I am always glad when I can help someone, because to "just hang in the air" is not good. This is what I am experiencing myself right now.

Munich, 28 April 1945
I guess today is the last day I will be working in the hospital for a while. Munich is more and more becoming a Frontline city. The Fronts close in. The food and clothing warehouses are being disbanded, with all the materials being distributed. There is one special allocation after another. Today was a really emotional day. At 7:00 in the morning, the voice of a traitor sounded over the radio, inciting the people against the *Führer* and announcing a special peace agreement between Bavaria and England-America. The entire situation was a blown-up "bluewhite" [colors of the Bavarian flag; a reference to local NS opposition] and a lie from A to Z. By 11:30 Giesler and Fiehler took their stand to demand fighting and opposition until the end. Everything in the ward was taken to the basement, leaving upstairs only the few patients who are able to walk.

Medicines, instruments, etc. were stowed away below. Aside from this, it is very quiet in the city, even if the mood is not the best. Every bit of gossip is believed and passed along. One only makes oneself crazy and reaches a state of panic. At home, all the necessities of life, especially food, are in the basement. We wait, to see what time will bring.

Munich, 29 April 1945

I sit here writing as the earth shudders from the thunder of gunfire. They are thought to be in Ismaning already. One volley after another is shot through the barrels. In between one feels the detonation of the bombs. It is all so unique. Here the thunder of guns causing the window panes to shake; there the blooming flowers speaking of spring. The chestnuts blossom in their candle-like white. Lilac, tulips and almond trees are in bloom. Everything would be so nice if one could enjoy it. Another hit.   Each one seems to be closer. The street cars continue to run; the traffic goes on in the Frontline city of Munich. What must *Vati* and Manny be thinking? For weeks we have not received any news from them. It is the same case the other way around. In Berlin they are fighting until the end. I just want to know how the *Führer* is doing. Is everything supposed to be over, everything we believed in and everything that we lived for? Should all the sacrifices have been in vain? I can not believe it. As long as the German people live, they will pick themselves up and start again from scratch. Felix was here the day before yesterday. He is looking for his wife and their children, his mother, brother, sister and their little ones. They left Weissenburg on April 17th and have not yet arrived in Munich. We have to assume that something happened to them on the way. It would be awful, seven lovely people. Gretl with four small children is supposed to be near Weissenburg; Theo fights in Silesia, so the entire family is torn apart. I wonder if we will live to see our 300 year anniversary in 1948. Sounds of the dueling artillery duel grow ever stronger. Tonight we will sleep in our clothes so as to be immediately ready if there is an "enemy alarm." Deep down inside I wish it would just be over. But we still have to fight and offer resistance, so as not to shame ourselves before the other cities. *„Nur die Sache ist verloren, die man aufgibt!"* ["The only thing lost is what one gives up!" – quote from Gotthold Ephraim Lessing, 1729-1781] And yet, these hours of waiting wear one down. One is torn back and forth between one's feelings and beliefs. *Reichsmarshall* Goering has resigned. What is this step supposed to mean? They say it may be health. Does the *Führer* have to drink the cup to the dregs? What will the Occupation be like? Foreign troops in Munich, in all of Germany. It is hard to believe and yet so unbelievably sad. We, who conquered territory from the Caucasus to the North Sea and the Pyrenees, held Tripoli and the Balkans, now have the enemy on our land ready to eradicate us. Though the Occupation may serve as a salutary lesson for many people, they had perhaps rather reflect on their Germaneness and realize that the American is not as humane as they today believe him to be. It is now 9 p.m. The sound of gunfire is almost non-stop. I close my lines and hope that we come out of this inferno healthy.

Munich, 30 April 1945

Allied troops marched into Munich today after the white flag was hoisted from the Cathedral at 3:00 p.m. This invasion into the city was the most unique experience I have ever had. There was a "war game" in front of our apartment building as soon as the first Americans walked our streets. Some people were waving their handkerchiefs. I would have expected a bit more honor from the Munich people. After a short while the tanks drove up. The infantry followed. "Now they are here." "Now it is over." These are the words heard over and over again. In the distance one can hear artillery, which had stopped here earlier in the day. The enemy is now in Munich. In the apartment building, we are all settled in. They were in our home also, but left us alone when they saw the broken down apartment.

Munich, 1 May 1945

May 1st. Memories of the past hold me prisoner. May 1st is National Day of the German people. Those times will probably never return. In the city, all the stores are being looted by the rabble. The police have been confined, so the people can do whatever they want. This May 1st is wet and cold as well as unfriendly. The enemy tanks and vehicles roll unceasingly through our city. They are made of such poor material that one cannot believe we had to capitulate before these weapons. The soldiers make grumpy faces and must be thinking to themselves, "What are we doing in this country, in this city?" They want to go home as soon as possible. Are the Russians going to follow them in now? May God keep us!

Munich, 5 May 1945

With all that is going on, I still had hospital duty today. We could dress in either civilian clothes or in uniform. In these hours, one forgets the calamity outside because the people that lie here need our help and the work completely engages us. Hilde sleeps in the hospital now because she cannot make the long trip every day and bike riding has been prohibited. Anyway, the residents are only allowed on the streets from 6 a.m. to 7 p.m. The foreigners — Ukrainian, Polish and Russian prisoners — are free. They do not work anymore and loot all the stores, factories, etc. They are all supposed to be leaving now, which will be a true blessing. The Mayor and the Sheriff have already been voted in. The trams and small trains should be operating soon. We are waiting to see what comes next. Work does not make people happy because they ask themselves if there is still a reason. One has to have a job like in the Schwabing hospital where one has to really concentrate, and where, also, results can be seen.

Munich, 12 May 1945

Today I would have worked at the hospital again but my hay

fever is being very hard on me. In this sneezing and sniffling condition, I am not a happy sight, and also of no help. We cleaned out our apartment of dust, mortar etc. and brought our suitcases and beds back up from the ground floor. I have arranged my books again, really went through my things. It could all be so nice, if our thoughts about the enemy and the future were not so depressing. Scharnagl, who has had this position since 1933, was named Mayor. This calms me because he knows his people of Munich and will know how to represent their interests. For three days now there is peace in Europe. Peace? Like mockery it rings in our ears. In America and England, the bells resound for a victory that, even according to Churchill, was won only through continuous air raids on the civilian population. To me, that is not a victory. On a strictly military basis, we would not have been defeated. Now we have to bite into the sour apple and follow the orders of the Military Occupation. One can ride a bicycle again now. Soon there is supposed to be radio and newspaper again. Groceries, milk and meat are to be brought in. We have to stand in long lines for hours to get bread and meat. My thoughts constantly wander out; what are *Vati* and Manny doing? The cruiser *Lützow* was sunk by the English. We do not know whether or not Manny was still on it. This uncertainty is awful. What will Gretl do with the four little ones! I do not think that Theo will return. What is happening with Felix's family? Throughout these long war years our family has not had a casualty. At the end, this horrible uncertainty hangs over all of us. We have to pull ourselves together so that we can provide strong support for those who are coming in from the outside wounded in body and soul.

Munich, 5 June 1945

I have not written anything for a long time. Daily life has become monotonous. At 5:30 in the morning, one has to get in lines to get potatoes, many times for naught. The other gets in line for meat or bread. I had hospital duty on Pentecost Saturday and the following Saturday. Schwabing has become a hospital for foreigners and I no longer go there. I really have no desire to nurse Jews or Ukrainians back to health. Anyway, my cold has gotten worse than ever, a by-product of the beautiful weather. On Pentecost I reorganized my ethnic-costumes. Now I have fabricated a lamp shade for myself that still has to finish drying. I am also making baby clothes for Mrs. Niegele who is expecting her baby in August. She is alone and has lost everything. She was able to find shelter at Mrs. Umkehr's. One must fill the days with whatever work one can, so as not to have time to think, because the thoughts that come are so destructive and fatiguing. Everywhere one can see the hunger problem. The bread ration has been decreased to 700 grams. Most people do not have any more potatoes. All other rations are equally hard to come by. There is, however, still worse to come. The people will eventually see what it means to be a lost people, when the entire blame is placed on us.

Munich, 30 June 1945
The days come and go. Mornings I study, that means I am retrieving the knowledge I once had of Science and Latin. The University is supposed to re-open in the fall. That will be the second semester for the students studying medicine, so one has to re-learn what was learned in the first semester to be able to follow the lesson plan. Afternoons belong to my hobbies. I work from an arts and crafting book out of which I take my patterns. I can really use these things for the seven little ones in our family, among them the rascals from Berlin who lost their father and home. One doll is already finished. There is always something to make and to work on and this is good. No news from Manny or *Vati*. We hear that the Navy is still not releasing personnel. Work and more work.

Munich, 21 July 1945

Now it has really turned into summer. The skies are bright blue and the sun's rays beam down on us. We are in the best of summer weather, with the lakes tempting us to swim. It is best not to think about the past. It is better to look to the future which lies so open before us. I can not yet begin my studies so I have decided to take the midwifery class; then, I can take another look. We have arranged our small living room in a pleasant fashion. My bed room faces the front. Our piano is being brought upstairs. Gradually life is becoming more comfortable again. Where can *Vati* and Manny be? One is always expectant and, therefore, time passes quickly.

Munich, 7 August 1945

Finally some news from *Vati*! A woman brought us a small piece of paper with a greeting from *Vati*, informing us that he will be home soon. A soldier from Westerland had brought the news. Now we have that to look forward to. We hope that he will be able to handle the stress. He is healthy and he has felt good all along, so he can begin his voyage in good condition.

Munich, 8 August 1945

Today, after a very long time, my colleagues came by again. They are now employed in the nursing home in Schwabing. Dr. Feser is still there, as well as Hilde. Nurse Jugesia and Nurse Sigelana joined them. Otherwise, everything else has changed. Foreign patients, close accommodations, but it is working.

Munich, 9 August 1945

Irmgard Hellenbrecht got engaged. I wish her all the best for her union with a doctor. Now the *Beratungsdienst* [Advisory-Counseling Service], with a little help from me, has been brought to an end. I am curious as to what all she [Irmgard] will have to tell us when she comes. On Sunday we were at a concert again after a long time. It was truly a joy for me. The festively dressed people, the music, conductors, the soloist, the singer, the orchestra; all of this allows us to forget everything else for a few hours. We heard Mozart's *Overture to Figaro*, along with Hayden's *Symphony in B Minor* and three songs: *Caro Mio Ben*, an Italian Folksong and Mozart's *Hora Pastorale*. The finale was the *Sixth Symphony*, the *Pastoral*, by Beethoven. We now want to go to a concert at least once a month. I am making dolls and stuffed animals for a Kindergarten right now. The Americans took all the toys with them as souvenirs. This is wise use of my time, as seen by the fact that I am making a little extra money on the side.

Munich, 12 August 1945
Vati came home!! All the waiting has come to an end. He arrived early in the morning at 6:30 a.m. He looks great. Thank God he had been assigned to a good place. He traveled zigzag for 10 days through the whole German countryside, which lies there destroyed. The story telling has no end. Where can our Manny be? Our thoughts keep drifting back to him. Only God knows where he is.

Munich, 15 August 1945
I played housewife and mother for two days for Felix, who went to harvest beans with Erna. Waltraud and Wolfgang are two rascals who can really wear one out. I really enjoyed the cleaning up, shopping, cooking etc. because no one was there to criticize me. I could work as I wanted and it all came out all right.

Munich, 24 August 1945
Rosemarie was here. She has been released from the Army and, after her vacation, will begin working in a hospital. She knew a lot of interesting things from Garmisch and could tell us about the situation there.

Munich, 28 August 1945
This afternoon I visited Mrs. Beigele, who has given birth to her long awaited son. She feels well and energetic and has forgotten all about the pain now that the boy, Hermann Bernd, is here. She will give all of her love to this child as a memorial to her fiancé. I made her a small bunny out of a washcloth.

Munich, 2 September 1945
Today was a beautiful fall day, perfect for hiking. We really took advantage of it by hiking from Gruenwald to Grossdingharting where a wonderful meal in a peaceful setting awaited us. Then we went swimming in the Deininger Pond; swampy water, but still comfortable for swimming. On our return we went through Woehltal to Gruenwald. This hike reminded us once again about the beauty of our nearby surroundings. It is like being out in the country, but is less than 20 kilometers from Munich. Peace and quiet radiates out from Nature and draws the people into its spell. Life is still worth the effort in all this chaos of everyday life.

Munich, 9 September 1945
We went to Grossdingharting again. The path through the forest in fall was gorgeous. After breakfast, *Vati* and I went in the direction of the Ludwigshoehe to a scenic overview just beyond Kleindingharting. In front of us a panorama of the Alpine foothills; to the right, the Isertal; to the left, the Gleisental. Peace and quiet all around us. The bells of the Deininger village church announced the noon hour. After a short rest, *Vati* and I went to the Deininger Pond and found in our path elderberries, which we harvested. *Vati*'s handkerchief was filled so quickly. On the way home we gathered acorns which we will process into coffee. It was a beautiful Sunday.

Munich, 25 September 1945
Today I made a business transaction for the first time. Last

Sunday I read the advertisements and answered one in writing. I received a call today. I was invited to see Mr. Schnepper and show him my samples. So I took my animals and pocketbooks and went on my way. I sold the purse and briefcase right away. He kept the horse. He wants to keep it on consignment. Mr. Schnepper also gave me another order. He wants a colorful Pasbol belt. I am supposed to sew other belts as well, to be made from old military cloth and other materials. Of course I took them with me. I am already so excited about the work I will be doing at home!

Munich, 29 September 1945

Today I made my second delivery of homemade craftwork. This time it was 10 Pasbol belts, some finished off with rickrack. My next assignment is to make stamp and letter holders out of beautiful green artificial leather, also book covers made of plush and with all kinds of decorations. The work brings me a lot of pleasure and it also allows me to earn a little something. I make the beautiful things and other people find pleasure in them. I am very curious as to when our business will open.

Munich, 27 October 1945

I have not written anything for a long while because time has just been rushing by, one day after another, bringing work and more work. But I enjoy my work because I work at home and can manage my time as I choose. It is nice and warm here. I can welcome guests, while not allowing them to disturb my work. They have become used to this and now bring their own work to do. One Sunday I visited a colleague with whom I spent a nice afternoon. Everyone everywhere asks about Manny, from whom we still have not received any news. Helmut is looking for work as a tradesman, anything which can still be of use later. Most of us expect to eventually reach our goals only after having to make wide detours. Inge is working at the Excelsior Hotel, Mopsi is interning with a dentist and Liese is working in the Census Bureau. At this time, Karin has been without a job ever since her father was arrested. Erna H. is enrolled in the translation school, Gretlies works at home and is trying to study, Lorle is at the high school in Wolfrathausen. Stupsi and Lotte work in pharmacies, Remptschperl is faking it as statistician. So, everyone has found the places which suit their tendencies, and all are trying to find their ways through the crisis. I am satisfied with my skill and hope that I can continue my studies soon.

Munich, 8 November 1945

I am celebrating my 20th birthday today. Yet I am not quite in the mood. We received the first news from Manny which was dated August 8th, which means that it was written three months ago. Back then he was lying in the hospital in Eilenburg near Leipzig. He is in the Russian zone, but thank God, as a civilian. The Russians have no use for sick people. Let us hope that he comes home soon; then he will get nursed back to health. He only weighs 120 pounds now, a second Gandhi. Hopefully he will be able to cross the border. I wish he was already here. For my birthday I got the book *Behring* by Zeiss and *Doctors Voices* by Zeller. I got a vase for decoration from Bertl. From Traudl I received an ethnic-costume picture and colorful trimmings for my ethnic-costume dolls.

Munich, 18 November 1945

Hanna bore a son. A magnificent boy of 8 pounds, 100 grams; 54 cm. long and a 34 cm. head circumference. He suckles as though in glory. She is overjoyed. The entire birthing process was over in just 12 hours. From the bottom of my heart, I wish her a lot of happiness with her son, Gerd Ernst.

Munich, 2 December 1945

First Sunday in Advent. Our thoughts go out to our loved ones, to our Manny. Where might he be? We have not received any further news. Today I handcrafted the pyramid back together. In renewed splendor, it will glimmer as it turns in the candlelight for the seventh time. All of our thoughts are on Christmas, the German holiday. This year no bombs will disturb this festival of lights and, more than ever, one seeks to bring someone else a bit of joy. I have to hurry and I have to work hard so I can make all of my clients' wishes come true. Everyone wants something; I should have ten hands. *Mutti* chopped into her finger, which means that I also have to take care of the household. But where there is a will, there is a way.

Munich, 5 December 1945
Tonight I went to see *Fidelio*. Eight days ago I saw *La Boheme* with *Mutti*. Both operas, each with its own uniqueness, are beautiful and gripping. The singers gave their best. These were two wonderful experiences.

Munich, 10 December 1945
Today I received the news of Irmi's engagement, which took place in October. The fourth young lady of our group. I am wondering when she will come to tell me more. I can hardly visualize her as a housewife. My commissioned work load keeps me busy. I work all day long, managing the household on the side, and am always happy when a little time is left over for peace and solitude. Only 14 days until Christmas. Today we baked our first cookies, a really good way to get into the Christmas mood.

Munich, 21 December 1945
Christmas approaches in giant steps. Thank God that I am finished with all the presents and children's work. Actually I am happy that I am finally done with it because I am ready to get busy with some of my personal things, to put my collections back in order and, especially, to begin studying again. But it was good that I could spend this time usefully, to

my enjoyment and with a bit of financial gain. In the process, I acquired a certain skill.

Munich, 24 December 1945

Christmas Eve. My thoughts go out to Manny, wondering where he might be as he celebrates Christmas. This uncertainty is the worst. But I am confident an answer will come soon. After our traditional Christmas Eve dinner, *Vati* lit the candles and the giving of the presents could begin. Next to the books, I found *Vati's* finely painted copy of a Spitzweg original. I received a charming scissor-cut paper silhouette from Miss Hahn, a book about fashion, and white paper onto which I can glue my collections. But I had still not unwrapped *Mutti's* surprise present. And what was it: a small *Schrühmerin* which I had admired so at Mr. Schnepper's and which *Mutti* had secretly ordered. *Vati* got a shaving mirror from *Mutti*; from me, a necktie and cigarettes. Miss Hahn gave *Vati* a wonderful paper cutout silhouette of a Maypole. *Mutti* was happy with a purse which I made for her, a tablecloth and a big piece of soap from Miss Hahn. We were all satisfied with these gifts. If all were so richly blessed, then all would be happy.

Munich, 31 December 1945

I am lying in bed with a small kidney attack. I will be able to get up tomorrow. Today we finally received news from Manny. He is still lying in the hospital in Eilenburg and has had to go through a lot. When he was admitted there on July 7th his head was bald and he weighed only 128 pounds. On his first day there, 200 cc of pleural fluid was taken out of the space between his lung and his rib cage; on the fourth day, 800 cc. His left lung had completely collapsed, meaning that it barely functioned. He can do easy jobs and so he helps in the different wards, is friendly with everyone—with sweets manufacturers, station girls from the country etc. He is counting on being released in February or March. In

November he suddenly came down with typhus. Where it came from is a riddle to everyone. Fortunately, he has recovered from it. We hope from the bottom of our hearts that he will be well soon so that he can come back to us.

1946

Munich, 8 January 1946

Eight days have already passed in the New Year. Today I received news of Baerbel's engagement. Her property needs a man. She and her fiancé made their escape together and went through further struggles rebuilding their lives. Should they wait for better times? I wish her all the best. To me she is the model of what a wife and a mother should be.

Munich, 22 January 1946

For the time being I am once again elated. I finally received my admission to the University, after having been first denied. Now I can get on with my medical studies. I am simply happy. And today we received news from Manny. Judging by the tone of his letter, he is merry as a cricket. His health is improving and he is still receiving great nursing care. Thank God things are going so well for him. Others report terrible things from the Russian Occupied Zone. We are happy that he is doing well and has found his sense of humor again. Karin Schuerholz came by this morning from Murnau. She went on to Reichenhall to see Oswald's mother. She will be moving to Hamburg in a few days to begin her nursing studies there. Karin is still the wonderful person she was.

Munich, 18 February 1946

I have not written anything in a long time. The days are just passing by so quickly. Each day brings with it something new. The admission process at the University has begun but the medical students have not had any lectures yet. It starts after Easter for us. I hardly believe anything anymore; instructions contradict each other. But at least something is happening now and that is a modest step forward. Now I am looking around for college books and notebooks. In the morning I study, do some shopping etc. and at night we often go out. We have seen all the pieces performed at the theater. *Mutti* is attending the Beethoven cycle. I went to the circus yesterday. Others are going to *Fasching* [*Mardi Gras/Carnaval*] parties, but I just do not enjoy that. One still cannot get any books. But to look for things is also fun; often one can still find something small, good wartime editions etc. Sometimes I have so many plans, while other times I just sit there staring into space, just waiting. If only things would get serious at the University.

Munich, 21 February 1946
Finally admitted. I picked up my class schedule and my identification badge. For the medical students classes will not begin until April or May. I will continue to work and prepare myself as best I can. In the afternoon I went to a lecture by *Geh. Rat* Dr. Vossler: "Research and Education at the University." This time they could not complain about a shortage of listeners; we had to move over to the big auditorium. Closing words were spoken by Minister of Culture Dr. Fendt. Soon I will be an official student-in-residence. If it would only start soon!

Munich, 26 February 1946
Yesterday we went to the cabaret *Bunter Würfel* [Motley Dice], which was simply magnificent. Brought to life was the slogan, "Munich is learning to laugh again." For two hours the wit and humor provoked in us deep, hearty laughter. Today we saw the movie *Paul Ehrlich*. The acting was good but it made me angry that facts were so distorted. Incidents were portrayed that, in truth, were totally different. I prefer to be content with our good old German films. [*Dr. Ehrlich's Magic Bullets*, produced at Warner Brothers Studios with Edward G. Robinson as Paul Ehrlich, premiered in the US in 1940. The script was nominated for an Oscar. In 1945-1946 the film was shown, first in Austrian and then in German cinemas, under the title *Paul Ehrlich – Ein Leben für die Forschung*.]

Munich, 4 March 1946
Today we had a course about the profession of a doctor. It was truly very interesting. The lecturer, who is the head doctor of the Bavarian Medical Counsel, Dr. Steidele, found the right words to describe the occupation.

Munich, 7 March 1946
The University still has not opened its doors. One could jump out of one's skin. A variety of lectures are already posted but nothing is moving in the medical department. We are told to simply wait, but it is really hard, because one wants to move ahead, to finally get started.

Munich, 12 March 1946
One has to sign up for classes by March 23rd. At one time, a posting read that the opening date for the University would be moved up. Today, a different notice states that the opening of the University has been delayed because "the application papers were lost by the military authorities." Who cannot see through this maneuver? It is a shame for Munich that this University cannot begin. Prof. Dr. Rehm, the Rector, has stepped down from his post. *Geh. Rat* Dr. Vossler is his successor. A state commissioner has been designated to investigate relationships at the University. All talk; no action.

Munich, 16 March 1946
Today is Manny's birthday. He is 19 years old. He is slowly getting ready for his return home. If he were only here already! The crossing of the boarder can be a tricky situation. Let us hope that everything goes well and that he reaches us in good health. Whatever his future may be, will be determined then.

Munich, 29 March 1946
Today they announced the beginning of the semester at the University. It is supposed to start on Monday, April 1st. I just

hope that it is not an April Fool's joke. Finally I have reached the point where I stand firmly, albeit on the lowest rung of a tall ladder. This unexpected onset has upset my plans, though. I meant to visit Hanna. So now I have to put it off for during my vacation time. Manny left the hospital and is heading in the direction of home. Hopefully all will go well for him so that this worthy fellow does not get detained somewhere along the way and can reach home in good health.

Munich, 12 April 1946
Finally it has started. Four lectures are behind me. The Botany instructor is Suestengut; Zoology, Beutler; Chemistry, Wieland and Physics, Ruechardt. Some lecture times overlap each other. But Claire and I take turns and then we exchange our notebooks. It is just great to be studying again; to know you are moving forward – and towards a goal that is worthwhile. This semester will be over on June 9th. We can only hope the medical lectures will continue after the Easter break. The lecture halls, however, are overfilled. I always get there half an hour earlier and do some work there. Having to stand is most unpleasant, very hard to write.

Munich, 18 April 1946
It seems that classes just began but already we are having eight days of Easter vacation. We have learned a lot up through now because the lecturers move forward very quickly. We spend more hours than foreseen studying all the subject matter, but it is wonderful. I write down what I heard once I get home. One knows halfway what one has already written once. I want to use this method for as long as possible. I reported to the University for clean-up today, not willingly, but if I did not, then, as a "Nazi," I would not be allowed to continue my studies. They pay 79 cents per hour plus a bonus for heavy work. We female students get jobs for females. I was allowed to pick my duties since I reported at an early stage. I took a job

that falls during vacation time so that not too much time is lost during the semester. Once this is over, I will have peace so that I can continue my studies without interruption. I hope so anyway. Today the declaration forms for the "denazification" arrived. Every Party Member has to go on trial. Our atonement is pronounced either by fine or physical labor. It is all meanness that is played off only in Bavaria. Then they speak of Bavaria as the "Rural Model."

Munich, 21 April 1946
Easter — *Mutti's* birthday. When I think back to last year, it all seems to have been a bad dream, what was then and what is now. No one even wants to think about it; yet every conversation turns in that direction. "When" and "but" are discussed thoroughly but no point is ever reached. Outside, spring has arrived in a blaze of color. The trees, many of them in bloom, stand adorned in their fresh green leaves. The little spring flowers are all abloom. We went to the Botanical Garden where it was wonderful, the flowers, all the different kinds of trees. In the greenhouse we saw the tropical plants. Nature is so rich. I cannot understand Hermann M., how he can be a botanist. I enjoy the sight of the flowers but do not think about them in microscopic detail, the number of leaves etc. One really has to have great enthusiasm for this as a profession; otherwise it would drive you crazy! Manny has still not come back. His doctor will not give him permission to travel. His *Blutsenkung* [ESR, erythrocyte sedimentation rate] is still too high: 65/110. He is only gradually improving. It is better this way than if he were to collapse on his way back. He is being nursed back to health and, at least, he does not lack for anything where he is. Hopefully he will come in May, June.

Munich, 23 April 1946
Children, nothing but children. On March 29th Bertl gave birth to a baby girl. Christl, given her life history, is doing well so

far, even though her child was born four weeks too early. But it will all work out. Today I visited Irmi Koff in the home for mothers. She gave birth to a baby girl, Brigitte, on April 17th. She was not doing so well. The child was born breech. Still, no harm came to either the mother or the child. We were allowed to see the baby from behind a glass wall. Wayerlein [diminutive, endearing form of Wayer] announced that something small will be arriving for her in May or June. Hanna's son is thriving; he is the pride of the family.

Höttingen, 27 April 1946

Today I write from Höttingen, a small village near Weissenburg. Gretl lives here with her four children. Even though everything is quite small, it could be comfortably arranged. She is not a good housewife nor does she make any effort to become one. Everything is dirty. The children are a mess and are undisciplined but are still, actually, very nice children. Renate [the oldest of the four children] helps with everything. Herbert has Theo's stubbornness; otherwise he would be a nice boy. Helga was terribly afraid of us, only showed up every so often. Heinz needed a little more time to make friends with us. Now Gretl is waiting for her husband, and what happens then [if he doesn't return]? I am disappointed in some ways. She still speaks enthusiastically about her life as it used to be, without realizing that was the very life mandated by the Organization [Nazi Party], which is now so hated. She clings too much to the old and can only whine and complain when faced with raw reality. I will be happy when I am back in Munich.

Munich, 15 May 1946

The time just rushes by us in leaps and bounds. Mornings we study, afternoons attend the lectures. Every day is the same as the next in that it brings new experiences and new knowledge. Now I have to interrupt my studies for four weeks — to break stones. Tomorrow we have to report at 7:00 a.m. to the construction foreman. Curious to see what will that will bring.

Munich, 6 June 1946
Three weeks of my assignment have been completed. Time passed quickly but, at the same time, felt never ending. Now we only have three more days left, then we'll have it made. I was first put to work with a shovel. Then our construction team was sent to the Policlinic. We cleared the gardens and courtyards of debris, worked on dredging and shoveled. Our group was diversified and worked well together. My nose put a damper on things, which means that the gardens of the clinic are full of lime trees that are now in full bloom. This is why I was put on kitchen duty these last few days. The work here is not hard, but more boring. But even here we work well together. Manny's long awaited homecoming finally took place after I got home yesterday. Now there will be long hours of story-telling. He looks well, has recovered remarkably. Now he will be returning to school again so that he can earn his high school diploma, a goal which will yet cost him some sweat. But he is here, in his home, and that is the most important thing

Munich, 15 July 1946
The second semester started today. The vacation days in the mountains lay far behind us already. They are a lighthearted, refreshing memory. The weather was wonderful. Hanna's family members were all their usual selves, the youngest one, a delightful tot. I took a trip around the *Königsee* with Hermann M.; with Hanna and Herbert I went to the *Hintersee*. These days of relaxation in this beautiful area did me good. The last few days it rained as though coming down straight from heaven. The result was floods. The area from Inn to the city of Rosenheim became one big lake. People had to use boats to get to their homes. Everything was flooded. Even here in Munich the Isar River is very high. And today the new semester began.

This time I have no more than 12 hours, all of them in the afternoon. I would like to work in the mornings. I wonder whether or not my plan will succeed. First of all, we have to go through the enrollment procedures again but, at least, everything is moving in the right direction.

Munich, 22 July 1946
Today was the formal ceremonial opening of the University which now has all of its disciplines staffed and ready to go, including our medical studies. It is about time. We now have to study diligently 26 hours a week starting each day at 7:00 a.m. But all that does not matter. The most important thing is that it has started. I am one step further on the long way to my goal.

Munich, 20 October 1946
I have not written anything for a long time. Time moves on so quickly. The second semester in medicine barely took two months. There was a lot of material to master. Anatomy I and II were lectured, along with history. In addition, there were the science courses. I was kept busy all day long. On top of all this was the anxiety about the *Vorphysikum*[iv] [comprehensive examination which is mandatory after completion of the second semester]. There were so many applicants that only 50% could be accommodated. They wanted to solve this issue by delaying for one semester the admission of all students born after July 1st, 1925. That would have excluded me from taking the exam. For the first time, I witnessed democracy at work. The students protested so that now all the students who are qualified to take the exam will be allowed to take it, as originally planned. I will, after all, be taking the examination on schedule. And now three weeks of vacation have gone by. They were filled with preparations for winter, getting clothes ready, Christmas presents and other small personal things. The new semester will begin soon: the biology dissection and

microscopy course, physiology and physiological chemistry. Along with that we have to study for the *Vorphysikum*. But learning is a joy. Step by step we move ahead. Hanna and her husband visited us on October 6th. Hermann was with them also. Hanna took another look around Munich and we spent some exciting hours together. There is always so much to talk about. The Nuremberg verdict was carried out on October 16th. Goering did not allow them to triumph; he poisoned himself the night before. The others that were sentenced to death are Ribbentrop, Rosenberg, Frick, Seyss-Inquart, Streicher, Sauckel, Keitel, Jodl, Frank and Kaltenbrunner. Doenitz got 10 years; Neurath, 12; Speer and Schirach, 20 years. Raeder, Hess and Funk received life sentences.

Munich, 8 November 1946
Today I am of legal age. Through 21 springtimes I have been here on earth. They have brought both happiness and sorrow; albeit, more happiness than sorrow. I was allowed to live a happy childhood, sheltered by an understanding mother to whom I give thanks for everything. Even during those most difficult times, we were in harmony. Both of us really try to avoid any confrontation. What for, anyway? Life offers enough adversity; why make it any harder? Now I am waiting once again for the University to open. The outlook is not promising. Schneider and von Lang were dismissed without notice, along with another 31 lecturers. This leaves us without the anatomy class. What will happen next, no one knows. The only sure thing is that time is being lost. My colleague took the comprehensive exam and did well on it. I wish I were that far.

Supplement to the *Diary* 1939–1946

by Emanuel Von Koenig

as recalled in 2005

1940. Summer with *Vati*, who took the picture, in Rum, Austria, which two years earlier had become part of the *Reich*.

1941. Manny, *Vati*, *Mutti*, Lulu.

Boyhood Interest

As I grew older, I developed an interest in model building. My mother was very supportive as long as I cleaned up. In high school I and a few other fellows who were quite good in chemistry learned to make explosive compounds with materials available in pharmacies. So I thought about developing a miniature, functioning depth charge for a model. The finished product was about ¾" long and half that width in diameter. I told my mother I would try it out in the bath tub. She nixed that idea and suggested I use a bucket, fill it with water and try it out on the back balcony. I did. The effect was dramatic. The noise was deafening. The bottom of the bucket blew out and the black water dripped over the edge of the balcony. What I did not consider was the fact that the lady on the first floor was airing out her feather beds. Both parties were furious, my mother more so because she had to do the washing.

Other things I did when I was a teenager:
- Was certified as a Life Guard.
- Attended a three-week intensive training course in dealing with incendiary magnesium and phosphor bombs.
- Instructed 12 year olds in firing 22 caliber rifles.
- Assisted in moving household goods from bombed out families to rural areas.
- Fire department runner: during air raids identify damage to buildings and determine status of inhabitants and immediately report to neighborhood fire department control center.
- Fire-fighting and salvage work when required.
- Twice a week I slept in the basement of our High School (with 15 others) to act as fire guards during air raids.
- Clean up and make repairs to our apartment if damaged during air raids. And of course, be a good boy, go to school and get good grades.

Hitler Youth

There were two age groups. The junior group was from 10 to 14; the senior group was from 14 to 18, at which time one was expected to become a member of the party.

The junior group was relatively non-political—or so it seemed to me at the time. During the bi-weekly meetings we learned about the glorious history of the *Vaterland,* its heroes etc. We had many opportunities for sports and weekend camping trips. In a way, it was like Boy Scouts.

In the senior group one had choices; there was a general group but also specialized units such as communication, motorized, flying, pioneers and naval units. These units were, in a sense, all pre-military training. Since I had the plan to ultimately have a career in the Merchant Marine I joined a naval unit. On Lake Starnberg, near Munich, we had a variety of boats at our disposal and trained there about every third weekend during the summers. During our regular meetings we would learn seamanship, various types of knots, signaling with flags, rules of navigation and so on. In our unit there was very little political indoctrination.

**1942. Manny assigned to clean-up
after bombings of Munich.**

There was a brief period of time when I had the additional duty of teaching junior troops the use of rifles and supervised their target practice. We used 22-caliber equipment.

In April 1943, at age 16, I graduated out of the Hitler Youth by becoming a member of the LWH, *Luftwaffenhelfer*, and was assigned to the Munich Air Defense Sector of the German Air Force Auxiliary. At the beginning, air raids were by British bombers which flew their missions at night. In the morning we would take the streetcar to go to school and at noon returned to our battery positions. American Air Force primarily flew daytime missions and when they began to include Munich as a target, we no longer left our battery position. Each day a different teacher came and taught school. Interruption of classes increased because of attacks. As the public transportation system became unreliable all school activities ceased.

January 1944. Manny at left, seated next to life-long friend Peter Gluck; all wearing uniforms of the *Luftwaffenhelfer*.

In June of 1944 I was transferred out of the LWH into the RAD, *Reichs Arbeits Dienst,* and sent to a base in Prague, Czechoslovakia—the "Protectorate," as we called it—where I served as an 88mm heavy anti-aircraft gunner.

Late in the summer I was given a two-week home leave. Happy reunion with mother and sister, nice meal, warm bath, my own bed. Then at 11 p.m.—Air Raid! This was the beginning of a series of air raids which lasted through my leave period. Never got out of my uniform. Activities: rescue, firefighting and salvage. Statistic of bombs dropped during this period: 23,400 high explosives (250 lbs. to 2000 lbs.); 77,900 liquid-phosphor fire-bombs; 1,235,000 stick type fire-bombs. By then, city ¾ destroyed.

October 1944 I began training at the German Naval Academy in Mürwick-by-Flensburg. On 2 January 1945 I reported on board the Heavy Cruiser *Lützow*. Peace-time travel time by train from the Academy to port of Pillau, where the ship was located, ordinarily took about five hours. It took us four days. Many stops, much retracing and finding new routes to avoid contact with advancing Russian troops. Several times strafed by Russian aircraft, casualties. Many times within hearing range of Russian artillery.

Manny in the *Kriegsmarine*.

Heavy Cruiser *Lützow*: displacement 10,000 ton, primary armament two triple turrets 11" guns, secondary armament eight 6" guns in individual mounts., many anti-aircraft guns of various calibers. Area of operation: Baltic Sea. Primary objective: provide heavy artillery support to destroy tank concentration to slow the advance of Russian troops along the shores of the Baltic Sea, thereby allowing German army units to retreat. My primary duty station: engine room; secondary duty station: anti-aircraft.

When the ship was moored near Swinemünde on 16 April 1945, I disembarked to report to the Base Hospital at 10:00 a.m. for minor surgery. At 5 p.m. the *Lützow* was attacked by the British 617 bomber squadron dropping 5.4 ton Dambuster bombs known as "tall boys." Without a seaworthy ship to which I could return, I was assigned to the Infantry – just in time to participate in the Battle of

Berlin. My unit fought hand-to-hand in the western suburbs.

Russian Prisoner of War—April 1945-June 1946:
The Long Road Home.

A few days before being captured we were on patrol and stopped for a short rest in a wooded area. I noticed the body of a dead German soldier, lying face down. Since we were short on ammo and food, I went over to inspect his knapsack. No ammo but a piece of sausage and a pair of red and black knitted mittens. Since the nights were still pretty cold I kept the mittens—and shared the sausage.

On the day before my capture we held a position along a ridge and we were strung out relatively thin. In the late afternoon, our unit was apparently pulled back - but the order did not reach us at the end of the line. It became dark and there were the four of us, isolated.

From our location we could see a few burning farm houses and they gave enough light to be able to see Russian columns moving along a road. We decided on the direction to go and after a few hours we came to an abandoned village. We were exhausted, went to a farmhouse, went upstairs and found a place to sleep.

What woke us up in the morning was the unmistakable sound of moving tanks. Then it suddenly dawned on us that there was no German armor anywhere near. Russian tanks and infantry were moving through the village and we noticed patrols working their way down the road going from house to house. It was not long before one entered the house we were in. We heard, in German, the question if there was anybody there? I answered: Yes. How many? Four. Come down with your hands up.

I had learned from experience that in confrontation it is best to project a very positive attitude and positive thoughts. I was the first one and as I came around the landing to the staircase, at the bottom of the stairs were three Russian soldiers with three submachine guns pointing at my belly. All went well. They treated us kindly and even shared some food. We were taken to a collection point which was the fenced-in yard of a farm. During the day more prisoners were brought in.

Late afternoon we were taken individually to the back of the bam. Standing there were a Russian soldier and a German officer. I need to point out that after the defeat at Stalingrad a number of German officers formed a group to work with the Russians. They believed, at that point, that the war was lost anyway, and that their cooperation could shorten the duration of the war and save lives. He was one of these officers. His first order was for me to tum over any valuables—coins, wristwatch, rings and any other jewelry. When I opened my knapsack the Russian became very agitated and released the safety catch on his rifle. The officer apparently told him to calm down and then asked me how I came to have the mittens. It turned out that they were Russian Army-issue. After I explained how I got them and this was conveyed to the Russian, the safety went back on. Of course he kept the mittens.

The next morning we started marching and during the day the ranks of our column swelled. At about noon we had a short break. We were allowed to drink from a creek which was adjacent to the road. We all flopped down to fill up on water. When I had enough, I looked up and on the other side of the creek I saw the bloated bodies of two dead cows in the water. Too late to worry.

A few hours later we came to a small village. There was a knoll with a number of Russians standing around. We were ordered into a single file formation and led to a spot where there were many baskets full of scissors; anything from nail scissors to garden shears. A Russian would call two of us, take the next scissors and go through some pointing motions meaning "Cut each other's hair." We recognized that this was the beginning of a delousing operation.

To one side were picnic tables staffed by mean-looking Russian woman soldiers. Once sheared, we had to strip, put our clothing in a net-type bag and submit to being sudsed and close-shaved over every part of the body. Then into a mobile unit to be sprayed with some awful smelling stuff, followed by a cold shower. We spent the night in a fenced field.

The next morning I was called by name to be taken to interrogation. I wondered how they knew my name and then I noticed that all my papers were gone. I was still in Navy Blues and I figured that because of that they wanted to take a closer look at me. I was taken into a house where, behind a table in the interrogation room, sat a Russian officer. He spoke perfect German.

"Sit down. Your name is Emanuel von König?"

"Yes, Sir."

"The von in your name indicates nobility; therefore, your father is a Junker and Junkers have large land holdings. What I want to know from you right now is where those holdings are located."

"My father works for the State Railroad. He is a surveyor. We live in a rented apartment in Munich and I have never heard of any properties."

He changed the subject for a while and then came back to the same question. I gave the same answer. He then advised me of the penalties for lying to an interrogating officer. He repeated the question; I gave the same answer.

Then he made me an offer: "We will take you behind the German lines. If you can convince some German soldiers to surrender and come back with you, we will release you and you can go home." I saw that as just two more chances to get shot. I declined. Then, more questions. This went on for about 20 minutes before he handed me my papers and terminated the interview. At the door, I was reprimanded because I had not saluted the officer upon departure.

I rejoined the column of prisoners and the next afternoon we arrived at our first camp. Inside a large fenced-in area, several very large storage sheds became our quarters. The place must have been some commercial enterprise. In the buildings were some low platforms probably for storing something. There was no straw and we slept on the wood. The food was terrible. Once a day some thin soup, thickened with some starch and floating around were some kernels of barley. The bread was awful, very black and the center not baked through. It was not very long before I, among others, developed problems with stomach and intestines.

The system in the Russian camp administration was such that if you became sufficiently ill you were transferred to another camp which had only ill people. In the first of such camps I got an upper bunk and I noticed the wall smeared with blood. Squashed bed bugs!

As my situation deteriorated I was moved again to another camp. It had buildings with three stories and I learned that each building housed prisoners who had different infectious diseases. My building was for non-infectious people like me but even so, the death rate was appreciable. We slept on straw on the floor next to each other.

On some mornings you would wake up and find that your neighbor had died during the night. The idea that I could die never occurred to me. I was no longer in combat and there were no longer any bullets which had my name on them.

I had one more camp transfer. It was in Poland not too far from the German border. In this camp, once a week, there was a lineup of those prisoners where it was questionable whether or not they make it to next week. If the judgment was a NO, the prisoner received his release papers, a railroad ticket to his home town, a piece of sausage and 1½ loaf of bread. Once you walked through the gate of the camp, you were considered a free man and the Russians could care less what happened to you then. You were no longer their problem. If you died, the locals had to bury you.

One week it was my turn in the lineup. We had little tags with our name and a description of what was wrong. The person who made the inspection that day was a German Army doctor, also a prisoner. When he came to me he looked at my name and started asking a few question. It turned out that he and my father, at the beginning of the war, served in the same unit and used to play cards together. I will never forget his last words to me: "Son, I will never get out of here, but you will." He signed me off and I was released. Thank you, God. This was early in July 1945.

Back in Munich, in mid April 1945, a friend of my parents defied the threat of a death penalty and listened to a Swiss radio station, picking up the news of the bombing and the sinking of the ship I was on. He advised my mother. Shortly after the war ended in June of 45, my father returned from service. At the time of my hospital stay in East Germany there was no opportunity for mail to the West. Lacking any other information, my parents had to assume that I went down with the ship. Based on this assumption, they decided to apply all available funds toward enabling my sister to continue her studies and become a doctor.

Wolfhilde as student.

A small group of us made our way to the railroad station and waited for a train going in the direction of Berlin. There we found shelter for the night. The next morning we started walking to the station from which our next train would be leaving. People recognized us as released POWs and we were constantly approached and questioned if we knew anything about a loved one. On the continuation of my trip I had to transfer a few times and ultimately wound up in the town of Eilenburg on the river Mulde, near Leipzig. The train could go no further. The Russians had declared the river a demarcation line and one could only cross with a special pass. I wound up in a refugee camp and after a few days developed pleurisy. Twice a week the ambulance from the hospital, located on the other side of the river, was allowed to enter the camp and take the two worst cases with them. After about two weeks I was taken out. I must have been quite a sight, dirty and unwashed, down to about 130 pounds.

Once in the hospital, I only remember being undressed and lowered into a tub with nice warm water, then I passed out. When I woke up I found myself in a single-bed room.

It took three procedures to remove all the blood from my lung cavity. After some weeks I was moved to a general ward where I had to teach my spindly legs to walk again. As time passed, I regained my strength and put weight back on. After about five months things became quite boring and I asked to be given something to do. I started helping out in the Lab and in the office.

I was also encouraged to go on brisk walks to strengthen my leg muscles and give my lungs a work out.

Life had its interesting moments but I yearned to get back home and felt ready to leave. Then in January 1946 the hospital experienced a typhoid epidemic. I became infected and it hit me pretty hard.

Another patient, also from Munich, was released in March of 46 and through him my parents learned of my whereabouts.

After a total hospital time of 11 months I finally was able to continue my journey and I arrived in Munich in mid-June of 1946. I walked home from the railroad station. It felt good to see the city again. On the way I met an old school friend. He greeted me and I started crying. My nerves let go. After I collected myself I continued and when I turned the comer into our street I saw my father leaning out the window, smoking. I was halfway down the street before he recognized me and let out a holler. My parents and my sister were delighted to see me again. Happy reunion!

[Family-provided add-in.
Happy reunion! Even though this was the view of City Center,
the Marienplatz, in 1945.

When Christmas came, this was still the setting out of which rose the spire of Salvatorkirche.

This is how Manny appeared—excruciatingly thin!

End of add-in.]

After a few days I reported to the Veterans administration. Based on some of the tests made it was determined that I had a somewhat reduced lung capacity and what would today be described as Post Traumatic Stress Syndrome. I was temporarily classified as 50% disabled. I received an additional allotment of food coupons and within a short time I was also sent to a rehabilitation facility in Ambach on Lake Starnberg. I stayed there for four weeks. When I returned my parents told me about their decision regarding my sister's education. I understood their reasoning. Although I did not agree with what seemed an unfair arrangement—that they would continue to pay her schooling tuition but could not afford to pay mine, as well—I had to accept it.

Mid-August arrived and it was time to think about going back to high school. Nineteen years old already, with still my junior and senior years to complete before I could graduate. Pupils returning from service within an established grace period were allowed to complete the grade from which they left. I returned to Munich after the grace period had expired, therefore I had to repeat 7th grade to be able to advance to 8th grade [US equivalents: 11th and 12th].

Postlude Years 1947-1952

I returned to the *Luitpold Real Schule* in September 1946. By the time I graduated on 14 July 1948 from the eight-year course at

1947

this school, I had completed eight (albeit interrupted) years of German, History, Mathematics, Geography, Physical Education and Arts; six years of Physics, Latin and Biology; and four years of English, Music, and Chemistry (three years inorganic, one year organic). I was 21 years old.

Not until November 1949 could I afford to enter the University of Munich. I studied there only until July 1950 when a Fulbright scholarship was offered to me through the U.S. State Department. I sailed in August aboard the *S.S.Brazil* full of similarly selected students, all as happy as I.

1950

Manny at the University of Munich.

This concludes Manny's narrative.

Rosalyn Reeder picks up the story at this point.

In September 1950 my roommate at the University of Minnesota, Dorothy Johnson, who was also my childhood and high school friend, introduced me to her new friend Maung Khin, from Burma. Khin, in turn, immediately introduced both of us to his new friend, Manny von König. This took place in the house of the Delta Tau Delta fraternity, which was providing them both with board and room sponsorship.

This is a photo of Manny as he appeared then.

As winter approached, Manny—who had been as cold as he had been hungry for many years—bought himself this very warm coat.

1950-1 Winter. Manny In front of the Delta Tau Delta house.

By Christmas 1950, Manny's 23rd, he and I—pictured here on the right with (left to right) Sheffi Hossain, Mickey Kane, Dorothy Johnson and Maung Khin—were considering marriage.

1951: a bow-tie phase.

1951. We hit the Twin City beaches; Manny still abnormally thin.

**1951. Manny & Rosalyn on ship *S.S. Washington* with
Werner Prange and Max Klägel.**

August 1951 we sailed to Bremer Haven with hundreds of returning German students—Wolfgang Schleich among them—aboard the *S.S. Washington.*

Manny's family welcomed me.

1951 Christmas; Manny's 24th.

| 1951 | 1951 Christmas | 1951 Christmas |

In 1952 Wolfhilde became fully certified as a medical doctor, having earned the title *Dr. med.*

Frau Dr. med Wolfhilde von König

Manny went to the Police Department and declared himself "stateless," a prelude to emigration.

1952 Spring. Manny & Rosalyn stroll the gardens of Nymphenburg Castle.

Early in 1952, Wolfgang, working for Radio Free Europe in Berlin, found himself transferred to Munich, which enabled us to become closer friends. When we left Munich, Manny this time as an emigrant, Wolfgang was there to see us off on the midnight train which would cross over the Brenner Pass to Genoa where we would board the *SS. Independence*. To accompany us on our journey, and on into the Future, he gave us a *Nürnberger Rauschgold Engel* which topped our Christmas trees for many years to come.

After Years 1953 – 2009

Manny arrived in New York as an immigrant in December 1952. He and Rosalyn returned to live in the Twin Cities area of Minnesota, where they had met. He immediately stepped onto the path of study leading to U. S. citizenship, which he acquired on 17 May 1956.

He then expressed his appreciation to his new country, and emphasized his loyalty to it, by joining the U.S. Active Army Reserve. He served with the 103D Infantry Division Reserve, becoming Chief of its Fire Direction Center. He was honorably discharged in 1962 at the rank of Sgt. E-6.

Munich, 1962. Last photo of the nuclear family before *Vati*'s death in 1968.

An inheritance from the Belgian *Tante* Margarete allowed Manny to take a one-year sabbatical from his employment at the Seeger Refrigerator Company to complete studies toward the degree begun at the University of Munich. Already the father of two sons, he obtained a degree in Business Science from the University of Minnesota in December of 1959.

Munich, 1985. Manny, *Mutti*, Lulu, Rosalyn. Last family photo before
***Mutti's* death in 1991 and Lulu's death in 1993.**

While her brother was still imprisoned in a Russian camp, Wolfhilde participated in the de-Nazification process. She adjusted to the new order and found happiness in her own country.

Manny—in haggard condition, struggling for months across the war-devastated landscape in order to return to Munich—was less forgiving. He felt that every level of his society, from the *Führer* on down through his parents and older sister, had misled and betrayed him. Throughout the Nazi years, Wolfhilde had been able to develop her passion for helping others into a health-service profession, while his projected naval career was literally blown out from under him.

The sibling Hitler Youths—as adults, able to make fairly frequent trips across the Atlantic to visit each other—eventually achieved full reconciliation. Wolfhilde became, to her nephews, possibly the best aunt the world has ever seen.

Frau Dr. med. Wolfhilde von König, specialized in anesthesiology, retired from the Maria-Theresia Klinik in Munich as its Chief of Staff. She died 16 November 1993 and lies buried in the family plot (pictured below) in *München Ostfriedhof* #116-2-36.

Manny retired in 1989 from his position as a Division Vice President of the Whirlpool Corporation. Upon his death in 2009 he was the father of four sons, proud father-in-law of his four sons' beloved wives, grandfather of six and great-grandfather of one.

His ashes rest beneath an Indian medicine wheel at his last residence in La Luz, New Mexico.

ACRONYMS used in the *War Diary*

BDM - *Bund deutscher Mädel*
League of German Girls, ages 14-18 (part of the Hitler Youth)

DLRG - *Deutsche Lebens-Rettungs-Gesellschaft*
German Life-Guard Club

DRK - *Deutsches Rotes Kreuz*
German Red Cross

GD - *Gesundheitsdienst*
Health Service

GDM - *Gesundheitsdienst Mädel*
Health Service Girl, part of the BDM

HJ - *Hitler Jugend*
Hitler Youth

HLV - *Heimatland Verschickung*
Homeland Evacuation

JM - *Jungmädel*
Young Girls, ages 10-14 (part of the Hitler Youth)

KBWK - *Kriegsberufswettkampf*
War Career Competition

KHD - *Kriegshilfsdienst*
Auxiliary War Service

KLV - *Kinderlandverschickung*
Children + Land + Evacuate; (See Endnote)

KVK - *Kriegsverdiensnstkreuz*
War Merit Cross

KWHW - *Kriegs-Winterhilfswerk*
War Winter Relief Program (sometimes abbreviated to WHW)

LWH- *Luftwaffenhelfer*
Air Force Helper; Manny was in it—see entries 8/15/43 and 7/10/44

NS - *National Sozialist*
National Socialist

NSDAP - *Nationalsozialistische Deutsche Arbeiterpartei*
National Socialist German Workers' Party

NSKK - *Nationalsozialistische Kraftfahrkorps*
Motor Transportation Formation of the NSDAP

NSV - *Nationalsozialistische Volkswohlfahrt*
National Socialist People's Welfare

OKW - *Oberkommando der Wehrmacht*
Supreme Command of the Armed Forces

RAD - *Reichsarbeitdienst*
Reich Labor Service

SA - *Sturmabteilung*
Storm Troopers, Brownshirts

SD - *Sicherheitsdienst*
Security Service, part of the SS

SS - *Schutzstaffel*
Defense Echelon, Blackshirts, begun as Hitler's personal bodyguard

WHW - *Winterhilfswerk*
Winter Relief Program

ENDNOTES

(i) - page 37

In spite of the circumstances which caused Manny to emigrate from his native land, as he did in December 1952, he remained proud of the formal education it had given him; with just cause, as things turned out. He explained in his writings of 2005: "About two years before anticipated graduation from the University of Minnesota, I had to have an evaluation of how many credits were yet needed to complete the requirements. I submitted all my educational documents from high school, the University of Munich and credits earned while I was an exchange student. The audit awarded me 24 earned credits I could not identify. I asked for clarification and was told that the teaching level and material taught in a German high school is acknowledged to be equal to that of the freshman year at an American University."

Manny left in his notes, also, a description of how the German School System functioned during the 1930s and 1940s when he was part of it.

Gender separation prevailed. There were separate schools for boys and for girls throughout all eleven or twelve years. Whether for boy or girl, the pattern was the same, beginning with the *Grundschule* (Grade School). At the end of the fourth year, a student might continue in this type of school for another four years and top it off with three years of trade school. Those who aimed for university educations took examinations at the end of their fourth year; those who passed were eligible to transfer into an eight year academic program that would prepare them for college entrance. For boys, these high schools were of two types: the *Gymnasium* which featured humanities, and the *Real Schule* which emphasized the natural sciences. For girls, there was only the *Lyceum* which, however, did a good job of covering both humanities and sciences curricula. Tuition for the eleven-year Grade Schools was free. Tuition had to be paid at the *Gymnasium*, the *Lyceum* and the *Real Schule*.

The *Real Schule* that Manny attended conducted classes from 8:00 a.m. until noon, sometimes 1:00 p.m., with one twenty minute break. Each student was expected to do a daily minimum of 2½ hours study at home. At school, pupils remained in the classroom; it was the teachers who rotated. Every teacher was highly qualified in at least one subject; all held either Master or Ph. D degrees.

The final week, including Saturday, of the final year was devoted to comprehensive testing, with three to four hours allotted for each subject. Test questions were established by the Ministry of Education, delivered in sealed envelopes and administered and supervised by teachers from other high schools.

A failing grade (F) in any one subject resulted in a mandatory oral examination by three teachers for other high schools. This system was in place to insure that a failing grade was not the result of personal problems between a teacher and a pupil. When a written-test result was one grade above failing (D), the student had the right to request an oral examination. Graduation was possible with one F or two Ds if the overall grade average met the established standard.

(*ii*) - page 59

Gau is a German Nazi-era political land division officially translated as "District." As in the US, the boundaries of a District are mutable and are sometimes changed according to such other changeable features as population; even federal and state districts are not necessarily conterminous. The current Administrative District (*Regierungsbezirk*) of Upper Bavaria (*München-Oberbayern*) —shown in the map: highlighted, set within the boundaries of the state of Bavaria; set, in turn, inside the boundaries of Germany—is almost identical to that of the Nazi-era *Traditionsgau*, or *Gau München-Oberbayern*.

This is the state of Bavaria (both shaded areas) with *Gau Oberbayern* (same as *Gau Munchen-Oberbayern*) shown in the

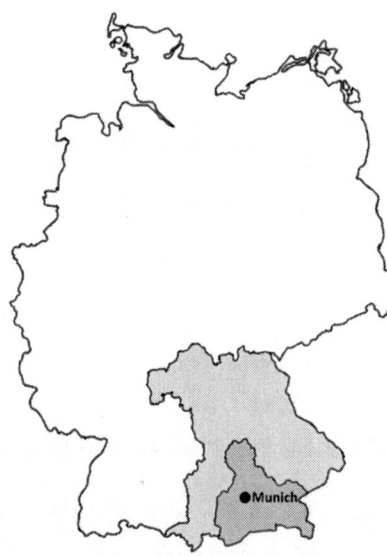

darker gray.

Gau München-Oberbayern was the heartland of the Nazi Party in its developing years. As the Party grew, so did the pride of this *Gau*. As Munich came to be officially known as *Hauptstadt der Bewgung* (capitol/birthplace of the "Movement") the *Gau*, of which Munich was also the *Hauptstadt*, elevated its title to *Traditionsgau*. The Party encouraged locales in resuscitating a kind of traditional patriotism; revival and enhancement of folk dances, folk art and music, folk dress, coats-of-arms. Each area's stimulated local pride was then channeled into support of the swastika and all that it had come to stand for.

(iii) - page 118

Kinderlandverschickung combines the words *children, country* and *evacuation*. It is the term for the German WWII program which evacuated school children, and mothers along with their smaller children, out of bomb threatened cities to the less vulnerable countryside. It grew out of the *Erholungsverschickung*, established by the churches and operating as early as 1900, which provided poor city children brief summer vacations in the country. In the context of *Erholung* (recovery, or respite), *Verschickung* had more the meaning of "to send" than "to evacuate." Children were lodged either with volunteering families or in camps.

By the fall of 1940, it was clear to German leaders that the British bombing of their northern cities would soon be greatly increased. As the British were evacuating their children out of London, Germany began evacuating from Berlin (200,000 from that city, alone) and Hamburg.

We read in Wolfhilde's 1941 *Diary* entries on March 6 and

12, and on May 27 that the von König family cared for little Liselotte. Munich was not "countryside" but was still, at that time, a safe location.

Relocation on the part of the evacuees was voluntary. In addition to quarters requisitioned by the government for their accommodation (for which compensation was provided) from inn and hotel owners, farmers and private homeowners, the KLV also established special camps complete with schools, medical facilities and food service.

Hitler ordered Baldur von Schirach to organize a comprehensive *Kinderlandverschickung*. Under his direction, an eventual 5,000 camps were set up in such far ranging areas as East Prussia, the Warthegau section of Poland, Upper Silesia, Slovakia, Bulgaria, Romania, Bohemia, Moravia and Bavaria. At peak operation of the program, 2,500,000 children were accommodated.

Under direction of adult leaders, most of the staff members were girls of the Hitler Youth, the BDM (*Bund deutscher Mädel*, League of German Girls). Wolfhilde began training in April 1941 as a Health Service worker within the BDM. Her first day of service at a KLV camp came on 3 August 1942 when she was three months short of being 17 years of age. She reports on 18 August 1943 that entire schools in the Hamburg area were shifting into KLV camps. Through the summer of 1944 she continued working with the KLV in the Berchtesgaden/Bad Reichenhall area with its concentration of 17 camps; and in Wolnzach, in the Holledau region where she simultaneously assisted with the hops harvest.

(*iv*) - page 280

Vorphysikum. Comprehensive examination which tests students' knowledge of natural science subjects taught during their first two semesters of study. Passing this exam is the first proofing stage toward becoming a physician. The second stage is the *Physikum*, administered after the students' completion of four semesters. Third and final stage is the *Klinischer Abschnitt*, the residency.

Lightning Source UK Ltd.
Milton Keynes UK
UKOW05n0723090114

224254UK00001B/8/P